D0132502

DESIRABLE
AND
UNDESIRABLE
CHARACTERISTICS
OF
OFFSHORE
YACHTS

Desirable and Undesirable Characteristics of
OFFSHORE YACHTS

By the Technical Committee
of the Cruising Club of America

Edited by John Rousmaniere
Illustrated by Stephen L. Davis

A Nautical Quarterly Book

W. W. Norton & Company
New York and London

Printed in the United States of America.

The text of this book is composed in Garamond Light, with
display type set in Garamond Light. Composition by Vail-Ballou.
Manufacturing by The Maple-Vail Book Manufacturing Group.
Book design by Marilyn Rose.

ISBN 0-393-03311-2

W. W. Norton & Company, Inc., 500 Fifth Avenue,
New York, N. Y. 10110
W. W. Norton & Company, Ltd., 37 Great Russell Street,
London WC1B 3NU

1234567890

Dedicated to the memory of
Lynn A. Williams,
1909–1985

Contents

Foreword by John Rousmaniere   11
Acknowledgments   15
The Authors   17

PART I: HULL DESIGN AND CONSTRUCTION

1. Trends in Yacht Design, 1920–1986,
by Olin J. Stephens II   23

Toward the First Dual-Purpose Yachts   23
Early Rating Rules   27
The Centerboarders of the 1950s   31
Modern Trends   36
Rating Rules   39

2. Some Thoughts on Stability, by Olin J. Stephens II   45

The Fastnet Shock   47
Stability   47
Recommendations   53

3. Avoiding Capsize: Research Work,
by Karl L. Kirkman and Richard C. McCurdy   57

The SNAME/USYRU Capsize Project   57
Sources of Research Data   60
Insights on Boat Size and Capsize Dynamics   61
Appendix 3-A: Roll Moment of Inertia   67
Appendix 3-B: Hull Shape, Ballast, and Stability   69

4. Avoiding Capsize: Practical Measures,
by Karl L. Kirkman and Richard C. McCurdy   75

Assessing Capsize Vulnerability   75
The Capsize Screening Formula   76
Sailing Tactics for Rough Weather   80
Using the Foregoing Material   81
Appendix 4-A: The Capsize Length Formula   82

5. Steering Control, by Karl L. Kirkman   83

Directional Stability   83
Control Effectiveness   88
The Trade-offs   88
Wind and Waves   89
Boat Shape   91

6. Modern Yacht Construction,
by James A. McCurdy   95

Loads and Stresses   95
Structural Systems   97
Meeting Concentrated Loads   98
Centerboards   99
Ballast   99
Electrolytic Corrosion   100
Quality Control   100
Rigidity   101
Merits of Construction Materials   101

PART II: ON DECK AND BELOW

7. The Deck, by Daniel D. Strohmeier   105

The Deck and Boat Strength   105
Keeping Out the Ocean   106
Keeping Out Drips and Dollops   109
A Platform for Gear   109
The Working Crew   110
A Cover for a Comfortable Interior   113

8. The Cockpit, by C. William Lapworth   117

Cockpit Types   117
Companionways and Dodgers   119
Design Details   122

9. The Cabin, by Lynn A. Williams   127

Interior Arrangement   127
Bunks and Berths   129
The Galley   132
Stowage   139

10. Ventilation, by Thomas R. Young   145

Ventilation Gear   145
Safety   155
A Note on the Dorade Vent (written by Roderick Stephens, Jr.)   156

PART III: SPARS, RIGGING, AND SAILS

11. The Sail Plan, Spars, and Standing Rigging,
by Roderick Stephens, Jr., and Mitchell C. Gibbons-Neff   161

Sail Plans   161
Spars   166
Standing Rigging   168
Lubricants and Tape   173

12. Running Rigging,
by Roderick Stephens, Jr., and Mitchell C. Gibbons-Neff   175

Rope Materials and Construction   175
Halyards   176
Sheets   182
Gear on the Boom   183
Fittings   187
Steering and Centerboard Gear   190

13. Sails for Cruising,
by Roderick Stephens, Jr., and Mitchell C. Gibbons-Neff   193

Sail Fabrics   193
Halyard Marks   194
The Danger of Luff-fed Sails   196
Recommended Inventories   198
Storm Sails   200
Roller Furlers   200

PART IV: AUXILIARY EQUIPMENT

**14. Navigation, Weather, Radio,
and Sailing Instruments,**
by Richard C. McCurdy and Thomas R. Young   207

Navigation-Pilotage Gear   207
Weather and Communications Instruments   215
Boat Performance Instruments   219
Instrument Packages   222
The Navigation Station   224
Suggestions for Radio Installation and Use   226

15. Ground Tackle,
by Clayton Ewing and Stanley Livingston, Jr.   229

Anchor Types   229
Anchor Weight   232
Recommendations   233
Anchor Cables   233
Buoys and the Stern Anchor   235

16. The Power Plant, by George D. Griffith   237

Diesel or Gasoline?   237
Performance   238
The Propeller   238
Engine Location, Maintenance, and Insulation   239
Engine Auxiliaries   241

17. Emergency Equipment, by Stanley Livingston, Jr.   245

Emergency Avoidance   245
Man-Overboard Gear   247
Fire Extinguishers   250
Damage Control   252
Abandoning Ship   252
Gear Location   253

PART V: FIVE GOOD BOATS

Adele, by Ted Hood   257
Compadre, by Bill Lapworth   263
Wissahickon, by McCurdy & Rhodes   269
The Pearson 386, by Bill Shaw   273
The Seguin 44 *First Light,* by Sparkman & Stephens   279

APPENDIXES

I. Checklist for Offshore Sailing   289
II. Illness, Injury, and Accidents at Sea:
     Recommended Procedures, Basic Medical Supplies and
     Their Use, by George H. A. Clowes, M.D.   293

Further Reading   301
Index   303

Foreword

John Rousmaniere

This book is the product of an extraordinary collaborative effort by a group of talented men who not only have thought deeply about the technology of offshore sailing but also have thoroughly tested their insights on the oceans and seas of the world. The sailing experience of the authors of these chapters is remarkable in both variety and sheer volume. Between them, they have been sailing for about 850 years, covered more than 750,000 miles offshore (the equivalent of 30 circuits of the globe), and owned 43 cruising-racing sailboats. They have sailed a total of 147 Newport-to-Bermuda Races, 36 transatlantic passages, and 11 races to Hawaii. Five of them—Olin and Rod Stephens, Jim McCurdy, Bill Shaw, and Bill Lapworth—are widely respected yacht designers; Karl Kirkman is a naval architect who works at the interface between hydrodynamic theory and sailing practice; and most of the other authors are engineers who have taken a special delight in applying their professional skills to their sport. In sum, the expertise of this panel is remarkable in both breadth and depth.

For many years, these men have sat together on the Technical Committee of the Cruising Club of America, where they have debated the wisdom or folly of trends in yacht design, construction, and rigging. Since it is under the CCA's aegis that they have written the papers that make up this volume, any reader who wishes to understand their assumptions and approach must appreciate what the Cruising Club stands for.

The CCA was founded in 1922 by the first generation of amateur sailors to regularly venture out of sight of land in relatively small sailboats. One of their goals, which was written down in the club's constitution, was to encourage the design and construction of suitable boats for offshore sailing. By "suitable" the founders did not mean what the word has come to suggest in some sailing circles today: an overweight tub of a hull under a stubby rig and a mere cloudlet of sail—in brief, a vessel unable to get out of her own way except when running before half a gale of wind. Rather, by "suitable" those men meant a real *sailing* yacht, a boat with a good turn of speed, especially upwind. As one CCA founding member wrote, "I am convinced that it is our duty to stimulate the production of fast, as well as comfortable, boats for long-distance work."

For these men, as well as for many other experienced blue-water sailors then and since, decent speed was an essential component of good seamanship. Certainly, a boat should be a comfortable home when at anchor. But she should also have legs long enough to allow her to reach a distant harbor before the arrival of a gale and—should the gale catch her—enough close-winded speed so she can beat off a threatening lee shore to the safety of deep water. Of course, by "speed" nobody meant wild breakneck wave-jumping; as Karl Kirkman and Richard McCurdy point out at the end of Chapter 4, a prerequisite for surviving storms without capsize is to keep speed under control.

If speed made sailing safer, it also made sailing more fun. Alfred F. Loomis, the great yachting writer (and a passionate proponent of the CCA, of which he was a member), once quoted an old-time sailor's comments about a particularly commodious, ponderous boat. "She'll go a loooooooong way," this graybeard muttered, "an' take a loooooooong time gettin' there." To encourage the design and construction of boats that take a relatively shoooooooort time gettin' there, soon after its organization the CCA established an offshore sailing standard of its own, the biennial race to Bermuda. This is one of the few true ocean races sailed regularly. A 635-mile passage, often to windward, the race has for 60 years been a gut-wrenching, keel-bolt-shaking test of crew and boat. Only when you wring the Gulf Stream out of your socks as you sniff the fragrance of oleander wafting from Bermuda's coral shores can you honestly state that you have been offshore. And if the boat beneath you still seems comfortable and secure after four or five days of bashing into head seas, then you know that you have made the run in a yacht with more desirable than undesirable characteristics.

Thanks partly to its members' assiduous attention to the breeding of what came to be called the dual-purpose yacht, the Cruising Club became widely recognized as one of the world's most prestigious sailing organizations. Membership is by invitation only, and admission standards are demanding. For example, the proposer must honestly certify that he would gladly loan his own boat to the candidate anytime, anywhere. And "anywhere," for a CCA member, can literally be *anywhere*. The club's motto is "Nowhere Is Too Far," and the burgee—blue wave on white field—has flown over members' boats in plenty of far-distant anywheres: Cape Horn and Spitzburgen, Hobart and St. Helena, Suez and Bora-Bora.

Therefore, given the club's historic interest in encouraging the construction of good boats to be sailed long distances, nobody was surprised in 1977 when the CCA Technical Committee, chaired by Lynn A. Williams, published a booklet for private circulation called *Desirable Characteristics of Offshore Cruising-Racing Yachts*. In its 159 pages were packed hundreds of terse rules on designing, building, and equipping a proper oceangoing sailing vessel. As the title suggests, the stress lay on what was good and seamanlike; the bad and unseamanlike was generally ignored because, at that time, it made up a small part of the sport. In those days, a sailor could buy a boat larger than about 35 feet with the assurance that she could cross an ocean, survive a gale, and house her crew in comfort.

However, by 1983, Lynn Williams had determined that too much that was bad and unseamanlike had appeared in offshore sailing. Disturbing reports from races and cruising grounds alike indicated that something was wrong with modern yacht design, at least partly due to emphasis on racing. The first dose of hard news came in August 1979, when a storm hit the fleet participating in the Fastnet Race in England and dozens of boats were rolled over, five boats sank, and fifteen lives were lost. Not long afterward, several sailors were killed in a storm off the Australian coast. Sad statistics like these continued to appear. They have not stopped:

in August 1985, while the manuscript of this book was being prepared, two-thirds of the fleet in the Fastnet Race withdrew in a gale due mainly to damaged hulls and rigging, torn sails, and crew exhaustion; eight months previously, exactly the same proportion of boats had dropped out of the 1984 Sydney-Hobart Race, for many of the same reasons.

Questions began to be asked about the directions in which the sport was heading. While the trend toward complicated, highly specialized, fragile, and unforgiving racing boats and gear was obvious and disturbing, what most frightened many observers was the influence that these boats were having on the design of *cruising* boats. As Olin Stephens points out in his fascinating opening chapter on the history of yacht design, the type of boat that many people buy for cruising is often affected by the type of boat that is currently succeeding on the race course, and not always constructively. In the boats of the late 1970s and the 1980s, this meant that the things that people have always done with cruising boats—in particular, heading out on an offshore passage—were becoming increasingly risky.

Disturbed by developments that seemed to be harming the sport he loved (he had made eight Atlantic crossings and sailed in fifteen Bermuda Races), Lynn Williams proposed that the CCA Technical Committee update its pamphlet. Besides insights about desirable contemporary trends, he asked for criticisms of *undesirable* developments: those trends in design, construction, and equipment that run counter to the desire for the kind of safe, fast sailing that a suitable boat would provide. Working as volunteers, the committee members revised the old chapters or, in most cases, wrote entirely new ones that addressed issues that had arisen since the mid-1970s as well as many traditional problems. They circulated their papers among themselves and commented on them in the spirit of a highly constructive group editorial process. Throughout, they focused on the question, "What should the average person who intends to sail offshore know about his or her equipment?" After a while, Lynn suggested that instead of a pamphlet the new publication should be a commercially published book; if the committee's discoveries and conclusions were bound between hard covers and made widely available, its work could help the largest possible audience. The committee agreed, and Lynn asked me to be editor. My only regret is that he did not live long enough to see all his work bear the rich fruit that lies in these pages.

I cannot conclude without reporting a poetic justice. The draft manuscripts were delivered to me soon before I headed offshore on a 2000-mile passage to the Azores on Jim McCurdy's 35-foot sloop *Wissahickon,* commanded by Jim's daughter Sheila and with Alf Loomis's son Harvey in the crew. I am pleased to say that the preliminary editing was done under conditions that are every sailor's dream—in the cabin of a highly desirable, well-sailed vessel running truely and comfortably before strong fair winds, out there where the depth sounder shows no bottom.

John Rousmaniere
Stamford, Connecticut

Acknowledgments

W hile the editor thanks all the contributors for their hard work and support, he is especially grateful to the following people, who greatly eased his burden: Stan Livingston, chairman of the CCA Technical Committee, for his efficiency, patience, and understanding as coordinator of a complicated project; Bud Lovelace and Joe Gribbins, of *Nautical Quarterly,* for their support in getting the project off the ground and at several important steps; Marilyn Rose, for her skillful design work; Suzan Williams for her design assistance; Reg Reese, of Henry R. Hinckley & Co:, for the jacket photograph; the late Lynn Williams, for initiating the project as a book; Commodore Bill White and the other flag officers of the Cruising Club of America; and (as ever) Dana and Will.

Karl Kirkman and Dick McCurdy wish to acknowledge the help of the following technical collaborators on the SNAME/USYRU capsize project, described in Chapters 3 and 4: Susan L. Bales, Dan Blagden, G. Russell Bowler, Audrey Greenhill, Bruce N. Hays, John G. Hoyt III, Philip Kaiko, Joan Kimber, Andrew A. Magruder, James A. McCurdy, Toby Jean Nagle, J. N. Newman, Jay E. Paris, Robert S. Peterson, Joseph O. Salsich, George S. Schairer, Robert A. Smith, Olin J. Stephens II, Daniel D. Strohmeier, John W. Wright, Kenneth B. Weller, John J. Zselecsky, the Hydromechanics Laboratory of the United States Naval Academy, the David Taylor Naval Ship Research and Development Center, Hydronautics Inc., Massachusetts Institute of Technology, McCurdy & Rhodes Inc., M. Rosenblatt & Son Inc., Sparkman & Stephens Inc., and the Offshore and Publications Offices of the United States Yacht Racing Union.

The members of the CCA Technical Committee during the time when this book was being written were: Stanley Livingston, Jr. (Chairman), Mitchell C. Gibbons-Neff, George D. Griffith, Halsey Herreshoff, Frederick E. Hood, Karl Kirkman, William Langan, C. William Lapworth, James A. McCurdy, Richard C. McCurdy, Alan McIlhenny, William H. Shaw, Olin J. Stephens II, Roderick Stephens, Jr., Daniel Strohmeier, Lynn A. Williams, and Thomas R. Young. Former members of the committee include Robert N. Bavier, Jr., Mark H. Baxter, Gordon M. Curtis, Jr., the late Clayton Ewing, the late Patrick E. Haggerty, Charles Kirsch, and Wallace J. Stenhouse, Jr.

The Authors

George H. A. Clowes, M.D., author of the appendix on medical equipment and fleet surgeon of the CCA, is a surgeon and professor of surgery emeritus at Harvard Medical School. He has owned several cruising boats in which he has widely cruised in Europe and North America. He has made one voyage to Labrador and two to Newfoundland, and has sailed across the Atlantic three times and participated in ten Bermuda Races.

The late **Clayton Ewing** wrote the original draft of the chapter on ground tackle that has been updated by Stanley Livingston, Jr. The owner of several yachts named *Dyna,* Ewing made seven transatlantic crossings under sail and cruised and raced widely in Europe and North America. His name has become legendary for his performance in the 1963 Transatlantic Race to England, when he won a prize even though *Dyna* sailed the last 1000 miles without a rudder. Ewing, who did his early sailing on Lake Michigan before moving to Maryland, was commodore of both the CCA and the New York Yacht Club.

George D. Griffith, co-author of the chapter on engines, is a mechanical engineer living in Long Beach, California. A sailor for fifty-four of his sixty-four years, he has cruised and raced extensively in the Atlantic and Pacific (even as far as Fiji), frequently in one of the twelve boats that he has owned. A former commodore of the Los Angeles Yacht Club, Griffith has also served as chairman of the Technical Committee of the Transpacific Yacht Club, which sponsors the Honolulu Race, and on the Race Committee of the Cruising Club of America's Newport-to-Bermuda Race.

Naval architect and marine engineer **Karl L. Kirkman,** contributor to three chapters on stability and steering, is a researcher on sailing theory and yacht design who has done extensive work on 12-Meter and ocean-racing yacht development. Kirkman has owned two cruising boats that he has finished off or built himself, and races and cruises on Chesapeake Bay, near his home in Silver Springs, Maryland.

Naval architect **C. William Lapworth,** who wrote the chapter on cockpits, designed the famous Cal series of stock boats, among them the Cal 40 (one of the most successful ocean racers ever built as well as the first successful stock boat with a separated rudder), the Cal Cruising 46, and the Cal 39. The owner of his own 46-foot cruiser, which he sailed on the Pacific near his home in southern California before he moved to Virginia in 1986, Bill Lapworth has also raced and cruised extensively on the Atlantic, the Great Lakes, and the Caribbean.

Stanley Livingston, Jr., principal author of the chapter on emergency gear and co-author of the one on ground tackle, is chairman of the CCA Technical Committee and a former commodore of the CCA. A veteran of four transatlantic passages, he has also cruised extensively off the coasts of Africa, Europe, Canada, South America, Mexico, and the United States, often in his own boats, which have included a 39-foot Sparkman & Stephens sloop and a 50-foot Robb yawl. He was navigator of the 12-Meter *Weatherly* in the 1970 America's Cup trials. A manufacturing executive, he lives in Bristol, Rhode Island.

Author of the chapter on construction and commodore of the Cruising Club of America for 1986–87, **James A. McCurdy,** of the widely respected yacht design firm of McCurdy & Rhodes, has drawn the lines of many tough, fast offshore yachts—among them *Carina, Kahili II,* and several boats in the Hinckley line. A resident of Cold Spring Harbor, New York, he has chaired both the CCA's Bermuda Race Committee and the Measurement Handicap System Technical Committee of the United States Yacht Racing Union (USYRU).

Richard C. McCurdy, co-author of the chapters on capsize and instruments, is chairman of the USYRU's Safety at Sea Committee and a former CCA commodore. An engineer, he has long combined his professional talents and his love of sailing in work concerning sailing technology and theory, most recently in the area of safety and seamanship. Over a period of twenty-five years he cruised (and occasionally raced) along the Atlantic coast in his teak 52-foot yawl, *Mah Jong,* whose home port was Darien, Connecticut. He and Jim McCurdy are unrelated.

Co-author with Rod Stephens of the three chapters on rigging and sails, **Mitchell C. Gibbons-Neff** is sales manager of the yacht brokerage office of Sparkman & Stephens, Inc., in New York City, where he works closely with the firm's clients on equipping and rigging new and used boats. Though only in his mid-forties, Mitch Neff has accumulated tens of thousands of miles offshore in forty-one years of active sailing, including seventeen Bermuda Races and three transatlantic passages.

Wallace J. Stenhouse, Jr., who wrote the original draft of the chapter on the power plant, was World Ocean Racing Champion in 1972–74 in his 49-foot Sparkman & Stephens sloop *Aura.* Stenhouse, who lives in Chicago, has covered more than 25,000 miles offshore, including three transatlantic races, ten Bermuda Races, twenty St. Petersburg–Ft. Lauderdale Races, and twenty-seven Chicago-Mackinac Races.

Olin J. Stephens II, author of the chapters on design trends and stability, is probably the most successful and best-known yacht designer of the twentieth century. Among his products are many U.S. America's Cup defenders as well as a long list of successful offshore boats—among them *Dorade, Finisterre, Palawan, Dora IV,* three *Dyna*s, and a large number of popular stock boats, including many in the Swan and Tartan lines. After his retirement from Sparkman & Stephens, Inc. (which he co-founded in 1929, when he was twenty), he has lived in Putney, Vermont, where he has been developing computer programs for use by yacht designers. In 1965, Olin Stephens was awarded the Nathanael G. Herreshoff Award for contribution to sailing by the North American Yacht Racing Union.

Roderick Stephens, Jr., co-authored the three chapters on rigging and contributed to the chapter on ventilation. One of the world's authorities on yacht construction and rigging, and a partner of his brother, Olin, at Sparkman & Stephens, Inc., he for many years supervised the building of S&S-designed yachts all over the world. Along the way, he covered some 100,000 miles under sail, racing and cruising. In 1945, he was awarded a Medal of Freedom for his role in designing landing craft for use by allied invasion forces during World War II. Rod Stephens has served as commodore of the CCA.

To **Daniel D. Strohmeier,** author of the chapter on decks, belongs the unparalleled distinction of both winning the 1954 Bermuda Race and, twenty-four years later, finishing second in the 1978 race in the same boat, his 39-foot Concordia yawl *Malay,* home port South Dartmouth, Massachusetts. A graduate of M.I.T.'s department of naval architecture, he was for many years vice-president in charge of shipbuilding at Bethlehem Steel. He has cruised and raced widely for many years, and has served as president of the Society of Naval Architects and Marine Engineers and as a director of the Joint Committee on Safety from Capsizing.

As chairman of the CCA's Technical Committee, **Lynn A. Willliams** was the prime instigator of this book. Before his death in 1985, he oversaw its outline and wrote the chapter on cabins. In his long career he was at various times an inventor, a lawyer, a vice-president of the University of Chicago, and the first president of the Great Books Foundation. His sailing career was equally distinguished and varied. Based in Chicago, Illinois, he owned many yachts, small and large, and participated in dozens of Great Lakes races, fifteen Bermuda Races, and five transatlantic races (plus three return passages). His best-known boat was the 62-foot cutter *Dora IV,* which he commissioned from Sparkman & Stephens, and which, under his command and later as Ted Turner's *Tenacious* and Warren Brown's *War Baby,* has been one of the great dual-purpose boats of her time.

Thomas R. Young, who wrote the chapter on ventilation and co-wrote the chapter on instruments, has raced or cruised (often as navigator) over more than 100,000 miles of salt water on the Atlantic, the Pacific, the Mediterranean, and the Caribbean, often in his own two yachts named *Shearwater.* A chemical engineer who lives in Connecticut and Florida, Tom Young has served on the International Technical Committee of the Offshore Racing Council and the CCA's Bermuda Race Committee.

The Editor

John Rousmaniere has written or edited twelve books about sailing, among them *The Annapolis Book of Seamanship, The Golden Pastime: A New History of Yachting,* and *"Fastnet, Force 10,"* an account of the 1979 Fastnet Race gale, whose disasters helped stimulate much of the rethinking about trends in yacht design that is reported in these pages. He has made two transatlantic passages and a 2000-mile voyage from New England to the Azores, crewed in five Bermuda Races and the 1979 Fastnet Race, and raced and cruised in the Pacific, the Great Lakes, and Europe. He lives in Stamford, Connecticut.

PART I

HULL
DESIGN
AND
CONSTRUCTION

CHAPTER 1

Trends in Yacht Design, 1920–1986

Olin J. Stephens II

A yacht, I think, is any boat used for fun and providing accommodations for cruising. Since I first became acquainted with sailing some 60 years ago, I have seen several trends in the design of yachts, the most obvious of which is that there has been a big increase in the number afloat with a corresponding decrease in their size. But for a variety of reasons—mainly the effects of racing rules and of mass production—modern yachts also look very different, and are built in very different ways. The objective here is to consider some of these trends.

Toward the First Dual-Purpose Yachts

If one thing has remained constant over the years, it is that, then and now, the style has often been set by the current racing classes. In the 1920s, there were one-design racing classes of all sizes from the Star to the New York 40s and 50s (the numbers are their waterline length, which indicates how large many racing boats were then), which were designed by Nathanael Herreshoff (Figure 1-1). Herreshoff's Universal Rule was the most popular racing rule, with its heavy, narrow, long-ended sloops, and it was especially strong in Boston and Marblehead. But on Long Island Sound, where I sailed as a boy, that rule's popularity was nearing its end and the meter boats of the European International Rule were rapidly gaining acceptance, with 36-foot 6-Meters becoming popular "small" racing boats. Some of my first sailing was in the Sixes.

And yet to a cruising person's eye, there was little difference between the two rules. They both seemed to provide uncomfortable yachts for going to sea, with their narrow beam, skimpy accommodations, and combination of light hulls and deep lead keels, which made them fragile and pretty uncomfortable in rough water. As there were no standardized or "stock" cruising boats, anybody who wanted to go to sea had to commission a custom one-off cruising design. These boats tended to be beamier, heavier versions of racing designs. The only ones I remember as a type were designed mainly by B. B. Crowninshield of Boston. With their low freeboard and high cabin trunks and straight sheer, they did not appeal to me.

In the mid-twenties, when my family began looking for a moderately priced small cruising boat, our choice was between two different types of wooden hulls: a heavy and probably slow "proper" and comfortable cruising type, and a faster but cramped converted racing daysailer. My brother Rod and I liked to sail fast,

Figure 1-1. The Nat Herreshoff–designed 59-foot (LOA) New York 40 *Rugosa II* was typical of the converted day-racing boats that took part in early ocean races before the development of the dual-purpose cruiser. Converted from her original gaff sloop rig to a jib-headed yawl, she won the 1928 Bermuda Race. (Rosenfeld Collection, Mystic Seaport Museum, Inc., Mystic, CT)

and after trying several possibilities our interest in speed won out. My father bought a 30-foot (waterline) Crowninshield design of the Sound Schooner class, which had a racing hull and a small schooner rig for cruising. She was light and narrow, with a displacement-to-length ratio of just over 200 and a beam-to-waterline length ratio of .283. Her accommodations were limited, but she was a lovely boat to sail and fun without being extreme.

The Fishermen

Responding to the demand resulting from this limited choice between slow cruiser and uncomfortable racer, designers such as John Alden and William H. Hand developed the "fisherman" type of boat, which was the most distinctive and popular development in yacht design during the twenties (Figure 1-2). Of course, there were differences between individual boats as well as traits that they had in common.

These boats got their name from the sailing fishing fleet of New England, which had not yet died out. Like the working fishermen, they were schooners,

Figure 1-2. Very different from the converted racers like *Rugosa II* were the heavy fishermen schooners, the best of which were John Alden's *Malabar*s. The photograph is of *Malabar III,* the drawing and dimensions of the 58-foot fisherman *Malabar X,* winner of the 1932 Bermuda Race. (Photograph, Rosenfeld Collection, Mystic Seaport Museum, Inc., Mystic, CT)

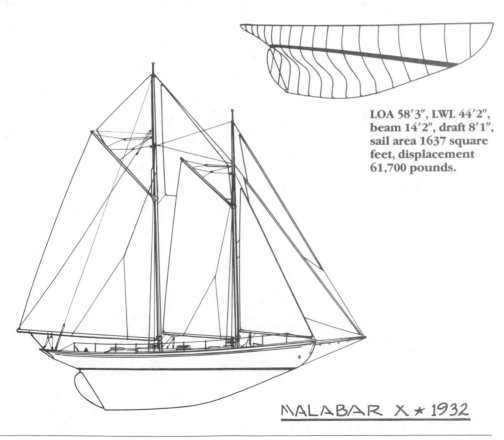

LOA 58′3″, LWL 44′2″, beam 14′2″, draft 8′1″, sail area 1637 square feet, displacement 61,700 pounds.

MALABAR X ★ 1932

they were finished plainly, they were roomy, and they were good boats to take to sea. Their great strength came from the use of plenty of wood. Frames were usually sawn, which required that the length of each piece had to be short in order to avoid cross-grain; the lengths were joined by overlapping side by side (called "doubling"). As the frames were heavy, they were not closely spaced, so rather sturdy planking was needed to bridge the span. This structure made for a heavy hull, and one that was relatively inexpensive. Unlike the racing boats, the fisherman schooner yachts found their stability not in deep, heavy ballast but in their wide beam. Their ballast was divided between an outside iron keel and concrete or iron in the bilge. Their generous beam provided room for comfortable accommodations and this, combined with the heavy hull and inside ballast, gave them an easy motion in a seaway. The fisherman-type yachts longer than about 40 feet were generally rigged as gaff-headed schooners. They had moderate freeboard amidships, which required trunk cabins for headroom below, and they had plenty of sheer, which was an advantage for offshore sailing, and it was good-looking.

Such boats should not have been fast, but the better fishermen—particularly John Alden's designs—not only behaved very well but also won a big share of the offshore and coastwise races that were gaining popularity after World War I. The Bermuda Race, revived by the Cruising Club of America, was only one of several long races for boats between about 35 and 70 feet long, and Alden's *Malabar*s did well. Interestingly, so did some converted Universal Rule boats, with their new tall jib-headed rigs. Alden fisherman schooners won the 1923 and 1926 Bermuda Races, while the yawl-rigged New York 40 *Memory* won in 1924. In 1928, I sailed on *Malabar IX* with John Alden, and I well remember how, in a light-air finish, another Forty, *Rugosa II,* showed up broad on our lee bow, which became our weather bow when the wind went to the southeast, giving her the race. So, although the racing type had the fundamentals of light hull structure and ample outside ballast (and the jib-headed rig), there was not all that much difference in performance between the two very different types, and everybody was entitled to form their own opinions.

The Schooner Niña

The 1929 stock market crash ended the wave of enthusiastic boat-building. The next decade was a relatively slow period that saw reactions to the fisherman type. Typifying this change was a boat that actually was built in 1928, *Niña,* which Starling Burgess designed for Paul Hammond (Figure 1-3). She had a tall staysail schooner rig and a rather light hull carrying a heavy lead keel. She won the 1928 Transatlantic Race to Spain in the last few miles on her windward sailing ability, and followed by winning the Fastnet Race in England later that summer. *Niña* showed clearly that a clean rig and a high ballast-to-displacement ratio, like those of Universal and International Rule day-racing yachts, could be successfully applied offshore.

But there is no such thing as a free lunch in yacht design and construction, and the detriments of this type of boat quickly surfaced. After her first great summer, *Niña* was bought by Bobby Somerset, the English owner of the pilot

Figure 1-3. Designed by Starling Burgess and built in 1928, the 59-foot jib-headed staysail schooner *Niña* had the deep keel and heavy ballast of the racing boats. *Niña* won the 1928 Transatlantic Race to Spain and 34 years later won the Bermuda Race. Burgess later designed three America's Cup defenders (on one of which, *Ranger,* he worked with Olin Stephens). (Rosenfeld Collection, Mystic Seaport Museum, Inc., Mystic, CT)

cutter *Jolie Brise* and commodore of the Royal Ocean Racing Club, who took her out from New York under winter conditions. Her quick motion and general wetness on deck and below prompted him to sell her soon after. Later, under DeCoursey Fales, *Niña* had a long and successful life, winning the Bermuda Race in 1962, 34 years after her first summer.

Early Rating Rules

Accompanying the reaction to the fisherman schooners was the development of rating rules in the 1930s. Searching for the good combination or compromise of characteristics has been the objective of rule-making committees, whether of the inshore or offshore variety, and it still seems worthwhile. This work has greatly influenced design.

In the early days, the boats generally came first and the rules followed. Owners had boats and made bets. The boat first to the finish line took the stakes. With larger fleets and smaller boats, however, handicapping became necessary. But how to handicap, and how much? Overall length was an early measure of speed, and it would still be fair if boats were alike in shape, construction, and sail area and different only in size. But if I like a boat that is long and slender and obviously fast, and if you, on the other hand, like more comfort, and if we both want to win, what do we do? A simple rule cannot give us both a fair chance. There are too many parameters influencing speed that must be accounted for in the rule, and if the balance between them is not almost perfect, people will find loopholes until eventually designs will show this or that feature and a certain trend or direction will turn up in boats built specifically to get the best rating out of a rating rule. So, in the end, I cannot build for speed or you for comfort. To win, we must study and build to the rule. Building to the rule has been a strong and growing trend that today has taken over the sport of ocean racing.

One opinion can be confidently voiced about rating rules: they have become more and more complicated. This is so for a number of good reasons, I believe. Going back, until about 1934 offshore rating rules on both sides of the ocean were pretty simple, taking into account only the parameters of length, beam, depth, and sail area—by far the most important speed-producing factors. Those rules did not measure stability, the next important factor. No boundaries were placed on proportions, which meant that the formula lacked perfect balance: one or another of the parameters could be exaggerated to produce a favorable rating but not a very good boat.

This fault in rating rules was identified about 1932 by Wells Lippincott of Chicago, who corrected it in the Lake Michigan Yacht Racing Association's new rule, of which he was the principal author. It incorporated a set of appropriate proportions adjusted for dimensions so that they applied reasonably well to all boats in the accepted size range. These proportions defined an "ideal" boat that was used as a base, penalized departures that were assumed to increase speed, and gave rating bonuses to features thought likely to slow the boat. Recognizing the merit of this new rule, the Cruising Club of America invited Lippincott to join its Rules Committee, and with minor changes the LMYA Rule became the CCA Rule, which was the major American rule until 1970, undergoing frequent modification over the years.

Formula and Measurement

A rating rule can be seen as consisting of two parts. The first part is its formula containing speed-producing and speed-reducing parameters. The second is the set of measurements of those parameters and the way that they are taken. This second area has a great influence on a boat's shape at or near the hull's measurement stations, or where the measurements are actually made by the measurer, since designers working to the rule may draw bumps or hollows simply to improve the rating and not to make a better boat. These small alterations can "fool the rule formula" into thinking that the hull is a different shape than it actually is and give it a lower rating. This second area is likely to give a rule committee as many headaches as the seemingly more important formula.

Another aspect of rule making that has greatly influenced trends in design is the question of freely changing or not changing the rule to close loopholes. This has been argued over the decades. The argument in favor of flexibility is that a change can control an excess in a feature before it gets serious (or dangerous). The argument against is that a winning boat represents an investment in time,

LOA 52', LWL 37'3", beam 10'3", draft 7'8", sail area 1150 square feet, displacement 37,800 pounds.

Figure 1-4. Olin Stephens' *Dorade* (photo on next page), designed in 1929 when he was only 20, brought the all-inboard rig and the narrow, well-ballasted, meter-boat-like hull to offshore sailing. Her racing record was superb; she also proved that a boat with a modern hull could be seaworthy as well as fast in the ocean. A comparison with the profile of *Malabar X* shows how original she was in both proportions and rig. She was quite narrow for her length, and Stephens soon began designing greater beam into his boats. (Photograph, Rosenfeld Collection, Mystic Seaport Museum, Inc., Mystic, CT)

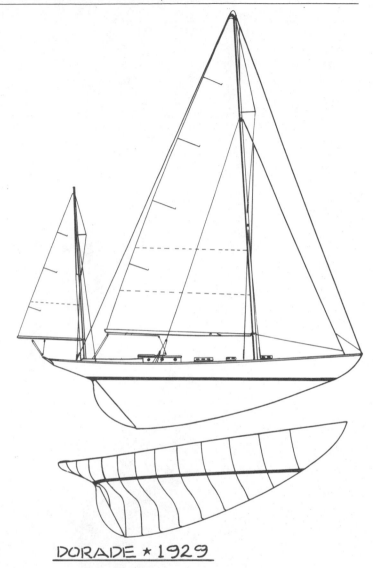

DORADE ★ 1929

effort, and money that may become wasted by a change in rating. After 1934, the CCA Rules Committee accepted the argument in favor of frequent change, the changes generally occurring in small increments.

Another influential rating rule in this early period was that of the Royal Ocean Racing Club, in England. The RORC Rule was tolerant of extremes in proportions except that, as the British have always liked narrow boats, the rule penalized wide beam, thereby encouraging deep, heavy keels to provide stability. In contrast, the CCA Rule encouraged generous beam, although a later development in the United States discouraging great stability tended to neutralize the beam bonus (as wide beam and initial stability often go hand in hand). Another aspect of the RORC Rule was that its method of measuring length virtually forced designers to

pinch the ends. Therefore, English and American ocean racers tended to have a very different look about them.

The Influence of Racing Success

Rating rules are not the only influence on racing-boat design. Racing success, luck, and weather conditions play a part, too. In 1931, our family boat *Dorade,* which I designed in 1929, won the Transatlantic Race by a big margin (Figure 1-4). She was (and remains) a good boat, but luck played a big part in our victory, for we sailed a completely different course from the rest of the fleet, approximating a Great Circle course to save a few hundred miles by staying far north in the area of icebergs in thick fog. With a win in the Fastnet Race that same summer, and again in 1933, *Dorade* along with *Niña* established the dominance of the racing-boat concept over the fisherman type and traditional boats like Bobby Somerset's pilot cutter *Jolie Brise. Dorade* was narrow—her beam was only 10 feet, 3 inches on an overall length of 52 feet—and had a deep lead keel and a modern all-inboard jib-headed yawl rig. In construction, she was lighter and more sophisticated than the fishermen, with hollow spruce masts and steam-bent white oak frames on close 9-inch centers.

Before long, the *Niña/Dorade* influence was spreading through the offshore fleet, although compelled by considerations of speed as well as space and rating, many boats had more beam than *Dorade.* Participation in offshore racing grew, as did a trend toward building boats whose main use would be for racing, not cruising. The yawl and cutter rigs and racing-yacht construction provided the basic pattern in the late thirties until World War II cut off development. As an indication of one of these trends, while sixteen of the twenty-five entries in the 1928 Bermuda Race were schooners, there were only seven boats of that rig among the thirty-eight starters in the 1938 race (Figures 1-5, 1-6, 1-7, and 1-8).

The Centerboarders of the 1950s

During World War II, the service of many new yachts in the Coast Guard's offshore patrol, watching for submarines in all types of weather, proved the seaworthiness of the newer type. Racing picked up promptly with peace, but new construction was slow until the early 1950s, when it came on with a rush.

The big trend in the next period was the enthusiasm for centerboarders. Relaxing after their years of war duty, many sailors headed south for winter vacations in Florida and the Bahamas, where the water is a little thin for deep keels. Several boats of the late thirties had shown that the moderate draft and wide beam needed for a centerboarder's stability were compatible with a fair turn of speed as well as roominess and comfort. Experience showed that these boats could get from here to there just as fast as their deeper sisters.

Rating Benefits

About here, the CCA Rule came into play to encourage the centerboard type. Because of the importance of stability in producing speed—a stiff boat gets more drive out of its rig than a tender one—the rule offered a bonus to boats that, with a low ratio of ballast to displacement, were assumed (wrongly?) to be tender.

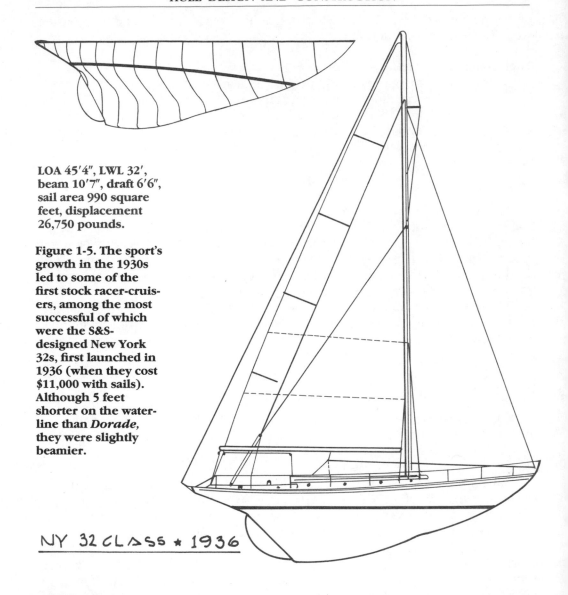

LOA 45'4", LWL 32',
beam 10'7", draft 6'6",
sail area 990 square
feet, displacement
26,750 pounds.

Figure 1-5. The sport's
growth in the 1930s
led to some of the
first stock racer-cruis-
ers, among the most
successful of which
were the S&S-
designed New York
32s, first launched in
1936 (when they cost
$11,000 with sails).
Although 5 feet
shorter on the water-
line than *Dorade*,
they were slightly
beamier.

NY 32 CLASS ★ 1936

Now, a centerboarder presents the designer with two inherent construction
problems: not only does the centerboard slot split the hull down the middle,
reducing much-needed support across its wide beam, but the shallow hull limits
the space available for the 'thwartships strengthening that this split requires.
Frequently, the best solution seems to be found in the use of metal, either galvanized steel or bronze, for the centerboard trunk, mast step, and floor timbers,
which are transverse members tying together the heels of the frames. Being
heavy and low down in the boat, all these structural members are actually effective ballast. But they are not ballast in a technical sense, and they were not so

LOA 72′, LWL 50′, beam 14′, draft 9′6″, sail area 2342 square feet, displacement 88,130 pounds.

Figure 1-6. The *Dorade* model inspired a new generation of offshore yachts like the 72-foot yawl *Baruna,* whose plans are shown here, and her near-sister *Bolero,* seen in the photograph at her launching in 1949. The reflections on *Bolero*'s black hull highlight a power, symmetry, and fairness rarely seen in the IOR racers of the 1980s, with their flat, light, wedge-shaped hulls and bumps at measurement points to provide better ratings. (Photograph, Rosenfeld Collection, Mystic Seaport Museum, Inc., Mystic, CT)

BARUNA ★ 1938

LOA 38'7", LWL 27'6", beam 11'3", sail area 713 square feet, displacement 22,330 pounds.

Figure 1-7. Carleton Mitchell's S&S centerboard yawl *Finisterre* holds the remarkable record of having won three straight Newport to Bermuda Races, in 1956, 1958, and 1960. She led a movement toward beamy, roomy centerboarders, many of them successful stock fiberglass racer-cruisers. She is 1 foot wider than the much larger *Dorade*. Her displacement is enormous compared with racer-cruisers built in the seventies and eighties—perhaps twice that of a 1986-vintage IOR boat of the same length. (Photograph, Rosenfeld Collection, Mystic Seaport Museum, Inc., Mystic, CT)

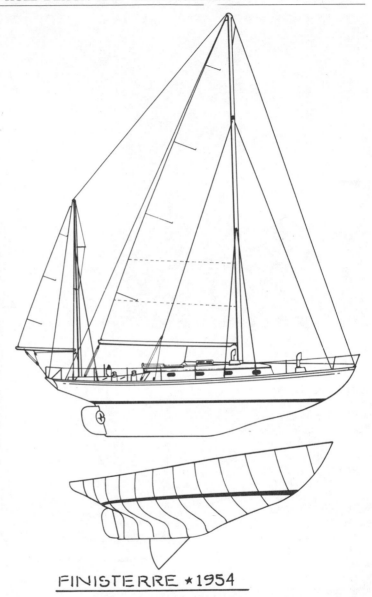

FINISTERRE ★1954

considered by the CCA Rule, and these centerboarders had low ratings. (Incidentally, this structural problem is much less acute with fiberglass or composite hulls.)

To anticipate slightly, this loophole in the rule was later closed, but only after a good deal of talk and study. It turned out to be difficult to define "ballast" fairly, so a technical solution was found in the inclining test. This is a method of locating a boat's center of gravity, and thus determining its stability, by heeling the boat in calm conditions and taking careful measurements. Because of the importance of the effect of stability on speed, this way of determining stability was in

due course substituted for the ballast-to-displacement ratio in the CCA Rule, ending the advantage of low ratings enjoyed by most centerboarders. Inclining is now routinely carried out by measurers under most rules.

One of the best known of these centerboarders was Carleton Mitchell's *Finisterre,* a Sparkman & Stephens design that won the CCA Bermuda Race three times running, in 1956, 1958, and 1960. I think it was primarily her low rating, second her excellent handling, and third her ability in strong winds that brought her through so successfully. It was her luck not to encounter much light weather, which is the bugaboo of this type because the ratio of sail area to wetted surface is so low. With a beam of 11 feet, 3 inches on a waterline length of 27 feet, 6 inches, *Finisterre* was a wide boat for her day. Many modern racing boats of that length are beamier, but have less than one-half her designed displacement of 22,300 pounds.

Modern Trends

The other, more lasting, trend of the postwar period was the development of glass-reinforced plastic (GRP)—or fiberglass—construction, which allowed for many more stock, standardized boats than wood could have. The advantages in relatively low initial cost and reduced maintenance expenses are significant, and fleets have grown beyond anything that I could have foreseen. For custom boats, welded aluminum construction provided long life, strength, and easy maintenance. By the mid-1980s, both stock and custom boats have come to be constructed of composites, including space-age materials such as Kevlar and carbon fiber, which provide great strength at a low cost in weight.

The Least Common Denominator

What has influenced the shape of the new fiberglass stock boats? In a word, the biggest influence has been what the builder (entrepreneur) and the designer (adviser) think will *sell.* There are many possibilities, but the direction tends toward the least common denominator: what will appeal to the widest possible audience of potential buyers. One reason for this is that, while a fiberglass stock boat may be relatively inexpensive to build in large numbers, the tooling—plugs and molds—needed to begin construction is costly. Unless the product can be sold in quantity, it can't be produced economically, if at all. So the design must please the many and offend the few.

Fortunately, there are a sufficient number of potential buyers to widen the spectrum, at least moderately. Choices are out there, but behind most standardized boats is the wish to please the whole family at dockside or on the showroom floor, rather than on open water. Since fiberglass construction requires thinner structural members than wooden construction, these boats have more room than the old ones. But in their effort to offer as much as possible with too little appreciation of general seagoing comfort, designers and builders tend to crowd the accommodations with too many berths.

The Separate Rudder

The separation of the rudder from the keel was one of the most radical changes

Figure 1-8. Among the successful designers of offshore racing-cruising yachts in the period of the CCA rating rule were Olin Stephens, Philip Rhodes, Aage Nielsen, and C. Raymond Hunt. In 1938 Hunt drew the lines for the Concordia yawls, which crossed oceans and won races well into the 1970s. This is the Concordia *Malay,* winner of the 1954 Bermuda Race and second in the 1978 race. She has been owned for many years by Daniel Strohmeier, author of the chapter on decks in this book. (Rosenfeld Collection, Mystic Seaport Museum, Inc., Mystic, CT)

to be found in the development of yacht design during the late sixties and early seventies, at the beginning of the IOR. Today, virtually all racing boats and a large proportion of cruising boats have this feature, although it remains slightly controversial as a feature on seagoing boats (Figure 1-9).

The separate rudder has a long history. It was widely used around the turn of the century, and for many years was familiar to us all through its use on the Star Class one-design. For whatever reason (evidently not a very good one), it was out of favor on larger boats from about 1905 to the late 1960s, although it was used on many New Zealand boats. Bill Lapworth, a yacht designer from California, pioneered the feature's return to favor in America with his highly successful Cal 40 racer-cruiser sloop. Dick Carter put a separated rudder on his *Rabbit,* which won the 1965 Fastnet Race, and our office took it up, with a trim tab as well, in the 12-Meter *Intrepid* in 1967. Before long, it was seen on many racing-cruising boats.

LOA 58', LWL 40', beam 12'5", draft 8'1", sail area 1316 square feet, displacement 46,060 pounds.

Figure 1-9. The combination of separated rudder and fin keel was the major innovation of the sixties. Developed first by Nat Herreshoff in the 1890s, it did not become popular until yacht designers Bill Lapworth and Dick Carter put it on their racer-cruisers. One of the first big boats to use it successfully was the S&S-designed *Palawan III,* **launched in 1966. A comparison of her dimensions with** *Dorade*'s **is suggestive. Slightly longer on the waterline, the more recent boat is much wider and lighter.**

PALAWAN III ★ 1966

The pros and cons of the separate rudder for offshore sailing will come out in Karl Kirkman's discussion of steering control in Chapter 5. However, as an active participant in the development of the feature, I must briefly comment on it.

In the context of speed, it has two real advantages over a long keel and attached rudder. First, it has less wetted surface, which means a faster boat, especially at lower speeds—for example, when sailing to windward in light weather. Second, a short fin keel with a high aspect ratio has less "induced drag," which is the drag resulting from the side force resisted by the keel.

More problematical is the effect on steering. The shorter keel is clearly conducive to quicker turning and the placing of more weight on the rudder, which combine to make it hard to hold a steady course and to self-steer. Separate rudders have also been all too prone to breaking off. I mention these problems in an attempt at objectivity, as I believe that there are very few requirements for strength or good steering that cannot be met by a well-designed boat with a separated keel and rudder.

Rating Rules

If the advent of fiberglass construction has brought a new factor to cruising-yacht design, one old wrinkle remains. There is still a tendency to adapt the characteristics of racing boats to the design and construction of cruising boats, whether or not the boat is intended for racing. Probably this is due to a fear of building a boat that looks different from other boats. This approach may be justified if, in fact, the design is a good compromise that has some racing potential as well as cruising amenities. For example, while centerboarders such as *Finisterre* had sufficient room and displacement for good accommodations, extreme light-displacement boats like those that became popular and successful for day and overnight racing in the late 1970s and 1980s do not readily accept the weight of decent cruising interiors without detriment to their sailing performance.

Ideally, the people who write and enforce the rating rules should take such compromises into account. They often do, but under some rating rules it is almost impossible to build a boat that can both win and meet cruising requirements. To editorialize, I think that form should follow the true function rather than some imagined version of function.

There were plenty of racing-boat models, as offshore racing increasingly became an international sport that was thoroughly covered in the yachting magazines. The Bermuda, Fastnet, Sydney-Hobart, Transatlantic, Honolulu, and other big races received many foreign entries despite the fact that different rules were used to rate them. A narrow, deep-ballasted English boat was at a severe disadvantage if she entered the CCA's Bermuda Race, whose rule tended to encourage wide beam and a low ballast-to-displacement ratio. And a typical CCA Rule American yacht participating in the Admiral's Cup in England found herself on the opposite side of the coin.

The Coming of the IOR

At the same time, dissatisfaction with the existing rules was growing in both the CCA and the RORC. In the mid-1960s negotiations to develop an international rating rule were under way. After some international and interclub maneuvering, an International Offshore Rating Council was formed to project a new rule with the potential for worldwide use. The International Technical Committee, which I chaired, was appointed to work out a new rule that would combine the existing CCA and RORC rules. Without going into detail, I can report that the task was not easy. The main effort was to eliminate old problems, especially the difficulty of measuring length and displacement under the CCA Rule and loopholes surrounding hull weight and scantlings under the RORC Rule. A One-Ton Cup sailed under the RORC Rule in the sixties was won by a Sparkman & Stephens–designed boat with a heavy steel deck and a very heavy engine. I didn't know that the owner had made these changes to our design to help his rating, but they were what the rule was asking for. It was a disgrace to the rule.

In the end, the new International Offshore Rule (IOR) combined most provisions of the RORC hull measurements with sail area measurements right out of the CCA Rule. Scantlings and stability were then, and remain still, very difficult to handle. We provided a center-of-gravity factor (CGF) to discourage excessively deep, heavy ballast. I am disappointed to realize that the CGF has worked opposite to what we intended. It now seems to encourage ballast so high that many boats have inadequate stability. This problem is now recognized (and discussed at length in Chapters 2, 3, and 4) and should be corrected. Despite this and other faults, since its inception in 1970 the IOR has been a powerful influence on international offshore sailing and the design of many cruising boats. It has also led to developments in construction using aluminum and exotic materials that have been passed on to designers and owners of cruising boats (Figure 1-10).

The new rule played a big part in bringing level class racing to offshore boats.

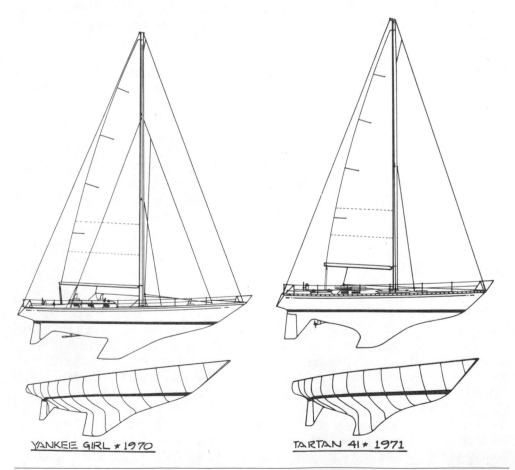

YANKEE GIRL ★ 1970   TARTAN 41 ★ 1971

Just as the IOR was taking form, the French sponsors of the One-Ton Cup assigned it for competition among boats rating 22 feet or lower under the RORC Rule. Later, an IOR rating of 27.5 was used, and participants usually were 34–38 feet long. Growing interest in level racing prompted the formation of a total of five level rating classes, from Mini Ton (16.5 feet) to One Ton (now 30.5 feet). Their world championships consist of two day races, one overnight race, and one long offshore race. This close, intense competition has had a great influence on yacht design because, while its short races strongly emphasize sheer boat speed over navigation, weather, and luck, the long race requires some degree of livability below (though not necessarily comfort). Still, few owners have used their level-rating boats for the dual purpose of racing and cruising.

The IOR was intended to foster international racing, and so it has. However, the intensity of this racing and certain characteristics encouraged by the rule have led to boats designed specifically to the rule. The goal is success in out-and-out competition rather than to come up with the kind of dual-purpose racer-cruisers that were popular before about 1970. The typical IOR boat is fast, fun to sail, and potentially roomy, due to its generous beam. But it has a large rig on a

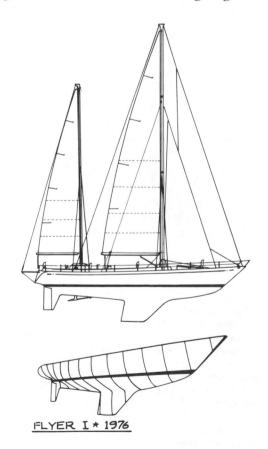

Figure 1-10. With time and the International Offshore Rule, separated rudders moved aft, keels deepened and became smaller, beams widened, and displacement decreased. Here are three IOR boats designed by S&S between 1970 and 1976.

(Left) *Yankee Girl* makes an interesting comparison with *Palawan III* and *Dorade.*LOA 55′8″, LWL 40′, beam 14′4″, draft 8′4″, sail area 1750 square feet, displacement 37,000 pounds.

(Center) The Tartan 41 was one of the most popular stock racer-cruisers of the mid-seventies; compare her dimensions with those of the New York 32 and *Finisterre.*LOA 40′8″, LWL 32′5″, beam 12′3″, draft 6′4″, sail area 725 square feet, displacement 17,850 pounds.

(Right) With her severely cutaway underbody, *Flyer* won the 1977–78 Whitbread Round the World Race. Though having almost the identical LWL as *Baruna,* she has about two-thirds her displacement.LOA 65′2″, LWL 49′9″, beam 16′4″, draft 10′, sail area 1827 square feet, displacement 55,300 pounds.

FLYER I ★ 1976

rather light hull, with a stability so limited that the typical boat must carry a big crew on the weather rail to keep it on its feet. Some smaller IOR boats may not be comfortable or even safe in heavy weather—a fact reflected in the 1980s by the diminishing popularity of long offshore races and the simultaneous burgeoning of short races. Many students of the rule, myself included, hope that further action will be taken to make these boats more stable for offshore racing and cruising (Figure 1-11).

The Development of the IMS

Concerns about one international rule for serious ocean racing have for many years been paralleled by interest in an alternative rule tailored to better suit the dual-purpose type of boat that an owner will feel good about taking on a cruise after a race. Even as the IOR fleet was growing during the 1970s, many people felt that a scientific, quantitatively directed approach to measuring could lead to a better balanced rating rule, which might spawn more and better all-round boats.

In a paper presented in Holland, Professor J. Nicholas Newman of the Massachusetts Institute of Technology suggested a method for meeting the aim. Afterward, H. Irving Pratt and other offshore sailors, many of them members of the CCA, subscribed to a fund to support studies by Nick Newman and his colleague at M.I.T., Jake Kerwin. Both are active sailors as well as naval architects and hydrodynamicists. Making the most of model testing and computer studies, they wrote a series of reports that, first, outlined a method of predicting a boat's speed for different points of sail and wind speeds from her lines and sail plan, and, second, established time allowances from those predictions. A device was developed for taking lines directly from the hull, thereby circumventing the bumps and hollows at IOR measurement stations.

The technical and political problems that this project overcame are too many to cover here. Fortunately, after Irving Pratt's death sufficient interest and support were maintained under the leadership of the late Lynn A. Williams, leading to a rule called the Measurement Handicap System (MHS). Under the aegis of the United States Yacht Racing Union, use of the MHS has spread, while technical problems are addressed by a committee chaired by Jim McCurdy. Although there was a period when feelings ran rather high between advocates of the two rules,

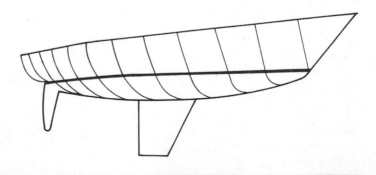

Figure 1-11. *Challenge,* **an S&S IOR ocean-racing boat from the early eighties, reflects the trend toward small keels and extremely beamy, light, shallow, flat-bottomed, dinghy-like hulls inspired by the IOR and fierce international competition.**

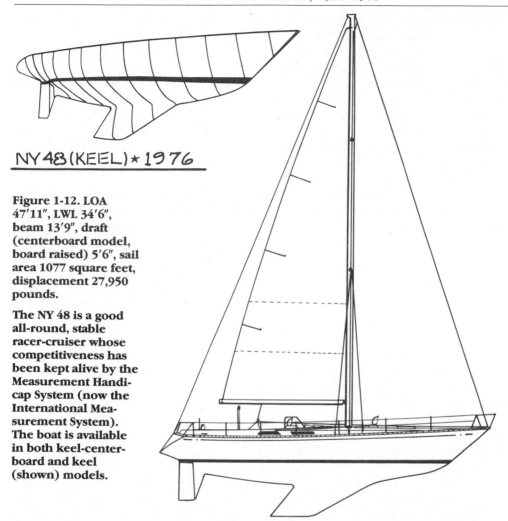

NY 48 (KEEL) ★ 1976

Figure 1-12. LOA 47′11″, LWL 34′6″, beam 13′9″, draft (centerboard model, board raised) 5′6″, sail area 1077 square feet, displacement 27,950 pounds.

The NY 48 is a good all-round, stable racer-cruiser whose competitiveness has been kept alive by the Measurement Handicap System (now the International Measurement System). The boat is available in both keel-centerboard and keel (shown) models.

now it seems to me that recognition is growing that each one can fill a need—the IOR for all-out racing boats, and the MHS for dual-purpose boats. For example, the CCA Bermuda Race now has IOR and MHS divisions. In late 1985, the Offshore Racing Council adopted the MHS as a second international rating rule alongside the IOR and renamed it the International Measurement System (IMS). Like the IOR, the IMS is administered by the International Technical Committee, which has been augmented by a group of members of the MHS technical committee.

While the IOR has been what is called a "type-forming" rule, producing a specific type of boat to the point that all IOR boats on a starting line look alike, the IMS gives promise of being more type neutral. Both IOR and late CCA Rule boats have done well in IMS races. Thus each fulfills its purpose. If the IOR boats were not so alike, the racing would not be so close. However, the question remains whether, without type forming, racing can be as good. My personal opinion is that, while the IMS speed predictions are remarkably good, turning them into time allowances and race results is difficult. More work should probably be done in that area (Figure 1-12).

In addition to these two measurement rules, there is a system called the Performance Handicap Rating Fleet (PHRF), in which handicaps are assigned by committees based on observed performance. Simple and inexpensive to administer (though not without its controversies), the PHRF is widely used in the United States for racing between cruising boats of different ages and designs.

Summary

There is today great diversity among small and large cruising yachts. Sailors frequently are individualists, as a yacht designer should know, and a visit to one of the ports that serve the long-range cruising fraternity is convincing evidence of the variety that exists. It is another certainty that cruising in deep water, for so many a dream, is not just a dream. Round-the-world voyages have become virtually commonplace, and in smaller and smaller boats. Fortunately, the sea is often kind, but it can be rough and cruel. The trend toward smallness must have a limit set by strength and stability, as will be discussed in later chapters. This limit should be pondered by all those going down to the sea in small vessels.

An essay on trends in yacht design should not fail to mention the multihull type, whose growth in numbers has been great. In this area I do not pretend to be an objective observer. The number of successful long voyages proves that multihulls can take you from here to there, and quickly, but any detailed comments on those boats would part company with the subject of this chapter.

The big trends have been toward greatly increased numbers of boats of reduced size; toward standardization through the use of fiberglass construction; and toward the separated keel and rudder. Multihulls and a great variety of small boats have gone into deep water. Offshore racing has grown, and, while leading to some questionable design trends, has to some extent become inshore racing. International competition has been active, but not unaccompanied by controversy.

Which all reminds me of one of the most important and innovative trends of the period covered in this chapter—the invention and growth of the sailboard, one of the most enjoyable of all boats. With all the activity, problems, and controversy, what we still find in sailing today, the popularity of the sailboard tells us that sailing is a lot of *fun*. And that is how it has been during my lifetime in boats, from the 1920s to the 1980s.

CHAPTER 2

Some Thoughts on Stability

Olin J. Stephens II

T he stability of many of today's yachts seems marginal, at best, especially in terms of range, although ample stability is an ideal characteristic in terms of speed, comfort, and safety. Most of us dislike a tender boat. Today, however, losses of boats over the last few years (most notably in the 1979 Fastnet Race) have forcefully drawn attention not only to the discomfort of sailing at a wide angle of heel but directly to the danger of tender boats, particularly those lacking a positive range of stability adequate to avoid capsize. Following on the heels of Chapter 1's historical survey of yacht design trends since the 1920s I think it is appropriate to consider some of the background of a very recent problem that can be summarized succinctly in these words:

> Some modern ocean racers, and the cruising boats derived from them, are dangerous to their crews.

In this chapter, I will touch on the nature of that danger and make some general comments about yacht stability. In Chapters 3 and 4, Karl Kirkman and Richard McCurdy will look at stability quantitatively and directly as it applies to the capsize problem and the kind of stability that is needed for reasonable safety. In Chapter 5, Kirkman will explore another kind of stability, the lack of which is a problem in many modern boats—poor directional stability coupled with lack of control.

First, some reflections. Growing up in the second generation of offshore racing and cruising, between 1920 and 1940, I had complete confidence in the ability of the normal boat to resist capsize and, more broadly, given good construction and proper handling, in its complete safety at sea. Many people did not share that faith, and there was considerable criticism in the twenties when the Cruising Club of America and the British Ocean Racing Club began to sponsor offshore races for boats smaller than about 70 feet, such as the Bermuda, Fastnet, and Transatlantic Races. It was in those races that my generation got their first taste of going to sea in small boats, and those races spawned the development and improvement of fast, seaworthy, easily handled yachts for long-distance cruising and ocean racing.

In those pioneering days, I avidly read *Yachting, Rudder,* the English *Yachting World,* and *Motor Boat* (despite its name a good sailing magazine). I followed the writings of Herb Stone, Sam Wetherill, Bill Nutting (the CCA's founder), Billy Atkin, and Jack Hanna. My bible was Claud Worth's book *Yacht Cruising.* Although these names may not be familiar to modern readers, each in his way was dedicated to advancing offshore cruising and racing at a time when the sport was very new and widely considered to be dangerous, and each preached the suitability of taking small boats to sea. (By *small,* they meant boats with waterline lengths of 40 to 50 feet; widespread offshore sailing in boats smaller than 40 feet on the waterline did not become popular until after World War II.) They debated the pros and cons of different designs and rigs—for example, the traditional gaff rig versus the new jib-headed or Marconi rig, the rugged fisherman-type schooners versus the prewar racing boats like Bob Bavier's converted New York 40 *Memory,* and long overhangs versus short ends.

Regardless of their shape, most of these early offshore yachts were thought of as good sea boats, and rightly so. Still, there were some near losses and losses. Most notably, in 1924 Bill Nutting disappeared off Greenland in an old-fashioned Colin Archer lifeboat-type cutter. Some losses had no known cause, since in those days there was no practical shipboard radio, but in the disasters whose causes were known, inadequate stability seemed to be the main culprit: the boats could not carry sufficient sail to claw to windward away from a lee shore. This poor stability was partially due to large amounts of inside ballast, which brought the center of gravity too high. Since those days, I have never liked more than a minimal amount of inside ballast, preferring to put as much ballast as possible in the keel to provide more righting moment.

However, the losses were few, and there were virtually none in offshore racing, which was fast becoming popular in the twenties. The competing boats were considered to be seaworthy, and the results confirmed that view. When

Figure 2-1. Her crew having abandoned her for a life raft and her mast badly kinked, a casualty of the 1979 Fastnet Race gale rolls in the left-over sea. (Royal Navy)

offshore, if I had any worries, they were about potential leaks and not the possibility of capsize. It was an article of faith that ballasted sailing boats did not capsize, however much they might heel.

The Fastnet Shock

Despite some criticisms, that confidence in the soundness of offshore boats held true until 1979, when I was suddenly shaken by reports from the unfortunate Fastnet Race, where fifteen sailors died, five boats sank, twenty-four boats were abandoned, and more than one-third of the entries suffered 180-degree rollovers (Figure 2-1). Although the storm was severe, this was by no means the first time that bad weather had struck a race. Here, as before, larger and more solidly built boats came through. That shocking incident made it clear that a change had occurred in the offshore fleet. We learned, for example, that, among the smaller boats, those built before about 1975 survived with few problems, while many new boats suffered badly. The 1979 Fastnet storm drew attention to other scattered losses, study of which confirmed worries about the character of the racing fleet (and the cruising fleet modeled on it). Something had changed.

Later statistical analysis told us how much things had changed. Boats everywhere were becoming lighter, beamier, and less stable. Figures 2-3, 2-4, and 2-5 show the results of analysis of a sample of ocean racers rated under the Measurement Handicap System (now the International Measurement System).

Stability

Before we consider the figures, a brief discussion of the term "stability" as used here may be in order.

Most often stability is taken to describe the difference between a "stiff" boat and one that is "tender." This has to do with the combination of hull stability, or righting moment, and the heeling moment applied by the rig and dependent on sail area and rig height. The boat will be stiff or tender depending on the relative power, on the one hand, of the hull in providing righting moment and, on the other, of the rig as it may provide heeling moment. Under steady conditions, the two moments must be equal and opposite in direction. The righting moment may be shown on a curve that, at small angles, increases in proportion to heel and, depending largely on the ratio of beam to depth and the height of the center of gravity, drops away from that line as the rail approaches the water. After reaching a maximum the curve normally returns to zero at an angle, usually between 90 and 160 degrees, which marks the "range of positive stability" (Figure 2-2). The curve usually reaches a maximum negative stability point at 180 degrees, indicating the strength of resistance to re-righting. If the heeling and righting moments are to balance, the heel angle will normally increase with increasing wind strength until the heeling moment equals the righting moment, unless the heeling force is so great as to heel the boat beyond the point of maximum righting moment, when capsize will occur unless the heeling moment is rapidly reduced by spilling the wind. Questions of inertia have some influence dynamically; these will be discussed later.

Designers often use a measure of stability known as a "Dellenbaugh coeffi-

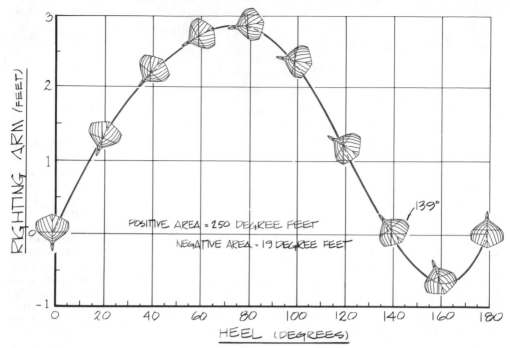

Figure 2-2. An illustration of the term "positive range of stability" using the racer-cruiser *Running Tide* as an example. Her stability range is 139 degrees, which means that she is able to recover from any knockdown so long as her angle of heel is 139 degrees or less. After that, she will keep on going and capsize.

cient" to define the heel angle under sail. This is essentially the righting moment per degree divided by the product of the sail area, the height of its center of effort, and an assumed wind pressure per square foot (usually 1 pound). The result, expressed as heel angle, is a useful index for the measurement of that aspect of stability that depends on the design of the rig. It should be clear that this angle does not, in itself, measure hull stability except in relation to the sail plan.

In what follows the role of the rig will be small. Primary consideration will be given to the hull. A boat's tenderness or stiffness has a great deal to do with its rig, but its stability lies primarily in the hull and is measured by its righting moment as it changes with heel angle. At a given angle the righting moment depends on the product of the displacement (weight) and the horizontal arm or offset between the centers of gravity and buoyancy. By inclining a boat, normally a part of rating-rule measurement, the righting moment is measured and expressed as that value per degree which, as mentioned above, holds through small angles and becomes smaller with increasing heel.

Figure 2-3 compares three factors: the year of construction (horizontal axis), the waterline length (diagonal axis), and the ratio of displacement to length cubed (vertical axis). The higher the asterisk, the heavier the boat is for her length. Note that, with few exceptions, boats—both large and small—became increasingly lighter in the seventies and eighties. Next, consider how this lighter displacement reduces stability.

Figure 2-4 compares displacement-to-length ratio (vertical axis) with the ratio of maximum beam to hull depth (horizontal axis). It shows that as boats become lighter they become wider and flatter, much like sailing dinghies such as the

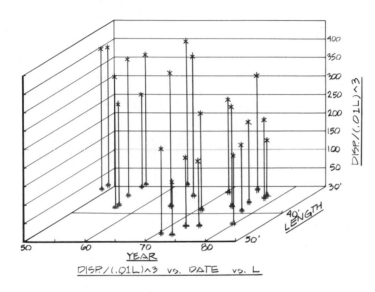

DISP./(.01L)^3 vs. DATE vs. L

Figure 2-3. This drawing compares three factors of a sample of racer-cruisers: year of construction (horizontal axis); LWL (diagonal axis); and displacement-to-length ratio (vertical axis). The data indicate that older boats tend to be heavier for their length than more recent boats.

Figure 2-4. A two-factor analysis comparing beam-to-depth ratio (horizontal axis) and displacement-to-length ratio (vertical axis), using the same boats as in Figure 2-3. It indicates that relatively wide beam tends to go with relatively light displacement.

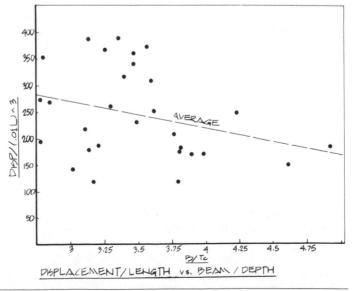

DISPLACEMENT/LENGTH vs. BEAM/DEPTH

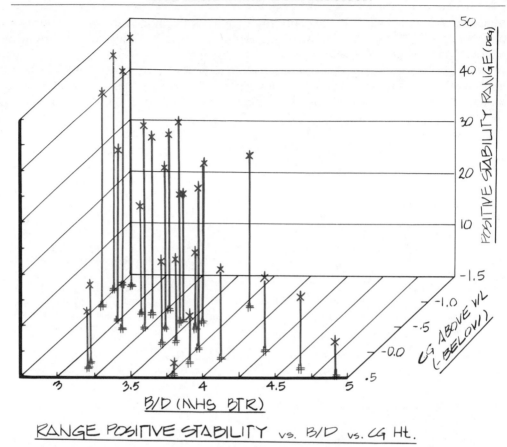

RANGE POSITIVE STABILITY vs. B/D vs. CG Ht.

Figure 2-5. Another three-factor analysis, using the same fleet of boats, this drawing compares beam-to-depth ratio (horizontal axis), the height of the center of gravity above or below the waterline (diagonal axis), and the range of positive stability over 100 degrees (vertical axis). The plot suggests that relatively narrow boats—ones toward the left end of the horizontal plane—tend to have centers of gravity below the waterline and thus higher ranges of positive stability. By combining these results with those of the other two analyses, one can make some generalizations about the effect on stability of trends in yacht design since the 1950s: more recent boats tend to be beamier and shallower, displace less, have higher centers of gravity, and have lower ranges of positive stability.

International 14 and Thistle. These proportions result from the need to maintain initial stability (stability at small heel angles) as weight is reduced, but the range of positive stability is sacrificed in the process by this hull geometry.

Figure 2-5 shows this effect as the characteristics are combined. The beam-to-depth ratio (horizontal axis), the vertical location of the center of gravity (diagonal axis), and the range of positive stability (vertical axis) are plotted. It is clear that both a greater beam-to-depth ratio and a higher center of gravity reduce the stability range.

Unfortunately, the range-enhancing factors—narrow beam relative to depth, heavy displacement, and low center of gravity—are all against recent trends, which have been accepted partly for reasons of speed, but also for rating advantage under the International Offshore Rule (IOR). During the period covered by the figures, there is a marked reduction in the typical boat's range of stability, which is a serious defect.

Righting Moment

As already mentioned, the conventional measure of hull stability is the righting moment. It measures resistance to heeling in foot-pounds. The righting moment can be measured by inclining, or heeling, the boat, usually by some form of shifting weight, and measuring the angle resulting from the application of a known moment. Most new boats are inclined to check the designer's calculations, as are all boats measured under either the IOR or the IMS. If the righting moment is known and the lines are available, the position of the center of gravity can be located, and a complete curve of the righting arms (the horizontal offset between the centers of gravity and buoyancy) can be plotted. The way this plot indicates the range of stability was outlined above.

Freeboard is an important design characteristic because it affects stability. It has several offsetting effects. Typically, high freeboard accompanies light displacement, because it provides living room below. With wide beam it keeps the lee rail out of water and thus allows a greater angle of heel before stability begins to fall off. Yet an excess of freeboard has the dual effect of raising the center of gravity excessively and adding to windage, thereby impairing windward performance.

Kinds of Stability

We know that the modern beamy, shoal-bodied boat has great initial stability, but it drops away. Older boats with relatively narrow, deep hulls will heel easily, showing modest initial stability, yet their ultimate resistance to capsize is greater than the beamy type. This is due to their greater range of positive stability. A good offshore boat must have a good range. This is insurance against remaining inverted should capsize occur under extreme conditions. This wide range of stability is inherent in the form (low ratio of beam to depth and low center of gravity) that best holds an increasing righting arm with increasing heel angle.

The contrast between this type and the light beamy type is great. The latter type loses stability much more drastically as the rail goes under, and the heel angle increases, as Figure 2-5 illustrates. Smaller boats of this sort have to depend on crew weight to carry their sail and remain upright. In this they are like the racing dinghies on whose hulls they are modeled. Those which are extreme capsize much more easily than the narrower, heavier type, and if inverted they are much more stubborn in staying there. Thus, extremes of the three relationships (low displacement-to-length ratio, high beam-to-depth ratio, and high center of gravity) are to be avoided.

Stability's Benefits

How does stability generally affect the performance and general usefulness of a boat? The Fastnet experience gives an important if partial answer: lacking stability range, the boat may capsize. The ultimate stability failure is that, once capsized, the boat cannot right itself. Chapters 3 and 4 discuss these problems in considerable detail. We do not need to stress further the danger of a design characteristic that limits stability range. So we will look at some general considerations.

First of all, ample stability, in providing a stiff boat, surely contributes to crew comfort. A boat that sails on her side is not a comfortable home at sea. Even worse is one—like many racing boats of the eighties—that requires her crew to sit on the weather rail to keep her going (Figure 2-6). All hands should be able to move about the boat to do ship's chores or to be comfortable.

Figure 2-6. This photograph shows three dubious characteristics of boats designed to the International Offshore Rule in the early and mid-1980s. Crew weight is needed on the rail for stability. The bottoms of their light, shallow, beamy hulls are quite flat. And when they heel, their rudders lift up and out of the water. (Rosenfeld Collection, Mystic Seaport Museum, Inc., Mystic, CT)

Good stability also contributes to a boat's speed, and speed is an altogether good quality for cruising as well as racing yachts. A fast boat will be more fun to sail and will have a greater cruising range than a slow one. Because it enhances speed, a good righting moment is penalized under the IOR and other rules. Because of hope that weight not put into the keel would go into strengthening the hull or rig, a high center of gravity was given a bonus under the IOR. Aware that stability spells speed, ambitious skippers use the movable ballast of crew weight on the weather rail. This has become a part of winning, and racing designs are done on that assumption. As usual, stock-boat design has followed along with that trend.

Because it offers good speed, good stability contributes to safety. Since most boats have reliable auxiliary power, we don't often consider this safety factor, but it is important. As weather conditions deteriorate, a stable boat will be able to continue beating to windward, perhaps to escape a dangerous situation such as a threatening lee shore. Because the windage of the hull and rig increases as the square of the wind speed, while stability grows only linearly with heel, a boat lacking power in the form of stability will run out of the safety margin of driving force over drag that makes her go.

Resistance to Sudden Forces

Recent studies of capsize have called attention to the importance of a factor that has often been overlooked in thinking about that problem. This is the transverse moment of inertia, which is the measure of angular acceleration around the center of gravity—in other words, inertial resistance to abrupt roll, such as sudden knockdown by a gust of wind or the impact of a breaking wave like the ones that swept the Fastnet fleet. These can occur anywhere in weather of the right (or wrong) sort.

Model tests have determined that the moment of inertia is one of the major parameters resisting sudden capsize, especially that caused by a breaking sea. By its nature, it is greater in large boats than in small ones. Naturally, breaking seas should be avoided whenever possible, and if this is not possible they should be met at the right attitude (probably the bow or stern quarter, but that is another story). However, avoidance of rough weather cannot be assured in the life of a boat that goes offshore. Anybody who buys a boat for offshore sailing should realize that, and so should race committees setting the size limits for an offshore race. It has been pointed out that most of the boats that got into serious trouble in the 1979 Fastnet would not have met the minimum size limit of the CCA Bermuda Race. Although based on other measurements, this is approximately 38 feet in overall length.

Other factors affect aspects of stability, power, range, and resistance to capsize. Surprisingly, a heavy mast will contribute to the last of these. Its weight represents an inertial mass that resists the sudden force of a breaking sea. A heavy hull has a similar influence, although not to the same degree. Modern racing boats, with their very light masts and hulls, again suffer. Comparisons, looking at both size and shape, will be made in the chapters that follow.

Recommendations

As a critic, I have had to deplore many characteristics of the present generation of offshore racing and cruising yachts. As I had a rather large part in the formulation of the IOR, which (given the intensity of the competition) has fostered many of the faults, I must admit my mistakes and try to encourage correction. Yet correction is not easy to accomplish, since rule constancy and close competition under the IOR have won wide approval. Happily, even as I write, recognition of these difficulties is growing. Some moves to improve both power and stability range have been made and steps that should bring better results are being seriously studied. If owners realize the importance of such issues, the answers will come.

Regardless of the rules, a potential owner looking for a suitable offshore yacht must try to evaluate and reconcile an often contradictory set of parameters, maximizing the favorable factors and minimizing the unfavorable ones. Here is a summary:

Increasing displacement builds inertia against sudden heeling forces and increases stability for sail carrying power. As a yacht designer, I have often found the addition of ballast to be good medicine (even in terms of speed) when too little beam or displacement has resulted in too little stability. Too much displacement can slow a boat down, especially when reaching or running in strong winds in the high-speed range. A buyer looking at a very-light-displacement boat should assure himself that it will provide good upwind performance.

Increasing beam contributes to righting moment, so it is good, up to a point. The way beam is used in combination with displacement and center of gravity is the crux of the stability question. Extremes are bad. Great beam with little displacement reduces stability range by lifting the center of gravity, and as the center of gravity rises both power and range are lost. Excessive beam can also slow a boat, especially in a seaway. The worst of all combinations is large beam with a light-displacement, shoal-bodied hull having necessarily limited ballast that is too high.

Increasing freeboard adds interior space and extends the righting-moment curve, but it also raises the center of gravity (decreasing the righting moment) and adds windage.

Lowering ballast lowers the center of gravity, thereby favoring every aspect of stability. It also reduces the danger of a prolonged inverted position. It demands strong construction, and to some degree it may reduce speed because it increases the longitudinal moment of inertia so that the boat less easily conforms to a sloppy water surface. Under many conditions this reduces speed (though under some conditions it can help).

Strong construction makes the boat and rig reliable and extends the life of the boat. To the extent that it means increased weight it improves resistance to dynamic capsize due to a breaking sea.

In tabular form, here is how the factors look:

	SAIL CARRYING POWER	RANGE OF STABILITY	RESISTANCE TO CAPSIZE
Great displacement	+	+	+
Wide beam	+	−	−
High center of gravity	−	−	−
Deep hull	−	+	+
Heavy rig	−	−	+

Note: + means favorable; − means unfavorable.

54

I see and have tried to emphasize the dangers of decreasing displacement and increasing beam because we know their part in producing characteristics that research has clearly shown to be linked to capsize. Other factors have been cited. Along with an understanding of such effects, every boat owner needs a reasonable understanding of his or her own requirements, a deep concern about safety, and a willingness to buck trends to find the boat that meets those requirements and provides safety for the inevitable difficult and testing situation.

CHAPTER 3

Avoiding Capsize:
Research Work

Karl L. Kirkman and Richard C. McCurdy

For reasons that are obvious, nobody wants to capsize while sailing offshore. Yet all too often, boats *do* get rolled in rough weather. What can be done about this—either by selecting boats with characteristics that are likely to serve well in such weather or by improving those that are vulnerable—is the subject of this and the next chapter.

This is a fascinating field of interest, and one that has borne fruit only recently via research aimed at understanding how boats act under severe conditions. Much of the work on which these chapters are based took place between 1981 and 1985 in a remarkable cooperative project involving sailors, designers, and naval architects and engineers functioning under an organization that will be described below. The conclusions should benefit all sailors who are interested in going offshore. While the project was not an activity of the CCA Technical Committee, all the project directors were members of the committee (and are among the authors of this book).

Here, we'll review the research efforts and in Chapter 4 we'll describe some practical measures that can be taken to lessen the chances, and the consequences, of capsize at sea. Some readers may prefer to skip first to the practical measures and then read about the research background; however, we feel that the best way to proceed is to learn something first about the project's history and the research.

The SNAME / USYRU Capsize Project

Until very recently, little was known about the mechanism of the capsize and recovery of boats exposed to violent wave action. This is in part because the phenomenon itself used to be quite rare. As Olin Stephens mentions in the previous chapter, the fear of a boat's capsizing in rough weather was very distant in the first 50 or 60 years of amateur ocean racing and cruising—that is, since the sport was developed in an organized way. In the mid and late 1970s, however, a whole new breed of yacht began to participate in ocean-racing events. These were light-displacement, dinghy-like boats that were fast and fun to sail, but that were also prone to various kinds of dubious behavior in severe wind and sea conditions. This development was disturbing to many sailors, and in America the CCA leadership was particularly concerned. The strong motivation to understand and to deal with stormy weather has long been a major goal of the club as an adjunct to one of its founding purposes—that of promoting the design and construction of good offshore yachts. Also, the club sponsors the biennial race from Newport to Bermuda, one of only a handful of regularly scheduled races in which the boats are offshore in the ocean almost from start to finish. Cutting across the Gulf Stream and finishing near extensive coral reefs, the Bermuda Race can be (and has been) extremely challenging, and sometimes outright dangerous.

All this general concern about trends in modern racing yacht design came to a head in August 1979, when we heard the reports of the tragic Fastnet Race. The 605-mile Fastnet is sailed around England's south coast and across the western approaches to the southern tip of Ireland and back. While it is not, strictly speaking, an offshore race (as boats are usually only 20 or 30 miles offshore except during the crossing of the western approaches), the Fastnet has always had a reputation as a rough race, and boats have been lost in it.

Nothing that had occurred in the history of the sport compared with the disasters that took place during the 1979 Fastnet, when a Force 10 (48–55 knots), and perhaps greater, storm swept across the 303-boat fleet in the western approaches. Twenty-four boats were abandoned and five sank. More than 100 boats were knocked over at least until their masts were horizontal and about 70 were rolled further. Approximately 18 boats performed 360-degree rolls and 5 capsized yachts reportedly spent periods of time from 30 seconds to 5 minutes in an inverted, or "turtled," position. Most tragically of all, 15 racing sailors were drowned or done in by hypothermia.

Obviously, those of us who were officials of the CCA and responsible for running the 1980 Bermuda Race wanted, first, to understand what had happened on August 13–14, 1979, in England's western approaches and, second, to see what, if anything, might be done to minimize such troubles in the future. Such concerns soon crystallized into an informal network in which ideas were circulated and pertinent data were collected, our main sources being the official 1979 Fastnet Race Inquiry and John Rousmaniere, who had been collecting material for his forthcoming book *"Fastnet, Force 10,"* which he kindly made available for study.

During the winter of 1979–1980, we at the CCA consulted with both our Technical Committee and the Technical Committee of the Measurement Handicap System (MHS—one of the rating rules we would use in the Bermuda Race, now called the International Measurement System, or IMS), asking them, in effect, "What can we do to keep Fastnet 1979 from happening to us?" These two committees included some of the most respected yacht designers and naval architects. While they had a general feeling that such characteristics as stability range and boat size were important in determining whether or not a boat would capsize, they told us that not enough research into the mechanism of yacht capsize had yet been done to allow our question to be answered definitively. So we tightened up the regulations for the race as much as we could, crossed our fingers, and ran the 1980 race. As luck would have it, the weather was perfect.

But of course the basic problem remained, and would continue to be around everybody's neck until the necessary research work was done. We were determined to do what we could to gain more knowledge. Karl Kirkman, chairman of the Sailboat Committee of the Society of Naval Architects and Marine Engineers, and Olin Stephens, a past chairman of that committee, began to study the problem from a research viewpoint. Meanwhile, Dick McCurdy, chairman of the Safety-at-Sea Committee of the United States Yacht Racing Union, and Dan Strohmeier, a member of that committee and a former president of SNAME, began to look for ways to encourage this work. We felt that the effort would be stronger and would reach a wider audience of both technical people and sailors if it was jointly sponsored by USYRU and SNAME through their relevant committees. The project was formally set up, and was called the SNAME / USYRU Joint Committee on Safety from Capsize. The directors were the four individuals mentioned above.

Since such research would necessarily require major facilities and a lot of highly skilled work, we did not think that we could raise the large amount of money needed as quickly as we would like. On the other hand, there were many able people willing to contribute their efforts, and we found organizations that would allow us to use major facilities on an as-available basis. As it worked out, the work was performed entirely by volunteers, and the main costs were for the printing and distributing of the reports. It was in every way a dedicated effort, with an esprit de corps rivaling the best that one is likely to see. The names of the participants in the work are listed in the Acknowledgments section of this book.

The project summarized its work in two interim reports, issued in 1983 and 1984, and in a final report, issued in 1985. These reports were made available worldwide through USYRU. The project workers also published seven technical papers. These papers can be pretty hard going for the general reader looking for an overall understanding of the problem and a general picture of what was discovered. What follows is a lay-language survey of the approach and the findings.

In considering the avenues of research pursued, and the way in which the findings are converted into useful results, one should understand that the research leads first to insights into the mechanics of the processes that are taking place. Then, based on this understanding, the practical uses to which the knowledge can be put finally come into view.

In our case, the *research work* was made up of model testing, both on our part and by others; analysis of actual capsizes; studies of the effects of hull form; oceanographic studies; and mathematical, statistical, and engineering analyses of the data.

Insights were gained into the mechanics of capsize, of recovery from capsize, of knockdowns and knockdown-induced foundering, and into the relative importance of boat characteristics in these processes, as well as the nature and formation of dangerous waves.

Practical results, which will be treated in the next chapter, include the development both of a method of ranking boats in order of their capsize resistance and of a method of predicting the length of time that a given boat is likely to be trapped in an inverted position. Characteristics that lead to a susceptibility to knockdowns and related troubles will be discussed, and we will offer a simple screening formula aimed at identifying boats that are likely to have certain desirable or undesirable hull characteristics, and which can be applied without knowledge of boat lines and other difficult-to-obtain data. Also to be covered in Chapter 4 are sailing tactics in rough weather.

Sources of Research Data

Model Testing

Testing of models in tanks equipped to make waves gave data of fundamental importance. The project's own testing was done in a tank at the U.S. Naval Academy on an "as-available" basis by volunteer workers. Other valuable data came from the Wolfson Unit at the University of Southampton in England, which was motivated by the same concerns over the Fastnet Race disaster. In addition, some published work by Japanese workers who were developing self-righting lifeboats added much to our understanding of the process of re-righting after capsize.

Model tests enabled us to understand that the basic mechanism of capsize by wave action is a dynamic one. The tests also yielded data that showed the relative importance of various boat characteristics in the process. Notably, we identified inertia moment as acting to protect against capsize, and unduly wide beam as undesirable. Model tests failed to show much significance of freeboard, nor did they indicate much sensitivity to appendages such as the keel or rudder.

The Southampton tank, being equipped to test free-running models while under way, gave the best data on sailing tactics to avoid capsize. Their tests also showed that longer-keeled models with balanced ends, in running before the seas, had less tendency to broach and capsize than shorter-keeled models with the unbalanced ends that are characteristic of the more "modern" designs.

Oceanography

There is a vast literature on oceanographic subjects, and we were fortunate in having a volunteer who is a weather expert to lead us through it. Through these studies, there were identified certain kinds of weather patterns that lead to the rapid formation of dangerous waves. This work also contributed importantly to two other phases of the research: probability data on the frequencies of arrival times of various-sized waves, which was an integral part in calculating the promptness of re-righting after capsize; and data on the buildup of seas, which enabled us to work out the probable wave situation prevailing in the various reported actual capsizes, so as finally to allow this body of data to be studied on a comparative basis.

Analysis of Actual Capsizes

Full-scale capsize data were of three kinds: a videotape of an actual capsize that occurred in Australia; a large body of data from the 1979 Fastnet Race, obtained by courtesy of the Royal Ocean Racing Club, based on questionnaires filled out by the crews of 235 of the boats that raced; and a set of miscellaneous capsize reports that we collected, and in which the data appeared to be well reported. This body of information proved to be of great value throughout the research, notably in furnishing an independent (albeit very rough) check on the insights coming from experimentation and analysis.

Mathematical, Statistical, and Engineering Analyses

Once we got insights from model testing as to the nature of the processes at work in capsizing and in recovery from capsize, we could begin the formidable task of expressing these in equations, and ultimately in numbers. In this, we had some measure of success, as the formulations in the next chapter will indicate.

We also subjected the Fastnet data to a "regression analysis," which is an approach designed to take such a mass of data and see what degree of correlation is present between hypothetical causes and effects. The result was to show that there were correlations between Fastnet events and the hull characteristics of the boats. The correlations were in the directions that might be expected from our research. The correlations were, however, weak—indicating that other factors were at work (perhaps storm tactics). We believe that there is more to be learned in this area, but unfortunately we lost our volunteer regression analysis expert and were unable to go further.

Finally, we wanted to see if very large computers, starting from scratch, could handle the problem of a breaking wave with an object such as a boat immersed in it. This is a task of truly immense complexity—but such computers have solved problems long regarded as too intractable. The attraction of computer analysis, of course, is that it gives another quite independent check. Professor J. N. Newman of M.I.T. (himself an oceangoing sailor) agreed to give it some study, and progress has been made.

Insights on Boat Size and Capsize Dynamics

Roll Moment of Inertia, Dismasting, and Capsize Resistance

An early finding from model testing was that, when the models were capsized by wave action, their behavior was controlled by dynamic principles rather than by the static flotation that normally controls a boat's attitude. Somewhat as with a football that has just been kicked, gravity takes a back seat for a while.

The manner of this discovery makes an interesting story. After the researchers had learned how to make breaking waves in the test tank and had begun to practice capsizing a model hull, they reminded themselves that the model was supposed to be a sailboat and really ought to have a mast in her. So they made a properly scaled mast and put it into the model. They then found that the model wouldn't capsize anymore when struck by waves that had readily capsized the mastless hull. This seemed quite bizarre to many people, and, when word got around, several disbelievers made the trip to Annapolis to see it with their own eyes. One even insisted on personally installing the mast in the model, fearing that some trick or joke was being perpetrated.

Clearly, this result could in no way be explained by the principles of normal flotation; after all, a mastless hull *has* to float more staunchly upright than when it has to hold up a mast. So it was evident that dynamics were at work, and that the rotation of the boat about her fore-and-aft axis during the capsize was fast enough that inertial forces were in control. We then wanted to know if real boats, when capsized, rolled rapidly enough to bring inertial forces into play. As luck would have it, we had managed to get a videotape of an actual capsize in Australia, which showed a roll of such extreme rapidity that doubt vanished. The boat was seen to roll from a floating position to an inverted one in about one second when struck by the white water. It is difficult to see such behavior as other than a dynamic process in which the roll inertia was acting against the capsizing impulse from the wave. (At this point, some readers may want to know just what is meant by roll moment of inertia. We offer a brief review in Appendix 3-A at the end of this chapter, for those not familiar with the term.)

In considering the makeup of the roll moment of inertia of an object like a boat, we should note that the heavier parts of the boat are located not very far from the roll axis, and may not contribute as much to the total roll inertia as one might think. On the other hand, while the elements of the rig are much lighter, they are a long way from the axis, so that they can bulk very large in the total roll inertia; and so it is. The project estimated the roll inertia of representative boats and found that the rig contributes over half the total roll inertia, in boats both big and small (Figure 3-1).

It should now be clear why the addition of the mast to the models prevented them from capsizing: doing so more than doubled the models' roll inertia, which was the factor supplying resistance to capsize.

In considering how this discovery could best be put to use, we needed a good way to approximate roll inertia without having to do the vast work involved in calculating it in detail from basic design data (even if the latter were available). A way was found to approximate roll inertia from measurement certificates, but we don't yet know how accurate this method is. We also found indications that there is a consistent relationship between roll inertia and displacement for the boats studied. However, we are not certain if this relationship exists for all boats, given the lack of availability of hard data; we are continuing to study this point. Apparently, the reason the relationship holds, at least in the boats we studied, is that the various weights (rig, hull, and ballast) that make up the displacement are arranged in a similar geometric way from boat to boat. A corollary is that if this broad geometric similarity is not maintained, the relationship between displacement and inertia will vanish. In particular, although losing the mast does not affect a boat's displacement greatly, *it will remove more than one-half of her inertia moment, and as a consequence will make her a lot more susceptible to capsize than she was before this happened.* We will come back to this point when we discuss the practical applications of the research.

The Effect of Boat Size on Capsize Resistance

That a "bigger" boat is less affected by a given wave than a "smaller" one is a fact of experience. The complication comes when one tries to define "size" for such purposes when the boats being compared are dissimilar in shape and other characteristics. From the beginning, since it was evident that boat size would be of basic importance in capsize resistance, we aimed to come up with a criterion that would rank boats in order of their resistance to capsize when struck by white water.

The problem is similar in principle to the familiar one of devising a formula

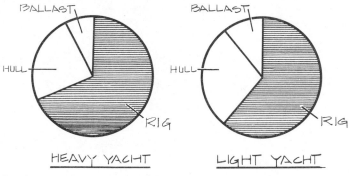

Figure 3-1. A comparison of contributions to moments of inertia for heavy and light yachts shows the importance of the role played by the rig.

for handicapping boats for racing. There, one starts with the known fact that longer boats usually go faster than shorter ones. But various other factors also are found to influence speed, so for purposes of handicapping boats in racing, a rating length *("L")* is calculated taking into account such other factors, the resulting *L* being intended to represent relative speed. In an analogous way, the project used its research findings to develop a formula for a "capsize *L*," intended to rank boats in order of their resistance to capsizing by wave action.

The derivation of the formula developed for "capsize length" is complex; however, the underlying ideas are not hard to follow. In brief, model testing demonstrated that roll moment of inertia is the main agent acting to resist capsize. It also showed that wider beam acts to favor capsize. To these can be added the certainty that the driver in the capsize is the force of the white water on the topsides, acting on an arm that is given by the distance from the center of wave pressure to the center of gravity of the boat. Analysis of model tests confirmed that the beam and centers of pressure and gravity in combination would represent the overturning force, while the roll inertia would provide the resistance to it.

The method used for actual calculation is, in effect, to compare the figures from the boat in question to those of a base boat of normal proportions, coming out with a "capsize length" that would rank boats in order of their relative resistance to capsize. The analysis is far from exact, which has to be accepted when dealing with a thing as disorderly as a breaking wave. On the other hand, we know of no other such calculation that is available to deal with this effect.

The project worked out the capsize lengths of a considerable number of actual boats where enough data were available to get at least a fair idea of the situation. The results show that there is a wide variation in capsize length as compared to physical length. The results of these calculations are shown in the next chapter.

The Problem of Being Stuck Upside Down

The idea that ballasted keel boats will float stably in a turtled or upside-down position seems novel to many people, yet just about any modern boat will do so. In the 1979 Fastnet Race, several boats did remain inverted, one reportedly for as long as five minutes. Since then, other boats have also stayed turtled for long lengths of time. The current sailing literature is increasingly filled with reports

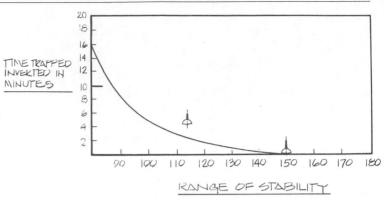

Figure 3-2. Test results (curve) and data from the 1979 Fastnet Race (hulls) shows that boats that remain upside down the longest after capsizes have low ranges of positive stability. If the stability range is 120 degrees, the boat probably will stay inverted for 2 minutes or less.

by survivors of such disquieting situations. One of the objectives of our research was to understand this behavior and to see what might be done about it. The boat characteristics related to how such events can happen are discussed in Appendix 3-B, which you may wish to read at this point.

A boat stuck upside down can be righted by rolling her enough to get her heel angle back into the range of positive stability, after which point she will come back up. If her range of positive stability is large (and the range of negative stability is correspondingly small), she need not be rotated very far in order to come back up. However, as the two ranges become more equal, she must be rotated farther and farther. A boat with a stability range of 90 degrees (meaning that she loses positive stability when heeled only 90 degrees) will be as hard to right as it was to turtle her in the first place. If the crew cannot manhandle the boat back up, and if outside assistance is unavailable, the only agent that can help re-right her is another wave that will roll her far enough. How big a wave is needed to do this depends on the boat's range of positive stability: the smaller the range, the bigger the wave required to right her.

The boat's time of maximum danger of attaining inverted equilibrium is when the biggest waves are just enough to roll her. When this happens, and she sticks in an inverted position, she is dependent on one of the lesser waves to bring her back up. The issues are, first, how big a wave is required and, second, how long it will be before such a wave comes along. The project worked this out for various ranges of stability by employing oceanographic "wave spectra" data. The result is shown in Figure 3-2, which gives actual data for two boats of known stability range that capsized in the 1979 Fastnet gale. The agreement between calculated times of inversion and the actual events is gratifyingly close. In Chapter 4, we will use some of these findings when considering appropriate stability ranges for offshore boats.

Knockdowns

Considerable dangers arise as the result of wind- and/or broaching-induced knockdowns extreme enough to place the mast near the water (or, in the presence of some wave action, in the water). In Appendix 3-B we present material that provides background for understanding this problem; you may want to review that appendix before reading the following discussion.

One defense against knockdowns is to make the boat stiff enough to resist sudden heeling forces due to wind gusts, seas, and loss of steering control. Since we see knockdowns occurring—especially to racing boats sailing under spinnaker—we have to conclude that many modern boats do not have the basic stiffness to prevent occasional knockdown. The issue then is how well a boat that has suffered a knockdown will re-right herself. This depends on her righting moment at extreme angles of heel—which in turn depends on her hull shape and ballasting. As is shown in Appendix 3-B, while boats with wide, flat shapes may have good initial stability, they may also have very little ability to re-right themselves at large heel angles. On the other hand, boats with rounder shapes can have a strong ability to re-right themselves from extreme heel angles.

If the heel angle at which the mast is in or near the water is close to the limit of the boat's range of stability, the boat will not have much righting moment left when she is knocked over that far and may take considerable time to struggle back up. The amount of time that a boat spends on her side during a knockdown is critical. As she tries to re-right herself, water may pour below through deck openings. Heavy objects below (including internal ballast) may shift to leeward. If the mast enters the water, it could provide considerable flotation if it is watertight; but if it has holes for internal halyards, it may quickly fill with water and so leave the boat with a mastload of water to be lifted as she tries to recover from the knockdown. Several boats have been sunk in such a way. A good defense against troubles of this kind is to increase the range of stability so that when the mast is in the water the boat still has considerable righting moment.

Oceanographic Data

Oceanographic findings played an important part in the capsize project's work. From them, we came to understand not only how some of the most dangerous waves are generated, but also how long a turtled boat is likely to be trapped. We were also able to satisfy ourselves as to the nature of the relationship between boat size and capsize vulnerability.

Consider first what kinds of waves are risky. As a rule, we believe, no nonbreaking wave is dangerous. A boat will capsize due to wave action not because the face of a nonbreaking wave on which she is riding is steep but rather because she encounters a jet of rapidly moving water from a breaker. As a wave grows and steepens, a point is reached at which the water at its top begins to move forward faster than the body of the wave and becomes white water. As the wave continues to grow, the white water becomes greater in volume and faster in motion, until its jet-like impact on a boat's side is great enough to roll her. Figure 3-3 shows a computer simulation of the growth of such a wave to the breaking point, based on a videotape of an actual capsize.

Some people believe that a wave with fast-moving white water is a shallow-water phenomenon. However, in recent years research has shown convincingly that such conditions occur in the deep sea at times when the wind is building relatively rapidly.

The machine that drives the formation of waves is, of course, the wind. If the

Figure 3-3. This computer simulation of a capsize in a breaking wave, based on a videotape of a capsize, shows how the breaker affects the boat. If the jet of white water on the wave's crest is large enough, its impact will roll the boat over.

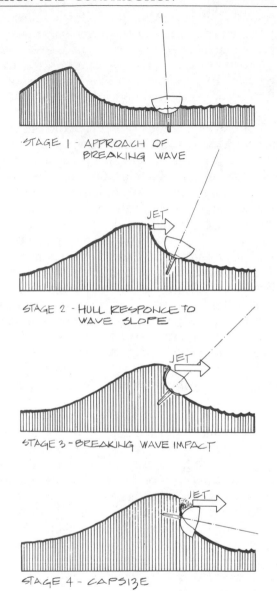

STAGE 1 - APPROACH OF BREAKING WAVE

JET

STAGE 2 - HULL RESPONCE TO WAVE SLOPE

JET

STAGE 3 - BREAKING WAVE IMPACT

JET

STAGE 4 - CAPSIZE

wind blows steadily from one direction over a long "fetch" (or expanse of water), the waves will gradually build up and lengthen until they are as high and long as they are going to get for that particular wind. The sea in this condition is called a "fully developed sea" at that wind speed (up to that point it is called "immature"). Unless the wind speed is very high indeed, fully developed seas are not likely to cause as much trouble as those arising from more rapidly changing winds. Also, with a wind of constant direction, the warning period will be long. The more usual condition, as sailors well know, is for the seas to be irregular, with waves and winds that vary in size, direction, and strength.

A very large risk of capsize comes from a sudden buildup of wind strength over seas that are moderately large but still immature. When this happens, great energy is pumped into relatively short waves, making them sizable and also steep—a combination that favors breakers. The worst scenario, we think, would come from a moderately sizable sea with a wind that quickly increases to 60 or 70 knots. Dangerous breaking waves could be expected to appear within hours of the onset of such a buildup. As is well known, contrary currents and a shallower depth of water can amplify these troubles.

Several kinds of climatological phenomena are likely to create this dangerous situation: a tropical depression or hurricane; a strong low-pressure system associated with a cold trough with intense convective cells and thunderstorms (convective cells are areas of up-and-down circulation of air); and what meteorologists have come to call a "bomb," which is a low that deepens rapidly, at a rate of 1 millibar per hour or more over a 24-hour period. The 1979 Fastnet Race disaster occurred because of a bomb—the barometer on the yacht *Eclipse* dropped 40 millibars in 24 hours while the wind shifted almost 180 degrees and increased from Force 4 to Force 11.

Appendix 3-A:

Roll Moment of Inertia

The purpose of this appendix is to discuss the meaning of the terms rotational inertia and moment of inertia. These may not be as familiar as linear inertia, which is the resistance that we feel when we push an object to start it moving in some direction. Rotational inertia is felt when we twist an object to get it to spin. If an object is spinning, the outside parts are moving more rapidly than the inside parts and so contribute more to the inertia than do the inside parts. Indeed, since the energy of a moving object changes as the square of its velocity, the outside parts will carry most of the energy. In either form of inertia, the object being moved resists the impulse either to start it moving or to stop it. How much it resists a given impulse is a measure of its inertia. In linear inertia, this measure is simply the weight of the object. In rotational inertia, the resistance to spin is called the moment of inertia, and it is found by taking each part of the total weight, multiplying it by the *square* of its distance from the axis of rotation, and adding all these up.

Many familiar actions are illuminating examples of the workings of rotational inertia. Consider an ice skater turning slowly with arms extended. When the skater's arms are pulled in, the spin becomes very fast. Why? Because with arms extended, the moment of inertia, and consequently the rotational energy, was concentrated mostly in the hands and forearms. When the hands and forearms are pulled in, the whole body then has a much smaller moment of inertia, and has to spin very fast to use that energy. We should remember this example when thinking about boats and, especially, the significance of the mast in resisting capsize (see Figure 3-4).

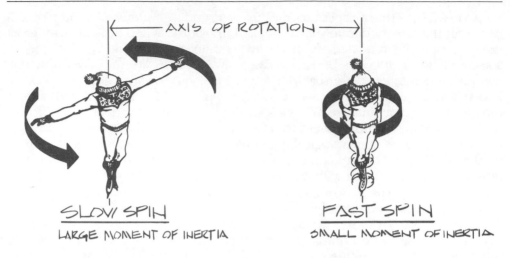

SLOW SPIN

LARGE MOMENT OF INERTIA

FAST SPIN

SMALL MOMENT OF INERTIA

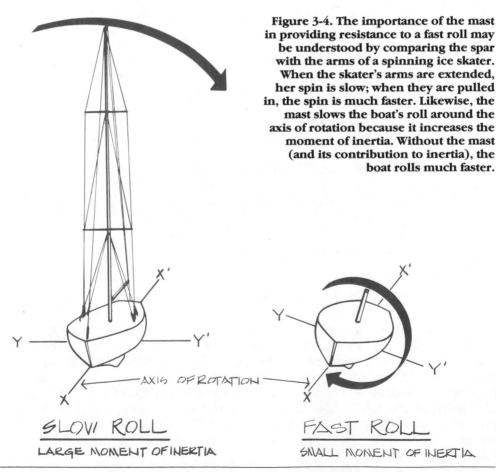

Figure 3-4. The importance of the mast in providing resistance to a fast roll may be understood by comparing the spar with the arms of a spinning ice skater. When the skater's arms are extended, her spin is slow; when they are pulled in, the spin is much faster. Likewise, the mast slows the boat's roll around the axis of rotation because it increases the moment of inertia. Without the mast (and its contribution to inertia), the boat rolls much faster.

SLOW ROLL

LARGE MOMENT OF INERTIA

FAST ROLL

SMALL MOMENT OF INERTIA

A boat has three axes about which she can rotate. The corresponding motions are familiar to all sailors. If the rotation axis is vertical, the boat is turning, or yawing; if she rotates about the athwartships axis, she is pitching; and if the rotation is about the fore-and-aft axis, she is rolling. Since this last is the axis about which she can most easily capsize, the moment of inertia about the fore-and-aft axis is the one of interest to us. It is called the roll moment of inertia, and it is the one that can resist a sudden impulse to roll the boat over.

The axis around which the boat rolls in this dynamic process is the fore-and-aft line running through the center of gravity. To calculate the roll moment of inertia, one takes each of the various pieces of the boat, determines the shortest distance of each piece from the roll axis, multiplies its weight by the square of this distance, and then adds these all together. This is most laborious, but necessary if one is to find the true roll moment of inertia.

Appendix 3-B:
Hull Shape, Ballast,
and Stability

Various features of a boat's behavior depend upon the relationship between the angle of heel and the rotational force that must be exerted to make her heel that amount. At normal sailing angles of heel, the size of this force determines her sail-carrying capacity, which is what sailors call "stiffness." The force exerted at small angles of heel ("initial stability") is routinely measured to approximate sail-carrying capacity for handicapping purposes. However, the force exerted at large heel angles ("ultimate stability") is not usually measured. This is not impossible; hull lines and weight distribution can always be analyzed to understand a boat's behavior at heel angles beyond those encountered in normal sailing. Yet this information was not routinely processed until boats began the modern trend toward light weight and beamy, shallow shape. With today's trends, ultimate stability has assumed increased significance, so there is good reason for us to understand the whole relationship between heel angle and the forces involved with hull shape and ballasting.

Hull Shape

In the following discussion we will use several technical terms. *Positive stability* applies to the situation where a boat, if heeled and left to herself, will come back upright. The term *negative stability* applies to the situation where she will turtle if left to herself. The term *range of positive stability* refers to the number of degrees of heel—from upright on over—within which range she exhibits positive stability. The terms *righting moment* and *righting arm* are technical ways of describing how hard she is to pull over to a given angle of heel. The following series of examples is intended to give familiarity with this nomenclature, and also to lend insights into the effect of hull shape on stability variations as the boat is heeled.

Consider first a simple example of the behavior of two quite differently shaped objects. Say that one is a round floating object with a weight attached to one side. However this may be turned, it will return to a position with the weight downward. Clearly, it has a range of positive stability of 180 degrees. Now consider a flat floating object, such as a raft. We can raise the side up until it is on edge, but if we go further, it will fall into an upside-down position and stay there. Its range of positive stability is 90 degrees, and its range of negative stability is also 90 degrees. Its behavior is similar to that of wide flat boats such as catamarans. This behavior is approached by some monohulled racers today.

Now, to introduce the way in which we illustrate stability data, consider Figure 3-5, which illustrates a situation very similar to the foregoing example, but

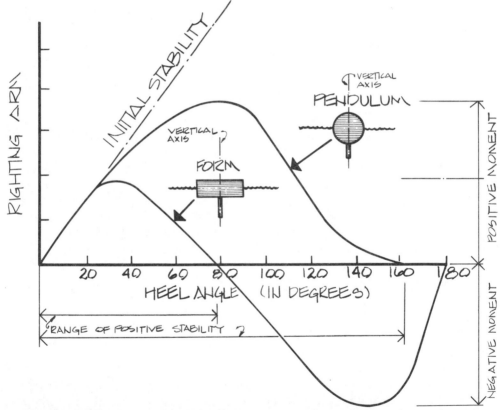

Figure 3-5. Hull shape greatly affects stability. Two extreme shapes with weights attached to one side—one square, the other round—provide very different ranges of positive stability. The round shape will always return to upright, which means that its stability range is 180 degrees. However, the square shape can capsize at a heel angle of only 80 degrees, which is its stability range. Since the square shape's stability is dependent on its shape or form, it illustrates a type of stability called form stability. The round shape illustrates pendulum stability, since it behaves like a pendulum.

employs a graphical form to show the stability variation with heel angle. Here are shown a round object, like a log, with a weight attached to one side, and a flat boxlike object which has been weighted internally so as to give it the same righting moment at small heel angles as the weighted log. The plotted curves show, for each one, the righting moment and the corresponding heel angle in degrees on the horizontal axis. Note that the log is stable at all angles of heel and that the maximum righting moment occurs when it is heeled 80 or 90 degrees, while the righting moment of the box declines at heel angles that could well be encountered in gusty or increasing winds and becomes negative at around 80 degrees. If heeled beyond that point the box will turtle. This example indicates that initial stability or "stiffness" gives little or no clue as to what will happen at large heel angles. The type of stability exhibited by the log is called "pendulum stability," and that of the box is called "form stability," for obvious reasons.

To show some actual boats whose characteristics illustrate pendulum and form stability rather well, consider those in Figure 3-6. One of the boats is a narrow, deep boat like those designed to the Universal and International Rules, the second is a modern, flat-bottomed IOR design of similar size and displacement, and the third is *Running Tide,* an extremely successful 1970-vintage ocean racer whose shape falls between those two extremes. The graphs show the righting moments and range of stability:

- The curve above the horizontal axis gives the positive moment, indicating the angles of heel at which the boat will come back upright if left to herself.
- The curve below the axis gives the negative moment—the heel angles where, if left to herself, the boat will turtle.
- The point where the curve crosses the line is the range of positive stability. At this angle of heel, the boat loses positive righting moment and gains negative righting moment. If she heels less than this amount, she will come back upright; if she heels more, she will not do so.

We can tell from the graphs that the meter boat will come back from any angle of heel, the IOR boat will turtle if she is forced down beyond 110 degrees, and *Running Tide* is safe up to 139 degrees—which means that she has a strong righting force throughout normal sailing angles of heel and well beyond. Note that the righting-moment curves for the two most extreme boats—the meter boat and the IOR boat—show a variation similar to that between the log and the box.

By studying the shapes and graphs shown in Figure 3-6, the reader should gain a feeling for the relationship between hull shape and stability characteristics. Obviously, wide beam, while it may lead to much "stiffness" at ordinary sailing angles of heel, will reduce the righting moment at very large angles of heel, and reduce the range of stability.

Ballast

In the foregoing we saw examples showing mainly the effect of hull form variations on stability characteristics. The other determinant is the amount of ballast and its location. Plainly, the more ballast that is carried below the center

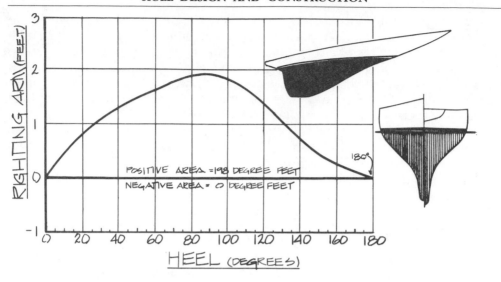

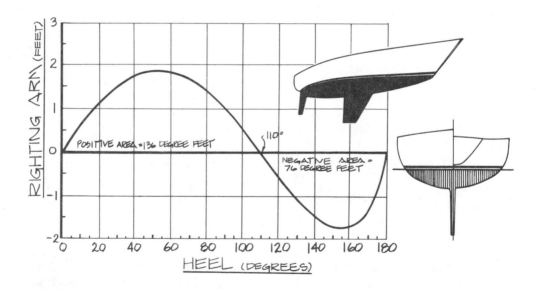

Figure 3-6. Here are stability curves for three very different types of boats, two on the extremes and the other a moderate compromise.

(Top) This narrow, deep, heavy boat could have been designed to the International Rule (which produces 12-Meters) of the Universal Rule (which produced the New York 40 Class). She could not have a better range of positive stability.

(Above) Light, beamy, and shallow, this typical IOR boat of the 1980s has a stability range of only 110 degrees, which is about when the mast hits the water.

(Upper right) Though somewhat beamier and shallower than the "meter-boat" type, *Running Tide* (built in 1970, as the IOR was being introduced) still has a relatively high range of stability of 139 degrees.

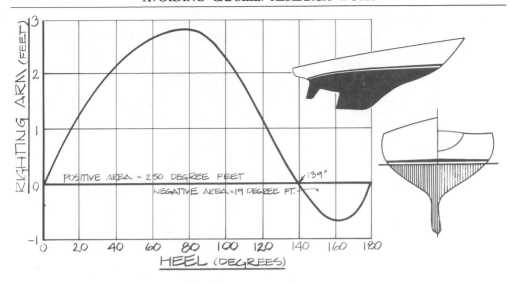

of gravity of the boat, and the farther below it is located, the greater will be the righting arm at various angles of heel, and the greater will be the range of positive stability. Ballast is of much interest because adjustments in the amount and position of ballast can be done after the boat is built if one wants to adjust the stability characteristics. In the case of the other determinants, such as beam and depth, the options are closed once the hull is built.

With a wide boat and a heavy crew on the rail, the actual righting moment while sailing can be considerably increased over the rated amount. This is widely done in racing, though it is a dubious practice in long ocean passages. However, note that after the boat reaches an extreme angle of heel the crew's weight on the rail will no doubt act in the direction of still further heeling.

Calculating Stability Characteristics

The stability versus heel angle relationship can be calculated by the designer, or from the hull lines and other data via the IMS system, in which the hull lines are measured by machine. The IOR system has determined to adopt machine measuring. One comment should be made in regard to measurements when the object is to determine the stability at large enough angles of heel so that the deck goes underwater. Raised parts of the deck structure, such as deckhouses, will increase the range of stability, while lowered parts, such as cockpits, will decrease it. The calculations for stability range that appear on certificates are figured as if the deck were flat. Therefore, the stability range that appears on the certificate will have to be corrected for the effects of deckhouses, cockpits, and so on, if the true range of stability is to be found. Ordinarily, this does not throw the calculation off much, because the raised part of the deck usually will more or less balance the lowered cockpit, but it is something to keep in mind.

Handicapping systems can't be expected to go to the trouble and expense of measuring the deck structure. The purpose of the rules is to handicap the boats while normally racing, rather than to deal with situations where the deckhouse is underwater.

CHAPTER 4

Avoiding Capsize: Practical Measures

Karl L. Kirkman and Richard C. McCurdy

B y virtue of the work described in Chapter 3, sailors and designers are now in a much better position to understand what can happen to different types of boats in severe weather, and to consider the features of a boat's design that relate to her behavior under such conditions. We hope that readers will have absorbed the insights presented in that chapter and will refer to them in the course of reading this one, where we outline the main practical findings from the research relating to rough-weather performance. This advice can well be kept in mind when planning voyages or considering the design of a new boat or the modification of an existing boat.

We emphasize that considerations of this kind are addressed to sailors who intend to go offshore, far from rescue and shelter. People who race or cruise in bays and sounds, or who sail in the ocean close enough to shore to find shelter when needed, have little reason to concern themselves with this work. They may prefer to sail light, sporty, beamy boats that may not do very well in extreme weather. Adoption of the measures that are indicated for deep-ocean work may well make such boats less fun to sail in lighter conditions. The most important service that the Capsize Project offers to boat owners is to caution them against going too far out to sea until they examine the suitability of their boats for that purpose.

Assessing Capsize Vulnerability

The sea can, and does (albeit infrequently), produce waves that are big enough to roll any yacht. Therefore, absolute roll-proofing is unattainable. There are, however, various yacht design characteristics that can render a boat better able to resist rolling, and quicker to re-right herself if rolled.

Boat "Size," and the Formula for Capsize Length

It is intuitively reasonable (and indeed a general fact of experience) that a bigger boat is affected less by wave action than is a smaller one, at least when the boats are similar in shape to one another. The complication comes when we try to compare boats that are dissimilar in shape and in other characteristics that turn out to be important. The project was determined to untie this knot, and finally did so after enough insight into the mechanics of capsize had been gained. These insights, described in Chapter 3, follow from the basic finding that capsize by wave action is a dynamic process, with the overturning impulse from the white water being resisted by the boat's rotational inertia.

The formula that was developed yields an adjusted length number that is called the boat's *capsize length*. The larger this number, the more resistant the boat should be to rolling by wave action. The formula is fairly complicated, so instead of giving it in this general discussion we are including it in Appendix 4-A at the end of this chapter.

From studying the performance of various boats in the ocean, the project concluded that an oceangoing boat should have a calculated capsize length of 30 feet or more. As Figure 4-1 indicates, capsize length can vary widely from other, more familiar lengths. Still, generalizations are possible. For example, the 30-foot target might be met by a moderately proportioned boat—one that is neither too light, too wide, nor too shallow—whose overall length is somewhat larger, say between about 35 and 40 feet. This is consistent with minimum size limits for various events (such as the Bermuda Race) that have been established over the years. Lighter and beamier boats having similar capsize lengths would be longer overall.

Important implications of the capsize-length concept are implicit in the formula. We note, first, that the capsize length of a boat is directly proportional to her total roll moment of inertia. Now (recalling material from Chapter 3), the latter is mainly due to the large contribution from the mast. If the boat is dismasted, her capsize length falls at once to a value less than half the original, and she becomes much more susceptible to rolling. In addition, the ability to steer is essential if the boat is to avoid the vulnerable position broadside to the seas, and to steer she must have a mast and a rudder. We should note at this point that, in the statistics that the USYRU has been keeping for many years concerning the reported causes of failure to finish races, mast failure and steering gear failure are the two most frequent reasons reported.

The first lesson to be drawn here is that *the mast of a seagoing boat should be stout enough to survive a roll.* This is not an impractical thing to do; many masts have survived rolls. It is, however, doubtful that the kind of mast now seen on most modern racing boats would qualify; indeed, many masts are lost during routine sailing. The rudder should also be built to survive.

At present, a lot of work is needed to calculate the capsize length of a boat from the basic data with which the designer works, and it is not yet known how accurate the alternative approximate calculating methods are, particularly for extreme boats. If the owner wishes to invest the money, which may be appreciable, he or she can have it calculated, along with the range of stability (discussed below), and thus make full use of the results of the research.

A Simple Capsize Screening Formula

We felt that it would be very desirable to get a general indication of a boat's survivability *using only data that come readily to hand.* After trying various ideas we came up with what we call the capsize screening formula. It offsets beam (excess beam favors capsize and frequently correlates to poor stability range) against displacement (a surrogate for inertia moment and consequently a reducer

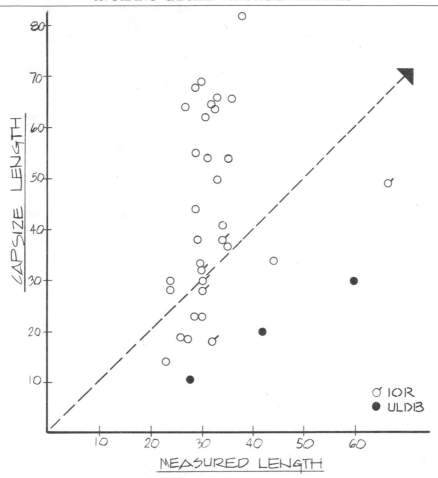

Figure 4-1. The capsize project concluded that the minimum capsize length of an oceangoing boat should be about 30 feet. This comparison of a varied fleet of racer-cruisers shows that measured overall length (horizontal axis) may have little to do with capsize length (vertical axis). Generally speaking, old-fashioned, heavier boats (white circles) have a capsize length greater than the LOA, while the two lengths are about the same with modern boats that have moderate displacement and beam. Wide, light modern boats (circles with tails) and ultra-light-displacement boats (dark circles) tend to have capsize lengths smaller than their measured lengths.

of capsize vulnerability). The formula is easily given in words:

1. Take the gross weight of the boat in pounds. Convert it into the volume of displaced seawater by dividing by 64.
2. Divide the cube root of this number into the maximum beam in feet.

If the result of the calculation is 2 or less, the boat passes the screen. (The derivation of this formula is given in Appendix B of the final report of the Capsize Project, whose publication information is given at the very end of this chapter.)

To be complete, a measure of capsize resistance should also include a minimum size. As a criterion, we suggest that a boat heading offshore should be big enough to be permitted to enter a major ocean race, say the Newport-Bermuda Race. If she is well enough built to satisfy the hull strength requirements of the American Bureau of Shipping, has a stout rig, and has ballast that has not been placed artificially high for race handicapping advantage, we believe that the chances of her coping with long ocean voyages are quite good, without needing a crew of experts to keep her out of trouble.

In 1985 and 1986, we tested the simple formula against data from several hundred boats on which we had estimates for capsize length (based on formulas for approximating moments of inertia) as well as against approximate data for stability range (provided by MHS and IMS certificates). The comparison is necessarily affected both by differences in the nature of the formulas themselves and by the accuracy (not well known in many cases) of the approximations being used. In spite of all this, and in spite of the considerable differences between the structures of the formulas, we are pleased that most of the boats either pass or fail both tests. In our judgment, for what it is worth, the results appear sensible.

We have no doubt that the future will bring much progress in the art of screening boats for capsize vulnerability. Meanwhile, we think that we have offered something that, while it may be rough, is the only known way to approach the problem using readily available data.

As regards stability range (see below), an approximation is obtainable from data provided either by the designer or by a measurement certificate. While the capsize screening formula places a limit on excess beam, which is important for good stability range, it does not control another main determinant, ballasting. With only simple data, this is as far as we can go.

Adequate Range of Stability

Boats that get rolled may not re-right themselves for some time. As we saw in Chapter 3, this very distressing behavior is intimately connected with range of stability. If the boat is turtled, remains upside down, and cannot be manhandled back up again by the crew or outside assistance, she has to await another wave big enough to roll her upright—or at least to roll her up far enough so she gets into her range of positive stability and can begin to re-right herself on her own. In Chapter 3, we explained how it was found possible to estimate how long this might be for various stability ranges. The calculations showed that, with a range of stability of 140 degrees or more, a boat that has been rolled by violent wave action should come back upright promptly. As the range decreases, however, the boat's probable time of inversion increases so that, at 120 degrees, the time is around 2 minutes, and at 100 degrees it is around 5 minutes. Since a "modern" racing fleet will have many boats in these latter ranges, being trapped inverted is a real concern for many sailors who go far enough into the ocean to have to ride out storms.

Surviving this accident will depend on the ability of the crew to resist panic, on how well the boat has been prepared, and so on. One needs to understand that capsize by white-water impact occurs so quickly that there would be no time for any action to be taken as the event occurs.

Having thought about this for some time, we agreed that the consequences will be much more survivable if the period of inversion is comparable with the time people can hold their breath, say 2 minutes. For this reason, a stability range of 120 degrees or more is favored for boats that go well out to sea, with still larger ranges for the smaller boats that are less resistant to capsize. The capsize project favors a range, in degrees, that equals 160 minus the capsize length. For example, if the boat has a capsize length of 35 feet, the stability range should be at least 125 degrees.

Improving Stability Range

These considerations naturally lead one to ask whether the range of stability of an existing boat can be improved. Such may well be the case in many instances— for example, when converting a boat that was designed for coastwise cruising into one for offshore passage-making.

Stability range depends on hull shape and ballast. While not much can be done to change the hull (narrowing the beam would require taking the whole boat apart and rebuilding her), adjusting the location of ballast may well be possible. This is particularly true in the case of a boat that was originally designed to a handicap rule like the IOR that tends to reward the raising of ballast. To test this hypothesis, the project, with the help of the designer, studied a 40-foot IOR One-Tonner that displaced 14,400 pounds and had a stability range of 118 degrees. The designer determined that by moving about 1 ton of ballast from her bilge to her keel her owner would improve her stability range to 130 degrees.

Knockdowns

Being knocked down with some regularity and even having difficulty coming back up again is a characteristic of modern light, beamy boats. When a boat has been turtled in this way, rather than by being rolled, there may be no seas running that are big enough to re-right her in the manner described in the preceding section. If far from rescue and particularly if lacking internal flotation, she is in dire straits.

The question of what range of stability would provide adequate righting after a knockdown, notably in a situation where there is also significant wave action, is a matter of judgment. A range of around 120 degrees (suggested above as a defense against roll-induced inversion of long duration) should provide a reasonable and probably satisfactory margin. Our feeling is that people who have boats that are susceptible to knockdown can learn the particular characteristics of their boats simply by sailing them around in severe weather in locations that are not too remote from aid. Then, based on what they find, they can decide whether to venture into areas in which the wave action is likely to be greater, and assistance less available. However, caution is in order in using this approach since it takes *many* hours in bad conditions to shake out the bad behavior of a boat which may be evident only in some particular combination of wind and waves.

Sailing Tactics for Rough Weather

In our tank testing we were able to verify that broadside to the waves is the worst position to be in from a capsize standpoint. We were not equipped to test free-running models under way; however, the tank at the Wolfson Unit at the University of Southampton, England, can do so, and their results are most valuable. They showed that models exposed broadside to a wave big enough to capsize them could survive better either by surfing down the wave or by going into it, up, and over. These findings lend support to the school of thought that favors keeping the boat moving during storms, and actively steering both to avoid particularly bad waves and to maintain the best attitude to the wave direction (Figure 4-2). Either steering down the wave or heading into it was found in the model testing to be quite demanding on the steering, which had to be both skilled and active. The risks involved in heading into the wave included not

Figure 4-2. Strong steering gear is a major factor in staying under control in rough conditions. This rudder blew apart during the 1979 Fastnet Race. (John Rousmaniere)

being able to get over it; those involved in running with it were broaching and pitch-poling.

A time can come in which sailing, however skilled, is no longer a valid option, and other tactics have to be considered. One of the classic ways (and in our view a good way) to cope is to tow something to slow boat speed and to maintain a reasonable attitude to the seas. There is a continuing interest in designing gear for this sort of maneuver, and there is a desire to see the results tested, as well as they can be, on actual sailboats involved in storms.

One such drogue-type device, shaped rather like a sea anchor but made of strong webbing sewn together in a way that leaves holes for water to run through, was recently given a trial in a survival storm and gave very good control of boat speed, as well as a degree of steering control. Encouraged by this good showing, an interested donor enabled the Naval Academy Sailing Squadron to equip their boats to carry these devices, which have been patented under the trade name Galerider by Hathaway, Reiser, & Raymond, in Stamford, Connecticut. Another device consists of a series of many small drogues positioned along an anchor rode, forming an assembly to be towed. Such devices are not heavy, bulky, or particularly costly. Anyone anticipating substantial sea time and willing to carry gear of this kind and to undertake trials as appropriate occasions arise would be performing a worthwhile service.

Using the Foregoing Material

The nontechnical sailor will find some of this material difficult to use. In addition, some of it requires data normally possessed only by the designer (although the capsize screening formula can be used by anybody who knows the weight of the boat). The best course for the individual who is in doubt about various technical issues is to consult with the designer of his or her boat, which is a good idea in any case if an ocean voyage is contemplated. It should also be understood that the findings presented here are the result of a quite recent breakthrough in research. Those of us who have worked on it believe that this research represents the best information that is currently available (that is, available in August 1986). The reader should realize that, as is always the case with such work, other researchers will add further knowledge in time. Therefore, those who wish to keep abreast of these subjects should check from time to time on the status of research in this area—which is another good reason to keep in touch with your boat's designer.

Appendix 4-A:

The Capsize Length Formula

This is the capsize length formula:

$$L' = \frac{LI}{I_B}\sqrt{\left(\frac{B_B}{B}\right)^2 + \left(\frac{C_B}{C}\right)^2},$$

where:

L' = capsize length, in feet

L = measured length (IMS "L"), in feet

B_B = base beam given by $\frac{L}{4} + 2$, in feet

B = measured beam (IMS "MB"), in feet

C_B = base center of pressure above vertical center of gravity given as 2, in feet

C = estimated center of pressure above vertical center of gravity given as 2-CGTOT, in feet

I = estimated roll moment of inertia (ft. ^{2}-pounds)

I_B = base roll moment of inertia given by .135 $L^{4.5}$ (ft. ^{2}-pounds)

For more information, see *Final Report of Directors* of the Joint Committee on Safety from Capsizing, available from the United States Yacht Racing Union, Box 209, Newport, RI 02840. Additional information about the International Measurement System (IMS) may also be obtained from USYRU.

CHAPTER 5

Steering Control

Karl L. Kirkman

There is a wide perception that the modern racing and racing-cruising yacht sacrifices a great deal in terms of steering control compared with its predecessors from the years 1920–1965. However, to say that all boats of the era of the fin keel and separated rudder have poor steering control is not quite accurate. Many of these modern boats actually have outstanding control effectiveness under all or most conditions. With a relatively low-resistance underbody and a rudder hung well aft, they can be turned easily and quickly under power and under sail. Yet the current standard of high daring in carrying excessive sail (especially off the wind) has led to accounts and photographs of extreme boats wildly broaching even when sailing upwind (Figure 5-1). All this enhances the fear that every yacht that has these design characteristics has severe and even dangerous control problems.

Many people mistakenly blame these problems on the International Offshore Rule (IOR). However, the tendency toward poor steering control predates the installation of the IOR and has little directly to do with rating rules. Rather, it is an offshoot of the long search by yacht designers for improved performance under steady conditions.

Although it had been noticed for several years, the tendency was first discussed in the technical literature in 1967, three years before the IOR came into effect. In a paper, reporting on some experiments with fin-keel boats, that they delivered to the Society of Naval Architects and Marine Engineers, Paul G. Spens, Pierre DeSaix, and Peter Ward Brown described the mixed results of combining a cutaway keel and a separated rudder. While its upwind performance was greatly enhanced, the boat used in the experiment was unmanageable when sailing off the wind. "In one race," they wrote, "it was reported that on a leeward leg the vessel could not be kept on course [and] rounded up and broached 33 times in three hours!"

Still, as Olin Stephens observed in Chapter 1, it is true that design trends in recent boats that were either built to or inspired by the IOR have tended to exacerbate maneuvering problems. In this chapter, I will look at some of these trends through the lens of hydrodynamic theory, and suggest some solutions to this rather dramatic problem.

Directional Stability

The scientific discipline related to steering properties is known as "stability and control." Like its name, it has two major branches.

Directional stability (in this context often referred to simply as "stability") is

Figure 5-1. Some modern boats are well known for their gyrations when carrying too much sail. Note here how two crew members are perched way aft to try to keep the rudder from lifting out of the water. (Rosenfeld Collection, Mystic Seaport Museum, Inc., Mystic, CT)

the property of a yacht, when affected by some external disturbance (such as a wave), to return to her original course without the helmsman's having to turn the rudder. In other words, a boat with good directional stability "steers herself" quite well under normal conditions. This is not the case with many modern yachts.

In principle, what is required for good directional stability is a system of forces and moments that will come into play to bring the moving object back on course whenever it is disturbed sufficiently to be pushed off its original path. In arrows, airplanes, and bombs, tail fins provide the compensating forces and moments that straighten the flight path. In yachts, keels and skegs serve the same purpose (some more effectively than others). The location, shape, and size of the stabilizing object, be it tail fin or fin keel, all have some effect on directional stability.

If the remainder of this chapter is to have meaning, this concept of directional stability must be understood. Let's look more closely at it, using the arrow as an example.

Figure 5-2 shows the important features of the arrow's stabilizing system. Looking at them from right to left:

- The direction of travel is the path of the center of gravity (CG).
- The location of the CG is the point at which all the parts of the arrow balance each other.
- The tail feathers are located *behind* the CG—that is, away from the direction of travel.

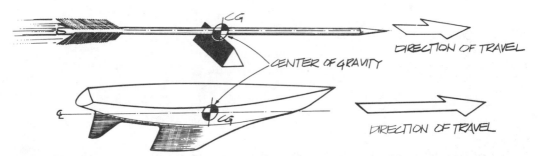

Figure 5-2. Like an arrow, a well-designed boat has its center of gravity at the balance point and in the direction of travel. The rudder—the yacht's stabilizer—lies behind the center of gravity, just as the arrow's feathers do.

Figure 5-3, looking down on the arrow, indicates how the tail feathers provide directional stability. Here are the steps:

1. At the first stage, as the arrow flies along its intended path, some sort of disturbance pushes the point to one side. The disturbance might be a gust of wind, a collision with a bird, a brush against a leaf—it does not matter.

2. At the second stage, the disturbance gives the arrow a yaw angle off the original path. As the arrow's head swings to one side, its feathered tail swings to the other. The tail feathers are now like a wing, with an angle of attack and a resulting lift force. This lift force serves as a "restoring" moment; that is, a torque develops that tends to line the arrow back up on the original direction of travel.

3. At the third stage, the alignment is complete and the tail feathers no longer generate lift.

What would happen if the feathers were located elsewhere on the arrow? To answer this question, we must use some technical terms: "stable," "unstable," and "neutrally stable":

- "Stable" describes an object that cannot be upset or affected by a slight disturbance, much like a cone sitting on its flat base.
- "Unstable" describes an object that is unbalanced, like a cone teetering on its point.
- "Neutrally stable" describes an object, like a stationary ball on a flat surface, that has no particular inclination either to return to its original position or to go to some new position.

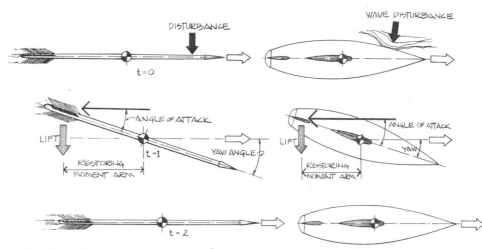

Figure 5-3. This overhead view shows how the stabilizers work. At time 0, the arrow and boat are in stable motion until disturbances affect them. At time 1, the arrowhead and bow have been pushed off to a yaw angle and the stabilizers (feathers and rudder) generate lift and begin to restore stability. At time 2, stability is restored and the arrow and boat are back on course. The circle is the center of gravity.

Now let's apply these definitions as we move the feathers around on our arrow. Figure 5-4 shows what happens with the feathers away from the flight path, toward the flight path, and over the CG:

a. *Stable.* When the feathers are far back, they tend to generate a restoring torque that turns around the CG, as was shown in Figure 5-3, and restores directional stability.

b. *Unstable.* When the feathers are far forward, the arrow is like the teetering cone: instead of generating a restoring moment, they generate an upsetting moment turning around the CG. This moment makes the arrow directionally unstable. In other words, the feathers create a torque that turns the arrow end for end. If and when the feathers are at the end away from the flight path, the arrow becomes directionally stable.

c. *Neutrally stable.* When the feathers are at the CG, they generate a lift force when the arrow yaws, but since that force is exactly lined up with the CG, no turning moment is generated. There is only a force without effect because there is no turning arm. The arrow will remain on its yawed path without correction.

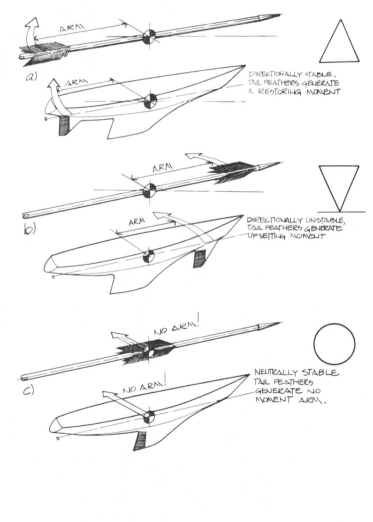

Figure 5-4. (a) Directional stability in an arrow and boat comes when the feathers and rudder are far enough back to generate a course-restoring torque around the center of gravity. This keeps the course from being permanently affected by a slight disturbance, much the way a cone is stabilized by its flat base.
(b) Directional instability results when the feathers and rudder are far forward. Instead of restoring the object, they upset it, much the way a cone tends to be upset when it teeters on its tip.
(c) "Neutrally stable" describes an object that has no inclination to change position or course, either in restoration or in upset. A ball on a table is neutrally stable, and so are arrows and boats whose feathers and rudder are right at the center of gravity—the arrow or boat can't be steered.

What this shows is that the greatest stability occurs when the feathers are well back of the CG. We will see how this applies to boats when we get deeper into our discussion of keels and rudders.

Control Effectiveness

Control effectiveness (or "control") is the property of the maneuvering device (the rudder) to overpower disturbing forces. On a boat, good control allows quick maneuverability during tacks, jibes, and less radical course alterations, as well as when the rudder must be used to compensate for large disturbances that cannot be handled by the keel and skeg alone. The position and size of the rudder affect its power to control the boat.

Compared with ships, yachts are relatively unstable and quite controllable: while yachts do not hold their course well, they have good rudder effectiveness. But as every experienced sailor knows, there are big differences between individual types of yachts, and a basic conflict exists between stability and control. A yacht with superb directional stability will strongly resist waves, rolls, and other turning forces and so stay on a given course extremely well without much steering. Yet such a boat is also hard to maneuver with the rudder. By "hard" I mean that a turn will involve large rudder forces to overpower the directional stability. Those forces create a physical problem for the helmsman, and they also cause high drag, which leads to a loss of speed. On the other hand, an easily controlled boat with good maneuverability, while it will turn quickly with little rudder action and loss of speed, will require assiduous (though probably not physically stressful) steering in order to be kept on a steady course.

To summarize in a sentence: boats that steer easily also run off course easily.

The Trade-offs

Inevitably, then, the designer and the client are facing a problem involving trade-offs. If the boat is intended for racing, directional stability can be very much a handicap, since each tack may cause the loss of a number of boat lengths to a competitor that tacks more easily. An extreme example of a boat designed purely with racing in mind is the model yacht. When sailing upwind these boats tack very often, sometimes as frequently as every few boat lengths. To minimize resistance they are rigged with a steering device that serves more as a stabilizing fin (like an arrow's feather) than as a rudder. When this device is more or less centered, the boat is perfectly balanced and sails a straight course. Putting the helm down takes the fin off center (much like changing the shape of one feather on an arrow). This causes the boat's center of lateral resistance (CLR) to move forward. With the sail area's center of effort (CE) now well aft of the CLR, the boat develops weather helm, rounds up, and tacks. The stabilizing fin is then recentered, and the boat sails off on a directionally stable course on the new tack. Model boats without this fine balance are noncompetitive.

Yachts—and not just model racing boats—can be made very maneuverable. On a yacht there is a live, presumably knowledgeable helmsman ready to correct course with rudder movement. If not, there may very well be a strong, sensitive, self-steering wind vane system. That being the case, we must ask the following question: "When a boat is designed for offshore sailing, what is wrong with strongly emphasizing maneuverability (control) and deemphasizing directional stability?" After all, the armed forces have developed highly maneuverable, highly unstable fighter planes that can be steered by computers.

The answer to this question is complex, but in terms of seamanship it involves two distinct problems that lead designers to build in considerable directional stability.

First, the control effectiveness sufficient for normal conditions may not suffice in very rough conditions offshore. The combination of helmsman or wind vane and rudder may be capable of handling, say, regular 4-foot seas, but when they encounter irregular breakers during a gale, they may need the help of a hull that is more directionally stable.

Second, no helmsman or wind vane is perfect even some of the time. Operating an inherently unstable vehicle, like a yacht running before a Force 10 gale, requires great concentration and invites mistakes. That's why most practical vehicles, such as automobiles and airplanes, are forgiving—which means inherently directionally stable. They must be able to "forgive" the driver's or pilot's inevitable errors. While steering a directionally *unstable* yacht on a gusty day is the equivalent of walking a swaying tightrope, with a directionally *stable* yacht it's more like driving a car.

Wind and Waves

Let's now look at the nature of disturbing forces in the sailing environment—the nautical equivalents of those gusts and obstructions that throw an arrow into a yaw—and why they cause problems in actual designs. These forces are the wind and waves, and their power can be larger than they initially appear. A gust of wind acting on the sails has much greater effect than the increase in velocity indicates. Instead of increasing in a straight line, the force of the wind increases as the wind velocity squared. Therefore, when the wind's velocity doubles, its force quadruples.

What that means is that a relatively small increase in wind velocity can have a big effect on the boat. That force—sharply increasing wind pressure on the sails—causes the boat to roll (or heel), and heeling stimulates another disturbing force, which is the yawing (or turning) moment. When a boat rolls or heels to leeward, she develops windward (or weather) helm; when she rolls to windward, she develops leeward (or lee) helm. Of course, the boat's characteristics play a vital role in determining how much helm is developed. Stiff boats heel less than tender ones. In addition, we know that, for the same angle of heel, boats with relatively narrow, symmetrical hulls, such as meter boats and old-fashioned racer-cruisers (whose underbodies are nearly double-ended), develop less helm than modern, tender, beamy boats (whose underbodies are wedge-shaped). Some modern-day racing boats with wide, flat dinghy-like hulls may suddenly develop uncontrollable amounts of helm when their heel angle changes—which is often the case because they have large sail plans over relatively tender hulls. A quick broach is always a threat in these boats.

Some heel—with the accompanying yaw moment—is beneficial because it helps develop just the right amount of weather helm for fast upwind sailing; on most boats, performance is best when there is a slight tug of helm, with the rudder turned 3–5 degrees. Recall for a moment how you were probably taught to sail a dinghy with a sharp forefoot. You rolled (or heeled) the boat slightly to leeward in order to build a bow wave, which pushed the bow to windward. In this common example of a roll-induced yaw moment, the effect is beneficial. But that is not always the case. If a boat—especially a beamy one—rolls suddenly and drastically to leeward, due to either a big wave or a wind gust, it may develop excessive and even dangerous amounts of weather helm that may surprise even a highly talented helmsman and lead to a broach.

Every sailor knows that waves, like sudden gusts, are acutely disturbing forces that throw the boat off course. Larger, heavier boats usually are affected less by waves than are smaller boats, and it makes a difference where on the hull the wave hits, but—upwind and downwind—no yacht goes entirely unaffected by the sea.

Figure 5-5. Broaching is often a risk when running in fresh wind. A roll to windward starts the process that often leads to a roundup to windward or, sometimes, a roundoff to leeward.

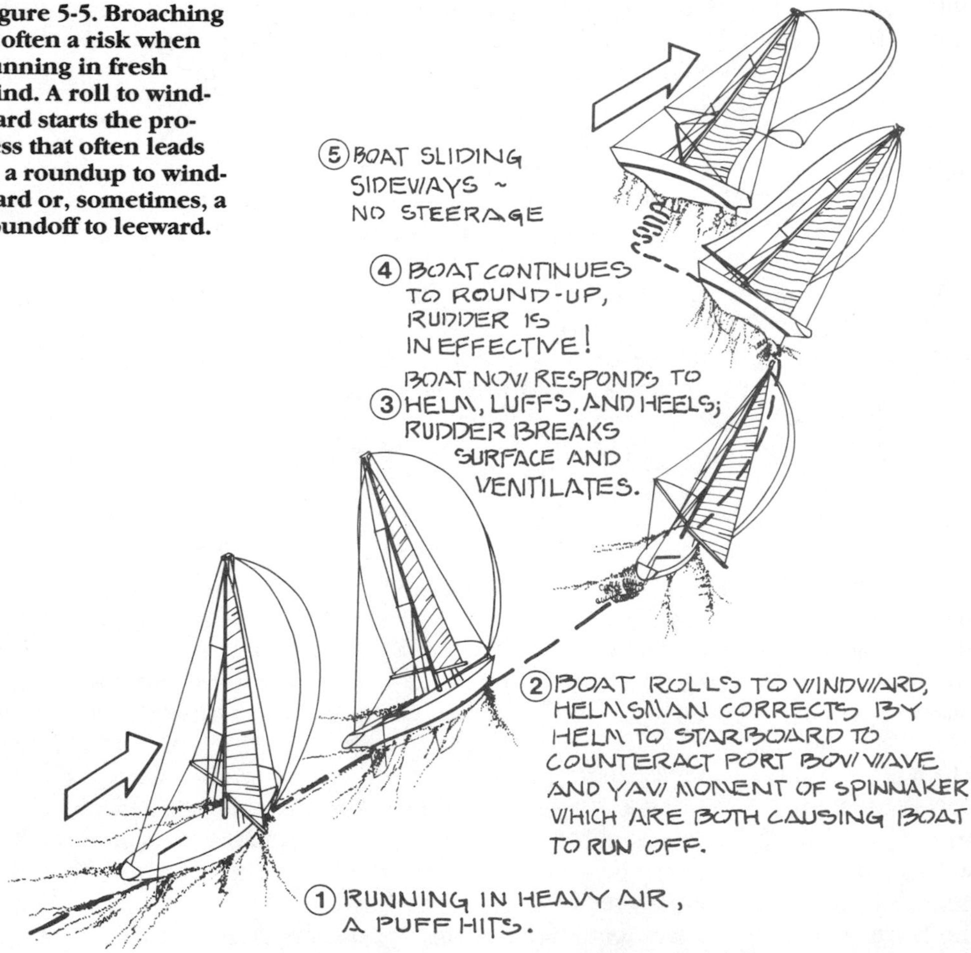

⑤ BOAT SLIDING SIDEWAYS ~ NO STEERAGE

④ BOAT CONTINUES TO ROUND-UP, RUDDER IS INEFFECTIVE!

BOAT NOW RESPONDS TO ③ HELM, LUFFS, AND HEELS; RUDDER BREAKS SURFACE AND VENTILATES.

② BOAT ROLLS TO WINDWARD, HELMSMAN CORRECTS BY HELM TO STARBOARD TO COUNTERACT PORT BOW WAVE AND YAW MOMENT OF SPINNAKER WHICH ARE BOTH CAUSING BOAT TO RUN OFF.

① RUNNING IN HEAVY AIR, A PUFF HITS.

The greatest danger may come when sailing downwind on a run or very broad reach, whether under spinnaker in fresh wind or under mainsail and/or wung-out jib in storm conditions. Then, if the boat is rolled to windward by a wave or gust, she may develop bad leeward helm and, before the helmsman can "catch" her, broach to leeward, perhaps suffering a dangerous accidental jibe as well (Figure 5-5).

In another way, boats with narrow bows and wide sterns are particularly vulnerable when sailing downwind in rough conditions. As the boat surfs at high speed down a wave, the fine, unbuoyant bow may root into the trough and the stern may lift. With the bow now immersed and the stern lifted, the underbody's center of lateral resistance (CLR) moves way forward and weather helm suddenly develops. The boat pivots around the bow and broaches to windward, simultaneously rolling to leeward and lifting the rudder up and out of the water so the helmsman loses steering control. If you're caught out in a storm in a boat like this, the only solution is to keep the speed relatively low by shortening sail or dragging a sea anchor or drogues. Under the same conditions, a moderate boat with fairly full, buoyant bow sections will be slower, but will stay level and more controllable.

Boat Shape

What does all this mean for the designer? Experience, theory, and experiment say that a yacht can behave much like the arrow.

- The hull tends to make the boat *greatly less* directionally stable. Change its underwater shape by heeling it, or slap its bow with a wave, and the boat will yaw.
- The keel makes the boat *slightly less* directionally stable because, like the feathers at the arrow's middle, it is at the center of gravity and so has little effect on returning the hull to its intended path.
- The rudder makes the boat *more* directionally stable. It is like the arrow's feathers; the farther away from the path and the CG it is located, the more effective it will be at developing a moment to restore the boat to its original course, whether she was thrown into a yaw by a sudden roll, by a big wave, or by a combination of the two.

We have looked at the trade-offs—ease of turning versus ease of staying on course—and at how wind and sea can throw a boat off course. Now let's discuss some approaches for designing a safe boat for offshore sailing. What attributes are required for good handling characteristics? Let's work through the three most important features—the hull, keel, and rudder.

The Hull

Hull shape for offshore sailing is given detailed attention in Chapters 1–4, and what is said there about one kind of stability applies generally to directional stability. It is enough to say that, for best directional stability, the hull should be neither too wide nor too wedge-shaped. If the after quarters are too wide, when the boat heels far over the rudder will break the surface and ventilate and lose its control. Of course, if the boat is stiff, she will not heel that far to begin with. Neither should the hull be too fine forward; otherwise, it will dig in and lift the stern and rudder. Good reserve buoyancy forward will keep the bow from rooting in, and so will a forefoot that is not too deep.

The Keel

The size and shape of the keel is a hot issue in discussions of cruising-boat design. Some people favor full-length keels with attached rudders because, they argue, long keels provide excellent directional stability (and can also provide good support during grounding-out). Other people say that that is *too much* directional stability; they prefer fin keels with separated rudders way aft because they allow acceptable stability as well as good maneuverability. They argue that quick steering is good seamanship: you need it to steer around bad waves in rough weather as well as to get around a race course or a crowded harbor. Of course, racing boats have very narrow, deep fin keels providing minimal directional stability but superb maneuverability (as well as excellent capability for catching lobster buoys and kelp).

Actually, the issue of keel length may be more complex. Certainly the longer length of a full-length keel provides more resistance to turning, but this is only part of the story.

I believe that a study of long keels will show that they tend to be only partly lead or iron (unlike solid high-aspect fin keels), and that this ballast is typically located in the keel's "toe." Thus, with the same ballast location, the full-length keel has its center of gravity quite a bit farther forward than does the fin keel. Now recall our earlier discussion of how the feathers affected the arrow. The farther back they were from the center of gravity, the more effect the feathers had on stabilizing. When they were at or near the CG, they had no effect at all even though they developed some force: like a farmer trying to wrench a big rock out of the soil, they need a long lever arm if they are going to have any effect. Remember that keels have some effect on directional stability. A keel whose center of pressure is far aft will have more effect on correcting yaw than one whose center of pressure is under or forward of the center of gravity. What this suggests is that a long keel is not as productive in stabilizing the heading as a fin keel located fairly far aft. A related consideration is that the attached rudder on a long keel is almost always farther forward than the separated rudder that is paired with a fin keel.

Whatever the size of the keel, it should be fairly far aft under the hull to increase directional stability. Putting it forward decreases directional stability, while moving it aft increases stability (unfortunately at some increase of resistance, which may hurt racing performance). One bad trend in racing-boat design has been to trim the boat bow-down (to improve the rating) by moving the lead in the keel forward.

The Rudder

The rudder should be well aft, it must be strong and have a reliable bearing and linkage system, and it must also project well below the water so it remains effective at all angles of heel. No matter what its shape, it must be symmetrical; even a small flat area on one side will cause the boat to be balanced on one tack but unbalanced on the other. (You can check for symmetry using straight edges or by making cardboard templates.)

There has long been a debate about whether the rudder should stand unsupported (the spade rudder) or should be mounted on a skeg. Let us examine the trade-offs. There are practical considerations. A skeg certainly can help to block out weeds or lines from lobster and crab pots. It can also be a good place to mount a propeller aperture leading from a short, unsupported shaft. Skeg construction can be tricky. If it is going to contribute its share of support for the rudder load, it probably should be molded to the hull rather than simply tacked on. Further, the construction of the lower end must be carefully thought out if you want to allow for removal of the rudder.

The hydrodynamic issues concern balance, directional stability, and control effectiveness. First, if they are properly designed, either type can be well balanced, but good balance is in some respects easier with a spade than with a skeg-hung rudder. Against this must be considered the large moment that develops in a spade rudder when the boat is moving astern. I know of a skipper whose ribs were broken by the tiller when he tried to back his boat down under power. Second, directional stability is improved by the skeg because it acts like tail feathers well aft of the center of gravity. The dorsal-type fin forward of many skeg-mounted rudders also acts as a stabilizing factor, allowing brief periods of hands-off sailing when the helmsman has to trim a sail; few spade rudders can be left unattended.

Finally, good control effectiveness is possible with both spade and skeg-mounted rudders, but in slightly different ways. The spade rudder can be quickly turned to large angles of attack, but may stall out (lose effectiveness at sharp angles because water ceases to flow attached to its surface). On the other hand, the skeg-mounted rudder will turn less quickly but will have camber—which keeps it from stalling at sharp angles of attack.

Summary

This overview of the problem of steering control has shown that this aspect of yacht design, like many others, involves several design compromises. There are few "correct" solutions. However, a number of unfortunate trends encouraged by racing are not suitable for good sea boats. Some of these, resulting from concern for pure speed and preoccupation with low ratings under handicap rules, fail to make any practical sense, especially for a boat that is headed out into rough weather.

CHAPTER 6

Modern Yacht Construction

James A. McCurdy

The hull is one part of the boat without which the boat does not exist. The importance of sound hull construction derives from this fact. The proper goal in hull construction is to produce the required strength and stiffness with the least weight of material. Unnecessary weight makes a boat more difficult to manage and less enjoyable to sail. It also makes for greater material cost. An example of inefficient hull construction is a fiberglass boat built without reinforcing bulkheads, stringers, or floors. In this case, the unsupported skin must be heavy enough to provide the required strength and stiffness by itself.

The structural arrangements and scantlings of the hull must combine to produce sufficient strength to survive the stresses of intended service. For an offshore racing-cruising yacht these stresses are not limited to those resulting from weather and sea conditions that the boat may be expected to encounter during her useful life. Rather, they are stresses caused by conditions rare enough to be met by the one boat in a thousand that is in the wrong place at the wrong time. Stated another way, there are combinations of circumstances that a boat could statistically be expected to encounter once during a service life of say, 1000 years. Whether this will occur during the first year or the thousandth year cannot be predicted, but if its occurrence is not allowed for in hull construction, the element of risk should not be acceptable to any owner who is not a gambler. (The reference here is not to a truly "freak" wave, which by definition has no statistical probability.)

Loads of Stresses

The entire hull structure is not uniformly stressed by the forces of the sea (Figure 6–1). Bending loads produced by waves and by fore-and-aft rigging stresses concentrate stresses amidships and high and low—at the deck edge and garboard area. Traditional construction systems took this into account by requiring longitudinal members to be made heavier or to be added in these locations. Tapering of these longitudinal members toward the ends of the ship was permitted. Similar variations in structure are desirable in new construction systems.

Under bending loads, the deck is heavily stressed because it functions as the top flange of the hull girder. For this reason the deck must possess strength of the same order of magnitude as the topsides of the hull along the deck edge. Deck strength should not be compromised by hatch or cockpit openings that are excessive in number or in size. This is particularly important amidships and near the deck edge. A deck that is only strong enough to support crew weight is woefully inadequate.

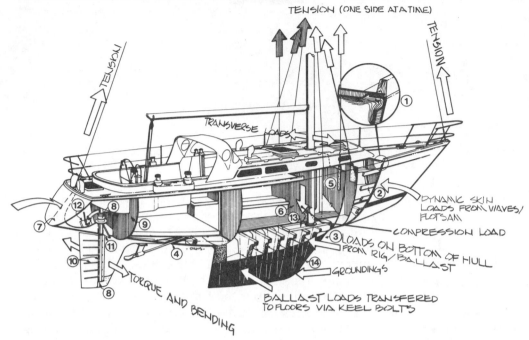

Figure 6-1. The loads on a boat and rig are varied and large. Here are some important construction details.

(1) **The hull-to-deck joint should be made with fiberglass bond as well as mechanical fasteners.**

(2) **Longitudinal stringers reinforce flat sections of the hull.**

(3) **Vertical floors help distribute ballast weight and mast compressive loads throughout the bottom structure.**

(4) **The propeller shaft bearing should be reinforced both to aid in shaft alignment and to withstand vibration forces should the shaft come out of alignment.**

(5) **Chain plates spread rigging loads to the structural bulkheads and brackets, and thence to the hull.**

(6) **Transverse bulkheads adjacent to the rig and cockpit help distribute loads throughout the structure.**

(7) **A vertical bracket in the transom helps to transfer backstay tension load to the adjacent structure. It also serves to stiffen the transom against the force of boarding seas from astern.**

(8) **There should be strong bearings at the top and bottom of the rudder.**

(9) **A transverse bulkhead both adds support to the cockpit and provides rigidity and support for the skeg attachment.**

(10) **The rudder stock should be large, with a reinforcement in the rudder to resist torque.**

(11) **The rudder stock should be reinforced to distribute lateral loads imposed by the rudder.**

(12) **All through-hull fittings should have extra reinforcing in way of the fittings.**

(13) **The mast step should bear on the floors both forward and aft of the vertical load. This distributes the compressive force to the bottom structure.**

(14) **External (rather than encapsulated) lead ballast is preferred in fiberglass boats, providing that the ballast is well engineered with a sufficient number of properly located keel bolts.**

The sea also produces severe local loads when a yacht is being driven to windward. These result from slamming into seas, and are concentrated on the lee side of the forepart of the vessel. Typically, this loading reaches a maximum halfway between the stem and mast. In this area, the hull surface is rather flat, and the lack of strong curvature makes the skin itself less able to resist the force it encounters. Here, structural stiffening is needed in combination with a thicker skin. Here, too, transverse and/or longitudinal framing both heavier and more closely spaced than elsewhere in the hull is required. Attention to the last requirement was noticeably absent in traditional scantling rules but is found in the more sophisticated of the newer systems.

Aluminum hulls that are grossly understrength in this forward area will have their plating permanently dented when encountering heavy going to windward. Understrength fiberglass hulls will exhibit extreme flexing under similar conditions, but the only permanent traces of inadequacy may be damage to the interior accommodations, as delamination is not visible. (Bear in mind that the stresses produced by *normal* heavy going to windward are quite small when compared to those resulting from the extraordinary conditions defined above, when deflection could translate into destruction.)

Impact loads resulting from contact with floating objects, including other vessels, and contact with immovable objects such as rocks and piers all require strength in the hull skin itself as distinct from the combination of skin and framing. The hull skin must be substantially more robust than the word "skin" would indicate.

Structural Systems

The forces of the sea that work on the hull of a sailing yacht are not subject to calculation with a useful degree of precision. Fortunately this lack is made up for by a long history of trial and error—experience that can be used to design hull structures in traditional, new, or yet-to-be-developed materials.

In the days before traditional wood and steel construction had been complemented and then largely replaced by more advanced techniques and materials, there were long-established scantling rules developed by designers and builders and by organizations such as Lloyd's Register of Shipping. These time-proven rules could be counted on, in combination with good workmanship, to produce sound hulls.

Today there are many systems employed in hull construction. Many of them are proprietary in the sense that they have been developed and are used by individual builders. Examples include the WEST system of epoxy-saturated wood, cold-molded wood techniques, cored fiberglass hulls, and composites using a variety of resins in combination with reinforcing materials of different types of glass fiber, carbon fiber, and Kevlar. While experience is required for proof of the efficacy of any new system, if its calculated strength approximates that of time-tested systems it can be accepted initially with some degree of confidence.

A new form of scantling rule with strength standards derived from various systems that have had satisfactory service experience has been produced by the American Bureau of Shipping. This is the *Guide for Building and Classing Off-*

shore Racing Yachts. It contains formulas for calculating the strength of elements of hull structure put together in a variety of ways from a variety of materials. The strength standards are the minimum acceptable for grand prix racing yachts, few of which see true offshore passages. However, compliance with the standards set by the *Guide* is an indication of a soundly engineered hull—about the only such indication available other than the reputation of the builder and designer.

The structural arrangements used by the manufacturers of production fiberglass boats are often dictated by considerations of end use and material and labor economy. Very few production boats are used as true offshore cruising-racing yachts, so it is perhaps unrealistic to expect all of them to be built to the exacting standards required by offshore service.

The scantlings and framing systems used for aluminum hulls are still largely proprietary but there has been an increasing standardization in the use of closely spaced longitudinal stringers in conjunction with rather widely spaced transverse frames. This is a rational development. Quality of welding is as important to the structural integrity of an aluminum hull as quality of fastening is to a wooden hull. Neither can be judged well except by destruction testing of sample welds.

Meeting Concentrated Loads

The hull must be locally strengthened to withstand concentrated loads imposed by the mast and rigging, the ballast keel, and the rudder (if skeg-mounted or spade). All these loads must be spread out over an area as large as practicable. Bulkheads and vertical floors are the best way to distribute the stresses from ballast weight and mast compression. The mast step must distribute mast compression fore and aft to floors. A bulkhead close to the mast is a desirable feature. Chain-plate loads should be spread by a hull attachment that is as long as possible—a structural bulkhead is ideal.

Bulkheads required by the interior accommodations can do double duty and will contribute greatly to the structural integrity of the hull and deck if they are installed as true structural members rather than simple partitions. Considerable strength is gained this way, at very little expense in weight.

Metal pipe stanchions can be used to tie the hull and deck together in locations where structural bulkheads are absent. Their use is particularly appropriate in metal hulls because of the simplicity of attachment by welding to deck beams and floors. At points where the deck structure concentrates loads, they are extremely effective as support members. In a metal hull a stanchion is a much superior substitute for the tie rod often installed just forward or aft of the mast.

The sides and tops of integral tanks can add to the longitudinal strength and stiffening of metal and fiberglass hulls if they can be arranged to be continuous over a reasonable distance, or at least between structural bulkheads.

The hull should be strongly reinforced around a propeller shaft strut attachment or stern bearing. The vibration produced by a bent propeller blade or shaft can impose severe stresses on the strut attachment or stern tube, capable of cracking the hull.

The hull/deck joint can be a weak point in fiberglass hulls. Mechanical fastening alone is often not adequate to keep these two essential parts of the hull from parting company. Fiberglass bonding across the inside of this joint can be used to bring it up to the same strength as the adjoining hull and deck surfaces.

A fiberglass hull laid up in a single rather than a split mold avoids potential weakness along its centerline because there is no suggestion of a centerline joint.

The skin of the hull should be reinforced in the way of all through-hull fittings, such as water intakes.

A spade rudder should have a stock large enough to support its cantilever load and it should have upper and lower bearings separated as far as can be accommodated. A skeg-mounted rudder can have a fair portion of its cantilever load taken by the skeg, providing the skeg itself is strong and strongly attached to the hull.

Centerboards

In general, a centerboard is not a desirable feature unless a boat is to be used in an area that requires shoal draft.

Centerboards can produce highly concentrated stresses on the hull in rough weather or grounding. These loads increase in proportion to the amount of centerboard exposed outside the boat as compared to the amount that remains inside the trunk. This is a simple leverage situation; as a rough rule the centerboard should extend up into the trunk at least half as far as it extends down below the keel when fully lowered. The centerboard trunk itself must be quite robust to withstand the centerboard forces and to give the crew confidence when the board is thumping.

The rudder on a centerboard boat should not extend below the maximum draft of the rest of the boat with the centerboard raised.

An extremely heavy centerboard or drop keel is not suitable for an offshore cruiser-racer both because of the large forces required to handle it and because of the loads that it imposes on the hull.

Ballast

Lead is the preferred material for ballast. Compared to iron, lead is 60 percent more dense, and it does not require protection against rust. Still, an externally mounted iron ballast keel will not be dented or damaged when it hits rock or coral.

Lead can be mounted either internally or externally. On aluminum hulls, internal casting by pouring in place is preferred. Since it is imbedded in the actual structure of the keel part of the hull, internal ballast is very strongly supported and concentrated loads from keel bolts are avoided. With external ballast, however, in the presence of seawater, electrolysis will occur between aluminum and lead, the aluminum being the metal under attack. Therefore, welded aluminum cover plates must be installed to seal internal ballast from bilge water, and an external lead keel must be isolated from all metal-to-metal contact with the hull. Keel bolts must be insulated with plastic sleeves and washers.

For fiberglass hulls, an external ballast casting is preferred, providing that proper attention is given to the size and distribution of keel bolts and to the strength of the bottom of the hull into which they extend. A problem with internal castings for fiberglass boats is that pouring in place is not possible. A separate casting must be lowered into the keel cavity and bedded in a resin mixture. In addition, with this arrangement, there can be no structural members running through the ballast to the hull; the ballast is attached to the hull only by the skin of the keel. And due to the thickness of the keel skin and the clearance required for insertion of the ballast casting, internal ballast will be undesirably higher than an externally mounted casting of the same weight. There is no electrolysis problem between fiberglass and lead.

Electrolytic Corrosion

Dissimilar metals in contact or electrically connected in a saltwater environment produce an electrolytic reaction similar to that of an electrochemical battery. One of the metals will be attacked by the other. This electrolytic attack will vary in intensity depending on the potential difference between the metals and their respective masses.

Just about every other metal will attack zinc. Therefore, zinc is often introduced to protect other metals by sacrificing itself. It must be in good electrical contact with the metal to be protected. Until the zinc is consumed, it will bear the brunt of the attack. Flush-mounted zinc plates can be used in this fashion to protect an aluminum or steel hull. The degree to which the zinc is attacked is an indication of the electrolytic forces at work; rapid wastage of zinc is a warning that a potentially dangerous corrosion situation exists and should be corrected. At the same time, the zinc will provide temporary protection.

The various ferrous alloys known as stainless steel have complicated reactions to electrolytic corrosion and can even attack themselves. It is safest not to use them in applications where they are continuously immersed in seawater.

Quality Control

In the case of custom-built boats, the experience and reputation of designer *and* builder provide the best basis for judging the quality of hull construction. For production boats, the experience and reputation of the builder should be given more weight because the designer, if not part of the builder's organization, often has only weak control over the actions of the builder.

The structural adequacy of a fiberglass hull is difficult to judge. The presence of reinforcing members is one encouraging sign. Their absence should raise questions. There are two simple tests that can identify grossly inadequate hull structures. Out of the water, the boat should be able to stand with its weight essentially all on its keel without visible hull distortion. In the water, hull deflection under the load of fore-and-aft standing rigging can be observed by running a taut string or wire from bow pulpit to stern pulpit touching one side of the mast. Start with the backstay slack and mark the point where the string touches the mast. Crank up the backstay to full tension (one-third breaking strength), tighten up the string if necessary, and see how far above the original mark it crosses the mast. This is the measure of hull deflection in way of the mast. By comparing deflection on similar-size boats, you should be able to evaluate stiffness.

Rigidity

Rigidity of hull structure is desirable in itself, a distinct from strength, but only in association with it. A structure that is both weak and rigid invites failure. A glass Christmas tree ornament is an example. A hull that flexes very little under rigging loads will permit headsail efficiency to be maintained by limiting jibstay sag as the wind increases. This can be quite important for racing.

If of equal strength, an aluminum alloy or steel hull will flex the least, closely followed by composites with high-strength unidirectional reinforcing material. Cold-molded wood comes next, conventional wood construction follows, and woven fiberglass (unless cored) brings up the rear. Cored woven fiberglass construction approximates cold-molded wood.

Merits of Construction Materials

Aluminum alloy is the material of choice for larger one-off custom designs. It offers a relatively rigid structure with the highest strength-to-weight ratio unless the hull is small enough for plating thickness to be in excess of strength requirements in order to be thick enough for welding. This is as one might expect from aluminum's use in aircraft construction. It is not suited to production boats because very little of the labor required can be eliminated by investment in tooling.

The marine aluminum alloys currently in use are resistant to chemical corrosion to the extent that paint is not required to protect them from attack by seawater. Paint is, however, required for appearance's sake, as is the application of surfacing compounds to smooth out plating distortion caused by the heat of welding.

On the other hand, aluminum is quite vulnerable to electrolytic corrosion caused by contact with dissimilar metals or imposed by improperly designed and installed electrical systems. With proper design, construction, and maintenance, all based on a thorough understanding of this vulnerability, aluminum is not a problem.

Aluminum alloy construction requires insulation under the deck to reduce heat transfer and minimize noise. Insulation of the inside of the hull is required for the same reasons and to eliminate sweating. Sprayed-on, flame-retardant urethane insulation can be applied quickly, easily, and permanently. Bilges below the level of the cabin sole should be left free of insulation.

Fiberglass-reinforced plastic is the material of choice for production boats. The material, commonly polyester resin reinforced either with fiberglass mat and woven roving or in a composite with Kevlar or other space-age materials, has been around for so many years that it has come to be defined by the simple term "fiberglass." The amount of skilled labor required can be drastically reduced by substantial tooling investment, the cost of which can be spread over a large number of hulls.

A fiberglass structure has a relatively high strength-to-weight ratio, but is extremely flexible for its strength. A fiberglass hull should be designed for stiffness. If it is stiff enough, it will be more than strong enough, barring poor detail design and construction. Careful design of bulkhead and stringer stiffening and local reinforcement can produce sufficient rigidity without requiring really excessive weight. Lack of attention to structural engineering in fiberglass hulls will produce boats that are undesirably flexible or heavy. Use of composite materials can stiffen and lighten the hull.

Composite and fiberglass hulls are not subject to corrosion or deterioration from age (except for surface effects). They can be repaired using relatively simple equipment.

Quality control of composite and fiberglass layups is not easy to maintain and flaws or lack of uniformity are difficult to detect in the finished product. The reputation of the builder is perhaps the surest, if not the only, guide in this connection.

Cold-molded wood construction is a term that covers wood held together by glues and resins rather than a complete reliance on individual fastenings, as in conventional wood construction. The word "cold" means that high temperatures requiring the special application of heat are not required for glue curing. Modern glues permit the construction of a wooden hull, the parts of which are permanently bonded together and essentially of one piece, with grain direction determined by lamination rather than steam bending or selection of natural curvature.

Cold-molded construction may be done by builders who have normal woodworking capabilities but who lack the experience, skills, and equipment needed for aluminum or fiberglass construction. It can produce boats far superior in strength and rigidity to those built with conventional wood construction, and with a strength-to-weight ratio second only to aluminum and a rigidity exceeding that of fiberglass construction.

While the product is impressive, at the same time one is forcibly reminded of the British cavalry, which on the eve of World War I reached a peak of perfection far exceeding anything ever seen, only to be quickly made irrelevant by the arrival of a radically different technology.

Conventional wood construction is an exercise of great skill utilizing the best materials available before, say, 1960. Today the skills are scarcer, as are the materials, and the virtues of the product are now largely sentimental or historical.

Steel construction cannot be considered as satisfactory for an offshore cruising yacht less than 75 to 100 feet in length. Steel is subject to chemical corrosion in seawater and an initial thickness of material beyond that required for strength is needed to ensure that sufficient strength will remain after some of the surface has been eaten away by rust. The extra thickness required for corrosion is the same for a small boat or a large ship. This means that the smaller vessel must carry a disproportionate and unacceptable amount of weight that is not required for strength.

Ferrocement is not satisfactory for yacht construction. Like a wattle and daub hut it can be useful when the skills and materials (including money) required for better construction are absent, but that is its only redeeming feature.

PART II

ON DECK
AND
BELOW

CHAPTER 7

The Deck

Daniel D. Strohmeier

Without a deck, an otherwise good offshore boat is just an open boat. But it is more than just a lid. A well-made deck is a structural member for the hull, a platform and protective cover for the crew, and a support for the rig. As such, the deck is capable of harboring a good many undesirable features. Let me count the ways.

My comments are pitched to the requirements of a dual-purpose offshore yacht. "Dual-purpose" means different things to different people, with the spectrum ranging widely from a ratio of about 10 percent racing to 90 percent cruising at one end, to about 90 to 10 at the other end. I'm assuming a scale tipped slightly toward cruising, which means that considerations of comfort and livability will take some priority over those of racing efficiency.

The deck has six functions that must be satisfied for safety, comfort, and efficiency:

- It should contribute to the overall strength and stiffness of the hull and rig.
- For safety, it should keep the ocean out.
- For comfort, it should keep drips and dollops out.
- It should be a good platform for boat-handling and navigation gear.
- It should provide a safe, comfortable working area for the crew and guests.
- It should provide good below-deck headroom, ventilation, and access.

Let's consider each of these functions, touching on undesirable as well as desirable features.

The Deck and Boat Strength

The deck makes several major contributions to the boat's overall strength and stiffness. First, it acts like the top flange of an I-beam, serving as the upper chord in the scheme of longitudinal strength. The deck resists the heavy longitudinal compression loads imposed by the downward thrust of the mast and the upward pull of the stays and sheets, which try to bend the yacht into the shape of a banana. At the partners it helps keep the mast in column and, therefore, in one piece.

The deck also serves the essential purpose of providing torsional stiffness to the hull, thereby converting heeling and twisting moments into righting moments and keeping the boat from changing shape under sailing load. Without the deck, a yacht's hull would have the torsional flabbiness of an open shoe box—giving and shaking like a jelly fish under every force. In any structure with a large opening, if you can find a way to preserve the shape of the opening, the torsional loads on the entire structure will be resisted. For example, an undecked dinghy would have almost no hull stiffness whatsoever were the shape of the large opening between the stem, gunwale, and transom not maintained through the use of brackets, breast-hooks, thwarts, and the like.

A deck works much more efficiently than those supports, even when it is broken up by companionways, hatchways, and cabin trunks. However, the stresses around those holes and structures can be large. Since these stresses tend to be concentrated at their corners—especially at the inside of sharp turns—the crew must be alert to signs of stress (cracks) in any opening. In fiberglass, aluminum, and other non-wood structures, cracks starting in these corners may propagate in the same way that a nick in a piece of cellophane can lead to an easy tear.

A valuable structural member is a bridge deck between the cockpit and the companionway. The bridge deck helps to hold the port and starboard sides apart while absorbing athwartships stresses. If there is no bridge deck, transverse stresses must zigzag across one side deck, up or down and across the cabin trunk or cockpit, and then across the other side deck. This places considerable strain on the cockpit and cabin, which, compared with the deck, are relatively weak torsionally. Another advantage of the bridge deck is that it is a strong, simple support for the main sheet traveler. If the traveler is put on the cabin roof, it will require a complicated support that looks like the Chicago Loop. On older boats with long booms, if the traveler is put abaft the wheel it may be dangerous to the helmsman; at least one life has been lost in a Chinese jibe when the slack main sheet snagged the helmsman overboard (Figure 7-1).

Keeping Out the Ocean

It is a matter of record that collapsing decks have been stopped by the inside of the hull. The deck must be stiff so it is not fatigued by continued flexing under the crew's feet, and it must be strong. The force of a breaking sea on a deck cannot be appreciated until it has been experienced. When water comes on board heavily, everything attached to the deck that is more than a few inches high will try to act as a breakwater and attempt to rip the deck itself off the hull at the rail.

Obviously, the hull-to-deck joint is critical. If it fails, not only will a lot of ocean be let in but the structural integrity of the entire hull will be compromised. In fiberglass boats, the joint should be composed of flanges secured by many bolts and much reinforcement. Short of a full-scale inspection by a professional boat surveyor, any inadequacy here may not be readily apparent.

On the other hand, if the deck remains bonded to the hull, any prominent object on deck may be either smashed in or swept overboard by a big wave. The greatest and most dangerous risks are to cabins and their ports, often on the leeward side when a yacht is rolled down by a cresting sea or falls off a wave. Inadequacy here may lead to loss of the yacht. Fiberglass boats are less likely to lose their cabin trunks than wooden ones because, in fiberglass construction, the trunk and deck are one piece. In wooden boats, where they are separate, the

Figure 7-1. A secure cockpit, clean deck layout (with plenty of grab rails), and wide, reinforcing bridge deck are demonstrated by Ted Turner's 62-foot *Tenacious,* which Lynn Williams built as *Dora IV*. Turner won the stormy 1979 Fastnet Race in her, and later sold her to Warren Brown, who renamed her *War Baby* and sailed her to the Arctic. (Rosenfeld Collection, Mystic Seaport Museum, Inc., Mystic, CT)

trunk should be well fastened to the deck with drifts or bolts.

Ports are especially vulnerable. The safest design for a cabin port is an elongated ellipse. Rectangular ports may seem more attractive, but they are structurally poor because of the abrupt transition between the gross and the net. Plexiglas storm shutters should be available to be bolted over the larger ports, with a small gap between shutter and window so that sudden wave impacts can be absorbed without damaging the window itself.

Earlier, I spoke of the bridge deck's value as a structural member. It also helps to keep the ocean out of the cabin after a breaking wave fills the cockpit. Another important barrier is a set of strong boards to be inserted in the companionway, which should be capable of being secured with a lock so they won't fall out in a very bad roll. Of course, one, two, or all three of these boards must be in place to keep the cabin dry when a wave comes aboard. I've noticed that whenever the sea gets a bit rough it is not until the first "freak wave" that the crew is prompted to the necessary discipline of inserting the boards. The reason for this, I think, is that when even one board is in place the crew must perform a considerable acrobatic feat to get below, thanks to the present-day trend of building the cabin so that its after side slopes forward over the companionway ladder.

No offshore yacht should have fewer than two paths of escape to the deck from the cabin. These openings include the companionway, forward hatchway, and skylights. Of course, all these deck openings should be capable of being closed tightly against the sea. The companionway is the most important of these. While it need not (and probably cannot) be totally watertight, its sliding hatch cover and hatch boards must be able to stand up against the dynamics of slamming seas.

The forward hatch calls for special attention in selection, installation, and use. There should be a provision for securing and releasing it both on deck and below. Even worse than a hatch cover that won't open is a hatch cover that won't close; in heavy weather, the open hole left by a broken hatch cover can sink a boat. The cover and hinge should be strong enough to take both a sea and crew mishandling, as well as tight enough to resist dribbling leaks. Some hatches will bend or break when stepped on while open or when a loaded line gets jammed under the lip. Strong supports, like the ones on my Concordia yawl, will handle the first challenge, and guards constructed of wooden blocks will protect the lips from flying jib sheets.

As the 1979 Fastnet Race storm proved, there is one very good reason why the deck should have watertight integrity and why those big openings should be sealable: the possibility of a modern yacht's being rolled over all the way is a very real one. This startling development has already been covered in considerable detail in Chapters 2, 3, and 4. Here, we should say a word or two about how capsizes are related to deck layout.

Many boats may, in fact, be quite happy in a stable, bottom-up mode for minutes at a time. But when a boat is upside down, a badly leaking deck is a poor substitute for her bottom. In the case of such an inversion, some ingress of water is unavoidable, but the yacht should stay afloat until the next kindly wave knocks her off dead center and she rights herself. Besides the hatches and skylights, smaller openings—including vents, hinged cockpit seats, blower openings, and Coast Guard–mandated engine ventilators—should be sealable.

Clearly, some gear that was considered safe for older, more stable designs should be viewed with some apprehension by the owner or potential owner of an unstable, beamy, light-displacement racer-cruiser. For instance, the Dorade ventilator, which for 50 years has worked so well in the roughest weather on boats that stay upright, may not be so effective at separating air and water when it is immersed upside down. Unlike a regular vent cowl, which can be readily removed and replaced with a screw-in plug, the normal Dorade has scuppers that cannot be easily sealed off on deck. The solution is either to rig a system whereby a screw-in cap can be inserted from inside the cabin or to dispense with the Dorade altogether.

There is a state between upright and inverted stability that can lead to down-flooding, when the water pours below through large openings. That may occur in a broach, where a yacht is heeled over on her beam ends. A good deck layout will position all openings to the interior close to the centerline. Off-center companionways are a poor compromise between convenient layout below and overall safety of the yacht. Companionways, skylight, vents, and hatches should be arranged so that they are well above the water when the boat is heeled 90 degrees.

An exception to this rule must be made for lockers under cockpit seats, which, unlike the openings mentioned above, are normally closed.

Keeping Out Drips and Dollops

An undesirable feature of almost all decks is that they have small leaks. I'm not talking about water sluicing through openings intentionally cut into the deck but about sneaky drips through unintended openings. Though not dangerous, they can degrade habitability out of all proportion to the amount of water that gets in. While serious risk from flooding can enhance crew morale in the common cause of survival, a deck leak that drips into someone's bunk every ten minutes has exactly the opposite effect.

Such water passes through the deck in several places. In fiberglass and metal boats, perhaps the most common leak is through the fastenings for deck fittings, such as jib-sheet tracks and inboard chain plates (which always seem to be over berths). The only solution is to remove the fastenings and rebed them and their fittings with silicone sealant or polysulfide bedding compound. Wooden boats often leak in the same places, but they also can suffer weeping through seams that are inadequately payed or areas where structural components don't fit. If you are unable to dry off the leaking area, a sealant called Life-Caulk will stick over a leak when bedding compounds peel away. If hatches and ports leak, it's often because their rubber gaskets have dried out; some extra gasket material should be carried along.

One way to keep water from seeping below is to prevent it from collecting on deck in the first place. On many boats, deck water is drained overboard through scuppers or limber holes let into the toerail, but the flow may be slow and may cause unsightly dirty streaks on the topsides. A proper yacht should be fitted with internal scuppers that pick up water at the low point of the sheer and drain it overboard below the waterline.

A Platform for Gear

The general arrangement on deck must be carefully planned to avoid undesirable features. To this opinionated contributor, a good dual-purpose yacht should cater to considerations for practical cruising at some compromise to purely racing features. In general, the deck should provide a relatively clear and uncluttered platform for equipment that is important to the boat's ultimate safety, such as mooring and anchoring gear, as well as boat-handling essentials, including winches, cleats, foot blocks, tracks, and padeyes.

Often, the chock and bow cleat arrangement on deck seems to have been laid out as an afterthought. Not only is the equipment insufficient for the job, but there are sharp deck edges or abrasive fittings in the way of the mooring lines and anchor rodes. On far too many newer yachts, bow chocks are either too small or nonexistent. The ones that are too small were obviously installed by people who thought that the boat would spend her entire life tethered to a marina's float with light docking lines. However, sooner or later the boat will find herself on a guest mooring as her owner struggles to fit a decent-size pendant through the tiny chock. It is gauche to accept the hospitality of a mooring by tying up to it in some Mickey Mouse fashion because your boat isn't properly equipped. The best bow chocks are the so-called Skene types, which have big channels in which the line is securely contained by large overlapping horns (Figure 7-2).

Small mooring cleats forward can save weight and expense, but they are a pain if they are not big enough for the lines they must handle. There should be two of them, not one; even with two cleats you may find yourself in situations— such as raft-ups—when you must lead two or more lines to each cleat.

A yacht that cannot readily launch a dinghy is not much of a yacht. As a rule of thumb, any yacht larger than about 35 feet overall should be capable of carrying a solid or inflatable dinghy on deck abaft the mast. The foredeck is no place for a dinghy, especially if it blocks the forward escape hatch. This means that the top of the cabin trunk should not be monopolized by mainsheet blocks, boom vangs, and go-fast equipment.

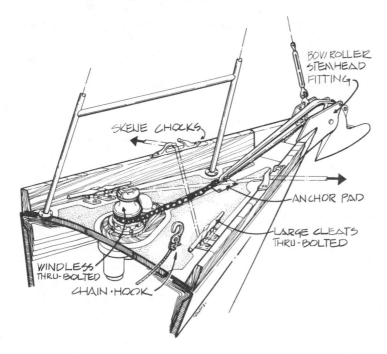

Figure 7-2. A fine foredeck arrangement. The chain hook is on the end of a length of heavy nylon line. Snap the hook over the chain forward of the stem, let out about 10 feet of line and cleat it, and then ease off the chain. The stretchy nylon will absorb shocks that the stiff chain cannot. Note that the rode and mooring lines are led across the foredeck in order to ease chafe through the chocks. The overlapping horns on the Skene-type chock keep the rode from leaping out of the channel.

The Working Crew

The deck must be a safe, comfortable place for crew to work and guests to sit. First of all, that means that there should be plenty of space on deck (Figure 7-3). On many yachts today, too much emphasis has been given to space below. Decks are so cluttered with encroaching cabin trunks, inboard chain plates, and tracks for jib sheets that the crew's path from the cockpit to the foredeck is an obstacle course that requires extraordinary agility if one is not to twist an ankle or peel an ear on a lower shroud (Figure 7-4).

To help crews get forward safely in rough weather, a line for safety har-

Figure 7-3. The sloping cabin trunk and clean teak-laid deck on this Swan 43 provide considerable living room below and a good working area on deck. In their recesses against the cabin trunk, the spinnaker poles are out of the way of feet and lines. Jack lines could easily be led aft from the stem fitting (out of the picture) to the brackets under the black foot blocks. The on-deck halyard winches are out of the way of jib sheets during tacks, and can be used with security in rough weather. Note the deck prism and the large Dorade vent forward of the mast.

nesses—called a "tether line," "jack line," or "jack wire"—should be rigged from stern to bow, secured to through-bolted fittings at either end. If inboard shrouds and the cabin trunk preclude a safe passage to the foredeck without having to unsnap the safety harness from the tether line, something is wrong. Safety harnesses should not be clipped to lifelines, since a hard fall may bend the stanchions. Around the cockpit, the harness may be clipped to through-bolted padeyes.

Transverse crew movement is often blocked by hatches, vangs, life-raft canisters, anchors, and other obstructions. In particular, on-deck anchor stowage

Figure 7-4. Here is a boat laid out solely for racing. Everything is all business. The genoa sheet is led to the windward winch so the crew can adjust trim without moving to leeward. The forward cockpit provides a secure platform for working the sheet and halyard winches; unfortunately, it also breaks up the cabin. Pouches along the sides of the cockpit are for loose lines. (Rosenfeld Collection, Mystic Seaport Museum, Inc., Mystic, CT)

does not often receive the attention it deserves. The best place for a plow is on a bow roller; otherwise, this anchor (whose odd shape can make it quite a nuisance on deck) should be stowed in a special chock, preferably under a dinghy where nobody can trip over it. The big yachtsman-type anchor is also best stowed under the dinghy. Danforth-type lightweight anchors must be well chocked and guarded on all corners. Some metal chocks for Danforths, available in many chandleries, only hold the crown, flukes, and shank, leaving the stock ends free to snag jib sheets and feet. What's more, unless the Dansforth's stock is supported in its own chocks, standing on it is like balancing on a teeter-totter.

Although Bill Lapworth will cover cockpit arrangement in greater detail in Chapter 8, I would like to consider it briefly in the context of decks. Actually, if our only concern were construction efficiency, there would be no cockpit, which exists only to take care of people. In it they work at steering and trimming sails; in it, too, they relax at anchor with glass in hand, taking in the magnificence of the Camden Hills fading away over Pulpit Rock in a Maine sunset.

Any feature that makes a cockpit inefficient for sailors and uncomfortable for guests is undesirable. There should be no interference between the sweep of the tiller and the working of a winch. People should be able to reach sheets, cleats, and winches without having to stumble all over the cockpit. The coamings should be high enough to keep out green water, low enough for comfortable sitting with elbows over their upper edges, and sloped outward for sitting comfort. The binnacle should be strong enough to support somebody lurching heavily in rough weather. The cockpit seats should be well thought out. Frequently, they are so far apart that comfortable seating is impossible when the boat is well heeled over. As a rule, the inboard edges of seats should be parallel to each other, a leg span apart. That is, they should not be parallel to the coamings. You should be able to open and close the cockpit lockers without moving all the lines out of the way.

As Tom Young will emphasize in Chapter 10, the cockpit dodger is an important component in the boat's ventilation system. Of course, it serves other purposes as well. It should be large enough to block spray from the hatch and cockpit, sturdy enough to serve as temporary handrail, and compact enough so the crew can see forward without straining.

A Cover for a Comfortable Interior

Finally, the deck should cater to requirements below as well as necessities above. Larger boats may be able to have a flush or nearly flush deck as well as good headroom throughout the interior, but the average yacht will need a decent cabin trunk. Because of excessive concern with efficiency on deck, plenty can go wrong with the underside to make the cabin uncomfortable.

Insulation is frequently left out, perhaps because it adds weight. Bear in mind that insulation works both ways. It keeps out the heat of summer and the cold of winter, giving the human critter below deck a degree of comfort. The need for under-deck insulation depends on the construction and where the yacht is to be used. Cored fiberglass, which is used on many modern boats, insulates quite well. Traditional wooden construction generally requires no special insulation, because nature imbued wood with a low coefficient of heat transfer. However, aluminum and steel transfer heat rapidly, and so insulation is a must for comfort on board boats built of those materials. Whatever insulating material you use, arrange it in removable panels to provide access to wiring and fastenings.

Another deck-related comfort factor that sometimes is not given due attention is the amount of light that passes below. Skylights, ports, and well-bedded flush deck prisms can provide adequate light in the cabins and head, particularly if the interior is mostly white.

Lynn Williams has much to say about headroom in Chapter 9, but a few comments are in order here. In a small yacht, headroom is generally some sort of compromise between what is adequate for comfort and the owner's tolerance of the skyscraper effect of high freeboard and towering cabin trunks. Some very ugly boats suffer from too much of each. A trend in racer-cruisers in the mid-1980s has been to build extremely narrow cabin trunks in order to allow more deck space for jib-sheet tracks for close-winded sailing. So, while these boats may have good standing headroom in the middle of the cabin, they may have none at all off to the sides. A limit on good headroom seen on many cruising as well as racing boats is the practice of securing fittings to the deck cabin top or

Figure 7-5. This is a good deck arrangement for cruising. The arrows show major rig forces. (Detail A) Windows should be oval and have storm shutters— either permanent, as shown here, or removable. (Detail B) The hull-to-deck joint at the rail should be made with bolts and fiberglass bonding.

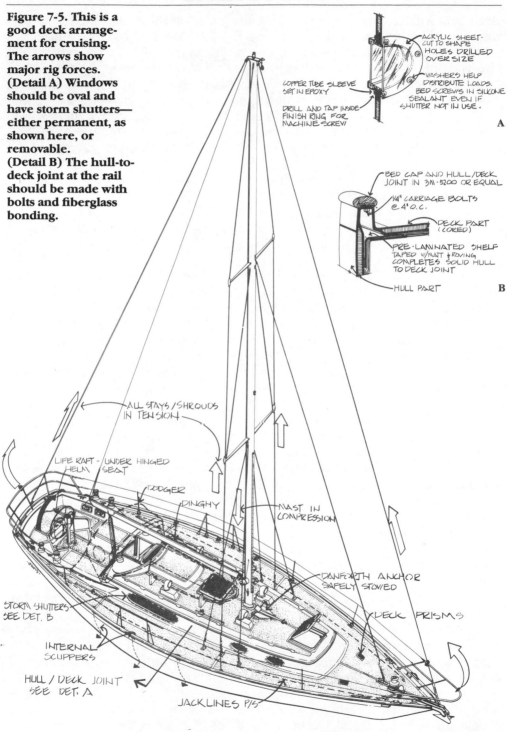

ACRYLIC SHEET-
CUT TO SHAPE
HOLES DRILLED
OVER SIZE

WASHERS HELP
DISTRIBUTE LOADS.
BED SCREWS IN SILICONE
SEALANT EVEN IF
SHUTTER NOT IN USE.

COPPER TUBE SLEEVE
SET IN EPOXY

DRILL AND TAP INSIDE
FINISH RING FOR
MACHINE SCREW

A

BED CAP AND HULL/DECK
JOINT IN 3M-5200 OR EQUAL

1/4" CARRIAGE BOLTS
@ 4' O.C.

DECK PART
(CORED)

PRE-LAMINATED SHELF
TAPED W/MAT + ROVING
COMPLETES SOLID HULL
TO DECK JOINT

HULL PART

B

ALL STAYS/SHROUDS
IN TENSION

LIFE RAFT - UNDER HINGED
HELM SEAT

DODGER

DINGHY

MAST IN
COMPRESSION

DANFORTH ANCHOR
SAFELY STOWED

STORM SHUTTERS
SEE DET. B

DECK PRISMS

INTERNAL
SCUPPERS

HULL / DECK JOINT
SEE DET. A

JACKLINES P/S

deck and leaving the nuts exposed inside. Even when acorn nuts are used, this can provide a painful experience for one's head.

A young, macho sailor who thinks that the nether regions are unimportant should switch his life experience to fast forward. When he is old enough to appreciate some of life's amenities, he will wonder why he put up with all those discomforts in the name of speed and racing efficiency (Figure 7-5).

CHAPTER 8

The Cockpit

C. William Lapworth

No matter how many people may be aboard, and whether it is being used during a cruise or a race, the cockpit is certainly the center of activity on deck. Under way, at anchor, or in a slip, the crew spends a great deal of time there, steering, trimming sails, or relaxing. Therefore, it is extremely important that the cockpit be well thought out (Figures 8-1 and 8-2). Deficiencies in a cockpit's design and construction can run the gamut from making it uncomfortable to making it downright unsafe. Here, I will discuss a few things to look out for when evaluating a cruising boat's cockpit so you won't be caught in, or somewhere between, those two unhappy categories. After examining the advantages and disadvantages of the two types of cockpits, aft and midship, I will discuss the companionways that connect them to the cabin. Finally, I will move on to some details of cockpit design and construction.

Cockpit Types

The arrangement and characteristics of a cockpit, and the companionway or companionways that connect it to the cabin, are dependent to a large extent on the cockpit's location in the boat, which is a function of the boat's size and shape. The traditional aft cockpit has a different set of advantages and problems than the so-called "midship cockpit," which is found on many cruising boats today.

Almost all boats up to approximately 40 feet in length have aft cockpits, which take up much of the space between the cabin and the stern (Figure 8-3). This is because the limited volume of a relatively small hull does not permit reasonable accommodations in the aft part of the boat, and an aft cabin would be quite small. On larger boats, with greater volume in their quarter sections, a cabin aft of the cockpit can be very commodious. This is why the midship cockpit (sometimes called the center cockpit) is usually limited to boats larger than about 40 feet.

The key ingredient for a safe installation of a midship cockpit / aft cabin arrangement is that the boat is big enough to provide a passageway from the main cabin under the cockpit seats to the aft cabin. For two good reasons, this passageway is preferable to a forward-facing companionway in the after cabin leading from the cockpit. First, this type of companionway is very wet in any kind of bad weather. Second, it provides almost no privacy for occupants of the aft cabin when it is left open to provide necessary light and air. It is possible to avoid these two deficiencies by having an aft-facing centerline companionway on the stern side of the aft cabin. However, entering this companionway would require leaving the security of the cockpit and going on deck to walk around the aft cabin, and this is not particularly desirable in inclement weather. Therefore,

Figure 8-1. The Lapworth-designed Cal 40's carefully thought out cockpit has a small foot well and plenty of seating space. The back rests are angled for optimum comfort when the boat is heeled.

with a midship cockpit arrangement, access to the aft cabin is best provided by the below-decks passageway. (Of course, there should be a hatch in the aft cabin's overhead to serve as an escape hatch in an emergency.)

While they allow for a private cabin aft, midship cockpits have some disadvantages. They can be somewhat wetter than aft cockpits, since they catch spray that, in a boat with an aft cockpit, would fall on the top of the cabin trunk (Figure 8-4). It sometimes is more difficult to locate cockpit drains so they will not intrude on accommodations below. And, with them, the area of the boat that has the most volume and least motion—around amidships—is given to the engine room and passageway, rather than to the galley, navigation station, and bunks, as is the case with an aft cockpit.

Figure 8-2. A high rail around the cockpit of the 46-foot _Zest_ provides security for the crew. The big winch forward is for the jib sheets. _Zest_ was owned by the late H. Irving Pratt, who initiated the research project that produced the Measurement Handicap System (now the International Measurement System). She was designed by McCurdy & Rhodes. (John Rousmaniere)

Companionways and Dodgers

The companionways should be on the centerline, although this may not be possible on boats where there is a stateroom aft. Unfortunately, an off-center companionway can be dangerous if the boat takes a heavy knockdown in its direction, since it is closer to the water than a centerline companionway. In the aft cockpit layout, if an aft "owner's" stateroom is important, the companionway can be located forward on top of the house, on the centerline. If so, sturdy handrails must be installed to allow crew members to get back and forth to the cockpit in a seaway. A reasonable compromise on an aft cockpit boat larger than about 40 feet is to have two companionways: the forward one (possibly slightly off-center) is used in normal conditions, and the aft one, leading from the aft stateroom, is used in rough weather, when privacy is sacrificed for safety.

If water can be kept out of the campionway, it will be kept out of the cabin. The usual way to block water is to install companionway drop boards (also called slats and batter boards) and, on aft-facing companionways, rig a dodger. Careful design here is important. Installation and removal of the boards is made easier if the boat is built with a wedge- or V-shaped companionway opening. With a

Figure 8-3. This aft-cockpit arrangement shelters the crew, who can handle the halyards without having to go forward. The transom ladder is a safety feature for recovering someone who has fallen overboard.

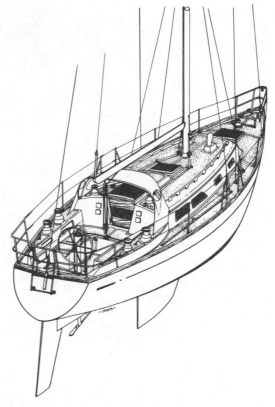

straight-sided opening, you must slide the boards all the way to the top in order to remove them, but if the sides slope away from each other, all you need do is lift them a couple of inches. Of course, care must be taken so that the drop boards do not come out too easily. Many people delay inserting these boards because they block out light, but that need not to be case. My own boat has a second drop board made of clear Lexan, which lets in light and provides a view of the harbor, but keeps out the wind, cold, and rain on those days when the weather is something less than ideal.

To prevent flooding of the cabin should the cockpit be filled, the sills of the companionways should be no lower than the lowest point of the coaming. The bottommost drop board should be capable of being secured into the companionway should heavy spray or waves begin to come aboard from astern. Participants in the Cruising Club of America's Newport to Bermuda Race are required to have a lock-in system for all the drop boards, so that the slats don't fall out should the boat be rolled.

Aft-facing companionways should be protected with sea hoods and dodgers so that rain, spray, and boarding seas do not find their way below. The dodger can simply cover the hatch or it can extend across the full width of the cockpit's forward edge in order to provide some shelter to people standing watch. On some boats, even the helmsman can duck his head under such a dodger when a

Figure 8-4. The midship cockpit / aft cabin arrangement works on boats large enough to have a passageway aft from the main cabin. A disadvantage is that the cockpit can get wet. For more plans of this arrangement, see the section on *Compadre* in Part V.

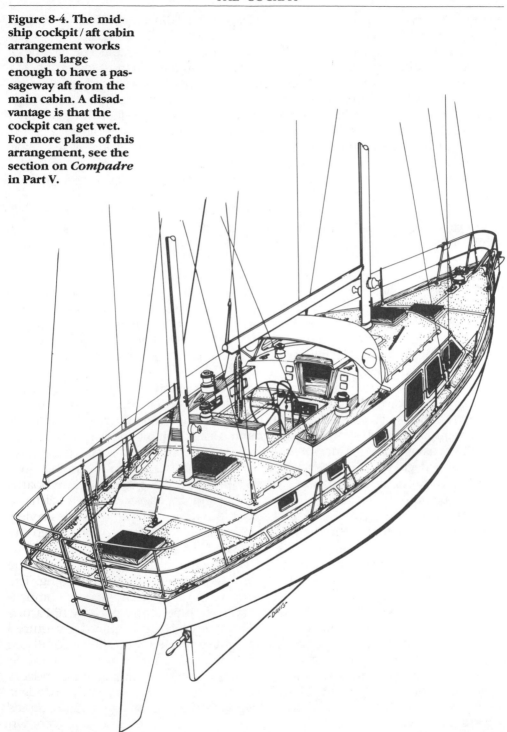

big wave is about to come aboard. (In Chapter 10, Tom Young looks at dodger design in considerable detail.)

The design of the cabin itself affects the utility of the cockpit. The aft side of the cabin should slope forward for the same reasons that, on most modern boats, the cabin side slopes inward: it improves appearance, allows more light below, enlarges the working area, and provides a comfortable backrest. In addition, the instruments on a forward-sloping cabin are easier to read than the ones on a vertical cabin. If the aft side of the cabin is sloped, it is still possible to keep the drop boards in a vertical plane if they are recessed into the companionway slightly. Unfortunately, while less rain may come in with such an arrangement, the ladder is pushed farther forward into the cabin, somewhat decreasing usable space below.

Design Details

Certain basic rules of thumb apply to the design and construction of both types of cockpits.

Cockpit Shape and Volume

The cockpit should be designed around the steering gear. Where wheel steering is fitted, consideration should be given to make fore-and-aft movement in the cockpit relatively easy. One answer to this problem is a T-shaped cockpit, where the helmsman's area is the crossing of the T. With tiller steering, the tiller's height, shape, and location will determine whether or not legs will be pinched against the edge of the seat.

As anybody who has taken a big sea knows, a cockpit may be too big. If the volume is excessive, the cockpit may be filled or partially filled with so much water that the boat's stability and buoyancy are threatened. Realizing this, the Transpacific Yacht Club specified a maximum cockpit volume for its race to Hawaii, and the Crusing Club of America followed suit for its Bermuda Race. These limits are now reflected in the Special Regulations of the Offshore Racing Council, which supervises the International Offshore Rule (IOR). Table 8-1 provides the ORC regulations that concern cockpit volume and drainage.

Regardless of the volume of the cockpit, the drains should be large enough to drain it completely in three minutes after it is filled to the coaming. The ORC specifies four drains totaling 1.77 square inches of area, but I recommend two 1½-inch drains, which have an area of 1.77 *each*. On the Cal 2-35, we used a single 4-inch-diameter drain through the transom, giving an area of 12.57 square inches.

It may be a good idea to try out the drainage time at the dock by filling the cockpit with fresh water. The Transpacific Yacht Club has required testing as a part of pre-race registration when the cockpit drainage time is suspect. During these tests, we have often been surprised to find that many "watertight" cockpits were anything but. On many boats, the cockpit will drain at any angle of heel. However, when some boats are well heeled, their drains will back up. Some years ago, I saw a nifty check valve in which a small ball floated up and prevented backing up.

A bridge deck is a desirable feature in any cockpit. In addition to contributing

Table 8-1
ORC COCKPIT AND DRAIN REGULATIONS

Maximum cockpit volume = .06LWL × beam × freeboard
  (where freeboard = freeboard abreast the cockpit).
Minimum cockpit sole height above loaded waterline = .02LOA.
Drains (for boats longer than 28 feet): 4 ¾-inch drains with a total area of 1.77 square inches.

to the overall strength of the vessel, it reduces cockpit volume, helps to raise the companionway sill to a safe level, and adds extra usable space in the cabin underneath. This is a good place for the main sheet traveler, not only because the deck is strong but also because, when the boat is on the wind, it allows the main sheet to function as a stanchion-like hand hold for people emerging from the companionway.

Construction

The scantlings and structure of the cockpit have received considerable and much-needed attention after an incident in Florida in 1983, where a boarding sea popped the cockpit right out of a boat's deck. In general, construction scantlings should match those of the main deck. Two types of structural stiffening are needed. One is the stiffening or support needed to carry the weight of the cockpit and its contents—its equipment, the crew, and any load of water that may decide to come along for the ride. This support is best provided by fitting longitudinal bulkheads at each side of the cockpit well or transverse bulkheads at each end. Each of these bulkheads should extend below the cockpit and be attached to the boat's floors. The other type of stiffening required is in the way of the winches and (if fitted) steering pedestal. Here, doubling of materials is usually required so that the deck or cockpit sole will not deflect from the large horizontal loads that are applied to this gear.

An important item that is often overlooked in stock-boat construction is the provision of a removable section of fiberglass in the cockpit sole to provide space to pull out the engine. This area should be bedded and bolted down so as to be completely watertight.

Seat Dimensions and Sole Height

One of the key considerations in the design of any cockpit is the height of the sole and seat. If either is too low, the crew will have to work harder to get their jobs done; if too high, they will not feel protected.

There are three limits on the height of the cockpit sole. First, it must be located high enough above the waterline so that the cockpit will drain automatically when the boat is either level or heeling at an extreme angle. Second, it must be high enough to permit the helmsman to see over the cabin trunk, preferably from a sitting position and definitely from a standing one. And third, it should not be so high that it raises the seats to the level of the deck. The reason seat height is important is that, when the seats are elevated above the level of the deck, people sitting on them will feel like they are perched insecurely *on* the deck rather than sitting safely *in* the cockpit (Figure 8-5).

Figure 8-5. These are reliable dimensions for seats and back rests for cockpits in an offshore yacht and a normal racer-cruiser.

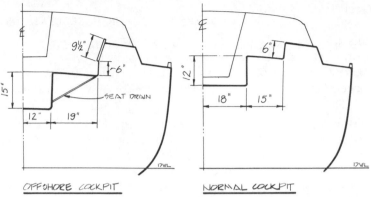

OFFSHORE COCKPIT   NORMAL COCKPIT

Since the height of seats above the cockpit sole—ideally 15 to 18 inches—is determined by the dimensions of the human body and therefore cannot be radically altered, the height of the cockpit sole determines the height of the seats. The sole should be lowered until the seats are slightly below the level of the deck. The feeling of security in this kind of cockpit seat is enhanced if the backrests are 12 to 15 inches high. The angle of the seat back should be such that a sitter is not pushed off the seat when the boat heels or rolls.

Some other key dimensions work in most cockpits, regardless of the boat's size. The seats should be 18 to 20 inches in width and at least 6 feet, 6 inches in length. And if the seats are parallel to each other and 24 to 30 inches apart, a person sitting on the windward seat can comfortably brace his or her feet against the leeward seat when the boat is heeled. Ideally, the cockpit should be sunken enough so that, when inserted in the winches, the distance from the cockpit sole to the tops of the winch handles should be about 42 inches, which is the most efficient working height for a winch-grinder.

Though unrelated to the dimensions of the cockpit itself, a design feature that can affect the utility of the cockpit is the arrangement of the lifelines. On boats that are relatively narrow aft, the lifelines and their stanchions can obstruct work on the sides of the cockpit or on the side decks. Some years ago, I had a Cal 29 that was fitted with the vertical stanchions that came with the boat from the builder. Later, the racing measurement rule was changed to permit stanchions to slope 10 degrees outboard in order to allow the genoa jib to be sheeted inboard of the lifeline for windward work. I fitted a new set of stanchions, whose tops were a bit more than 4 inches outboard of the top ot the old stanchions. This added almost 22 square feet of space inside the lifelines, which was most noticeable in the area of the cockpit and side decks particularly when a crew member went forward on the windward side when the boat was heeled.

The sole and seats should be surfaced with teak or some other suitable nonskid surface. It's a mistake to use long, thick cockpit cushions, which, while comfortable, can catch feet and turn ankles. If you must have cushions, try using a sheet of plywood onto which 1 inch of foam has been glued and save the soft ones for port.

Gear Stowage and Instruments

Stowage in the cockpit is needed for tools, winch handles, flashlights, and tails of sheets and halyards, all of which when strewn on the sole can make footing precarious, to say the least, and all of which should be easily located in the dark when necessary. Cloth sacks secured to the sides of the cockpit, small lockers in backrests, and winch-handle holders can be extremely valuable.

Hatches over seat lockers, where larger gear items can be stowed, should be made with care. They should be watertight, with gaskets and secure latches, and they should be scuppered so they drain onto the cockpit sole. Since a hatch can cause serious damage if it falls onto a head or hand, there must be lanyards or some other restraining devices to secure them in the open position. To prevent sheets and other lines from constantly jamming under the lips of hatches, follow three rules of thumb. First, stuff loose tails into bags. Second, keep the cockpit policed so that everything is stowed in its proper place. And third, to avoid opening lockers too often, stow gear that must be used frequently on deck, not in the lockers.

The compass and engine and performance instruments should be permanently mounted where they can be easily read, adjusted when necessary, and protected from possible damage. When mounting this equipment, be sure to preserve the watertight integrity of the cockpit by sealing all holes.

Emergency Gear

I will end this discussion with a few words about the emergency equipment that must be located around or in the cockpit. Installing man-overboard gear so it is both out of the way of normal sailing activity and accessible to the helmsman can be a challenge, and may require quite a bit of experimenting before you get it right. But it is time well spent. Another important safety consideration is to locate some securely mounted, accessible padeyes for hooking safety harness tethers on each side of the cockpit, aft for the helmsman as well as farther forward for the sail trimmers. To make hooking up even easier, secure lengths of ⅜-inch line between the padeyes, cleats, and other sturdy fittings so people won't have to fumble around looking for the padeye on a cold, windy, wet night.

The bilge pump usually involves the cockpit. I believe that the very best bilge pump is a diaphragm pump located just under the cabin sole; when it really becomes necessary to remove a lot of water, there is nothing like it. Still, bilge pumpers working below sometimes suffer from seasickness, so it's a good idea to also have a manual bilge pump that can be operated from the cockpit. The socket for the pump handle should be located so it can be inserted and worked without the necessity of opening a seat locker in rainy or rough weather—say, into the side of the cockpit well or on a cockpit seat. The pump's intake should be in a sump in the deepest part of the bilge and should have a screen to avoid clogging.

CHAPTER 9

The Cabin

Lynn A. Williams

C omfort, convenience, and practicality characterize many yachts (including some small ones) as a result of ingenious and careful planning of the cabin arrangement, including bunks, stowage, the head, and the galley. Unfortunately, many other boats are mediocre or worse in this department. Here are some suggestions about what works and what doesn't work.

The crux of the problem is that while the usable space usually isn't much larger than that of a big shoreside bathroom, the cabin must provide for the physical functions of several full-size people. They must cook and eat, wash dishes, and dispose of their garbage; they must wash and shave, sleep and sit; they must change into dry clothes and have a place to keep their wet clothes—all this in a small space that may be heeling, rolling, and slamming violently. Yet it can be done. In many cases, it is done very well.

Still, don't expect too much in the way of gracious living as it is advertised by boat builders in magazines and at boat shows. That glossy four-color, wide-angle photo may show a cabin table set with china plates, linen napery, and a vase of flowers. But only a few boat buyers ever really count on such amenities. The desire for gracious living may well be masking the need for practical, realistic consideration of the necessities of inhabiting the quite limited space that a sail-boat affords.

Interior Arrangement

Before we get to the specifics, here are a few guidelines for people looking for a boat to buy.

Form a clear idea as to how you will really use your boat. If you plan to sail by day and moor in harbors with nearby conveniences, such as grocery stores, you may need an interior in which bunk space for sleeping on the level takes priority over sea bunks, food storage, and fridge or ice-box capacity. But if you plan to sail offshore for several days or weeks, then you probably will want more stowage and fewer bunks (but ones that are better for seagoing). Do you plan to race with a big crew consisting of large, muscular bodies? Or is your goal to cruise with a small family crew that includes children? Whichever, the optimum layout for one type of sailing will not be the same as the best one for the other.

The obvious precept, then, is to match the boat's interior to her intended use. That is all too frequently forgotten in yacht design, construction, and selection.

Don't try to cram in more fixtures than you have room for. That is, don't miniaturize: don't make a dollhouse of your boat's interior. Accept the inevitable limitations of the small available space. For example, while a four-burner stove may be ideal for good cooking, you probably won't be able to fit it into the galley of a 35-footer. More realistically, install a two-burner stove.

Another example: any 30-footer can hold six bunks if they're stuck way in the ends, but they won't be very wide, they probably won't be very comfortable, and they will take up so much room that even if the boat can sleep six adults she won't have enough stowage space to hold the supplies they'll need to live aboard. For many crews, it would be better to have four good bunks located in the wide midsection, with the head and plenty of stowage located in the bow. (Still, if the boat is used for family cruising with children, a six-bunk arrangement with a forward cabin, for parental privacy, may be ideal. Once again, it's all in how you use the boat.)

Give account to the dimensions of the human anatomy. How tall, how wide, how thick, how long the shin and thigh bones—all should be considered, but most important, let people stand up below. One of the most common assaults on the anthropoid condition is lack of standing headroom. If crew members over 6 feet tall are to be accommodated with reasonable respect, the headroom, at minimum, must be 6 feet, 3 inches, and not just along the centerline.

The neglect of the headroom requirement is traceable to the influence of racing boats, whose shallow, flat hull bottoms raise the cabin sole and whose low freeboards and flush decks or sleek, narrow, low-windage trunk cabins compress the overhead. Except on the larger boats, many crews must crouch as they move around below. For purposes other than Grand Prix racing, it is better to accept the added windage and weight of higher topsides, crowned decks, and trunk cabins. The effect on speed is scarcely measurable except when sailing to windward. The appearance may be less racy, but, after all, you don't see much of your own boat's profile when you're on board. Meanwhile, other crews will

Figure 9-1. A good cabin arrange-ment for an offshore boat pro-vides plenty of stowage, a wet locker at the bottom of the com-panionway, a galley that can be used in rough weather, a sturdy dining table, and several sea berths for sleeping under way.

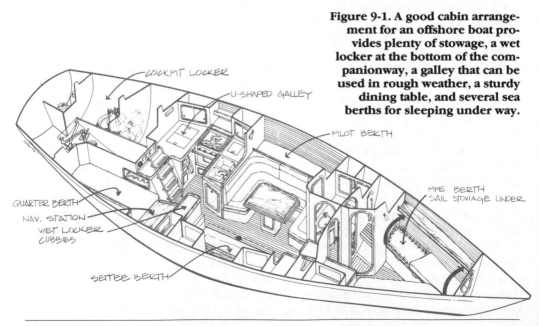

COCKPIT LOCKER

U-SHAPED GALLEY

PILOT BERTH

PIPE BERTH
SAIL STOWAGE UNDER

QUARTER BERTH
NAV. STATION
WET LOCKER
CUBBIES

SETTEE BERTH

recognize you as being an owner who is both knowledgeable and wise.

Pay due attention to details. Arrange and install plenty of grab bars and handles so crew members of all heights can support themselves when the boat is heeling. To prevent bad bruises and contusions should they fall against furniture, carefully round off all corners and edges with a full radius. Make sure the companionway ladder is safe, which means that it should not be too steep, and all steps and risers should be the same height. Not everybody goes down a ladder backwards, and severe spine injuries can be caused by a missed or slipped step.

With these general guidelines expressed, let us move on to discuss specific components of the interior, beginning with bunks.

Bunks and Berths

Good sleeping depends on having good bunks and berths aboard, in dry, relatively stable parts of the boat (Figure 9-1). Too many owners (and builders, too) take berths for granted, and look at them through the eye of an interior decorator rather than an exhausted sailor who must catch some rest at a 30-degree angle in the middle of a gale. Many of the details in a good bunk are not normally noticed. We will try to cover them in this section.

Bunk Types

There are several kinds of bunks, and each has a function on cruising boats. However, some functions are more suited than others to offshore sailing. A few berths—pipe, root, and pilot berths—make excellent sea berths for sleeping in rough weather because they are relatively narrow. Others—transom, settee, and V-berths—are best used when the boat is level.

Pipe berths are simple tube frames onto which a length of fabric is laced. They are commonly chosen for both simplicity and low cost, and are sometimes placed over sail bins and other stowage areas to allow quick and easy access. Often they are used without a mattress; the sleeper lies right on the fabric. Unfortunately, this is not very comfortable; it's not easy to keep the fabric taut and flat because the tubing in the frame usually is too small and may flex inward. Therefore, the bunks will be much more comfortable if they are fitted with foam mattresses that are about 4 inches thick.

Pipe berths can be pivoted on their hinges so they are level even when the boat is heeled. This usually requires adjustment of a small block and tackle when the wind comes up or the boat changes tacks, but the added comfort of staying in the bunk without having to rig a bunk board or lee cloth (which can cut off ventilation) is well worth this minor inconvenience.

These days, pipe berths are most often found in racing boats.

Root Berths are made of heavy fabric that is fastened to the hull or cabinetry at the outboard edge and to a stout rod of wood or metal at the inboard edge. The rod is inserted into notches in athwartships-running bulkheads so that the fabric serves as a seat back or as a bunk with the sleeper lying in the curve of the cloth. The bunk can be adjusted for various angles of heel by moving the rods up or down. As with pipe berths, root berths are more comfortable when they are used with foam mattresses. When the bunk is used as a seat back, some way must be found to keep the mattress upright—Velcro strips might do the job.

These ingenious bunks are rarely seen in post-1970 boats.

Transom berths (also called settee berths) are little more than seats for sitting at the cabin table that can be pulled out a few inches to make a bunk.

Hinged berths use the seat backs of transoms, which are swung up to horizontal and kept in place using some arrangement of locks or pins, which may be adjusted as the boat heels. In combination with transom berths, they provide Pullman car-type uppers and lowers, which can be converted back to comfortable seats by day. The hinged backs should be built strongly of plywood.

Pilot berths are permanent bunks above and outboard of transoms. They probably are the best built-in bunks for offshore sailing because, unlike transom and hinged berths, they allow daytime off-watch sleeping out of the way of cabin traffic without interfering with other cabin space. Unfortunately, there may not be room for them on smaller boats. On my 62-foot *Dora IV* (later Ted Turner's *Tenacious* and Warren Brown's *War Baby*), we had pilot berths that could be adjusted to offset as much as 30 degrees of heel angle so the sleeper would be level. With a light tackle, a crew member could lift either the outboard or inboard edge so that pins in the bunk corners could be inserted into notched plates in the end bulkheads.

A *V-berth* in the forward cabin provides two bunks that can be joined at the head using an insert in the notch of the V. Due to the bunks' orientation at a sharp angle to the centerline, sleepers always have either their heads or feet elevated when the boat is heeling, so these are not very good sea berths. Since this may be the only double berth on the boat, in the only private cabin, they do serve an important purpose for cruising couples.

Quarter berths are set under the cockpit, in the boat's stern quarters. Since they are next to the engine and are often poorly ventilated, they can be quite hot and stuffy in hot weather or when the boat is powering for long periods of time. Getting in and out of a quarter berth sometimes demands considerable gymnastic ability. On boats with skimpy stowage, the quarter berths often are catch-alls for loose gear. But at sea, a person can wedge his or her body quite nicely into a quarter berth for a good sleep well out of the way of cabin traffic—at least until somebody drops a winch handle on the cockpit sole overhead.

Berth Design and Construction

Bunks should not be placed too far outboard. If they are, they will be too narrow for normal use, too heavily tapered, and skewed well off the centerline. There is a tendency to push bunks way out to the side in order to gain floor space; this looks good at boat shows and in advertisements, but it produces bad bunks, and, anyway, floor space has little value except for being photographed. Indeed, under sail a narrow cabin sole may well be more comfortable and safe than a wide one, since the bunks provide support for people who are sitting or walking.

In fore-and-aft alignment, each bunk should be as nearly parallel to the centerline as is practical. Otherwise, when the boat heels, one bunk end will be lower than the other, putting your feet above your head on one tack and the

Figure 9-2. With lee cloths rigged, pilot (upper) and settee berths of the right dimensions are fine for sleeping at sea. They can be combined with stowage for clothes, books, and private items. Berths must be parallel to the boat's centerline.

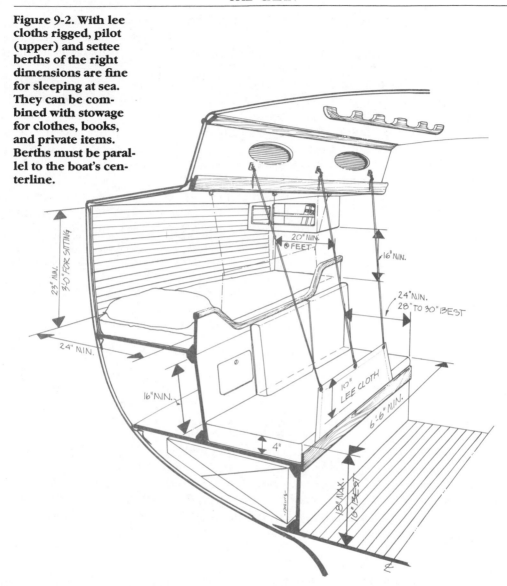

reverse on the other. The designer and builder should use the centerline, rather than the outer skin of the boat, as a reference point (Figure 9-2). You may remark that this leaves wasted space between the bunk and the skin, but that space is hardly wasted: it allows for a bookshelf or a small stowage bin for personal items, either of which will help insulate the sleeper from the clammy condensation on the inside of the hull as well as protect him or her from chain plates or framing. Make sure that the side rails keeping the mattress on the bunk do not extend above the mattress. If they are higher than the mattress, they will bruise or cut off circulation if an arm or leg slips out from under the blanket.

The minimum length for bunks is 6 feet, 6 inches, and the absolute minimum width is 24 inches (28–30 inches is best). Bunks should be as nearly rectangular as possible. If there must be taper, keep the foot no narrower than 20 inches. With that little space, sleepers may have to lie down with their ankles crossed. Blankets do not fit tapered bunks, either.

The vertical space between uppers and lowers (or uppers and the overhead) should be no less than 23 inches—and that is just for decent ventilation. Sitting up requires about 36 inches.

When the boat is heeling or rocking, a bunk board or lee cloth is needed to keep people in any bunk that cannot be leveled or that does not have barriers on both sides (like the quarter berth). The board or cloth should be 7½ to 10 inches high. Do not extend it to the end of the berth; leave about 18 inches at the ends for ventilation. The side should not only *be* strong, it should *feel* strong so the sleeper can nod off in full confidence that he or she won't end up on the cabin sole. Wooden bunk boards should be firmly supported with hinges, not just the edge of the mattress. Fabric lee cloth should be held up with several lacings of light, strong line passing through strongly secured padeyes. Since some people like more sag than others, leave a couple of feet of extra line and use of rolling hitch to adjust the tension. Climbing in and out of berths over bunk boards or around lee cloths can be difficult even in smooth sailing conditions, so locate plenty of grab rails around and over the bunks.

The Galley

Galley arrangements tend to be more standardized than they used to be. Before about 1970, galleys could be found almost anywhere in the boat—forward, along one side of the main cabin, or aft. Today the common location for the galley is next to the after companionway. This arrangement has much to recommend it: this is the part of the boat least susceptible to violent pitching motion; food may be readily passed to the cockpit; the cook is not isolated from the rest of the crew; and there is good ventilation through the hatch (perhaps with the aid of a small fan or exhaust blower over the stove). A detriment of this arrangement is that the cook may have to work in the traffic flow of people passing to and from the companionway. This may be overcome by setting the companionway slightly off the centerline and locating the galley in the wide side below (this configuration may be used only if the offset companionway will not be flooded at extreme heel angles).

The three major units—sink, stove, and icebox / fridge—should be close together so the cook can reach all three without having to move. A U-shaped configuration allows this, and also permits the cook to brace him- or herself against fore-and-aft motion (Figure 9-3). With a gimballed stove outboard in the turn of the U (a typical arrangement), a restraining belt or harness should be rigged to hold the cook in position close to the stove when it is to windward and away from it when it is to leeward. In addition, a stout metal bar should be set across the stove face to keep the cook from accidentally falling onto the burners.

There should be adequate counter space with well-raised edges and high, sturdy fiddles. Stainless steel is the best material for counters, since it will not be charred by a hot frying pan. Butcher block maple is both attractive and func-

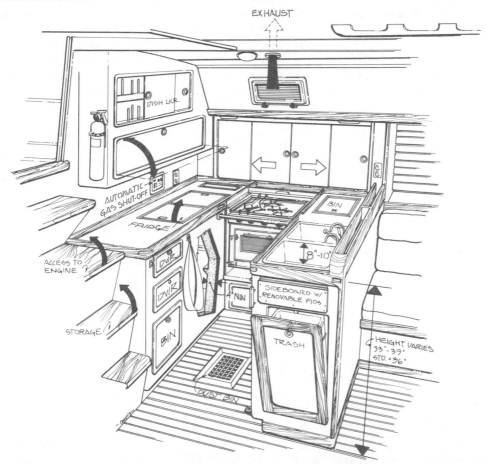

Figure 9-3. A U-shaped galley equipped with a restraining belt provides a secure work-ing space for a seagoing cook. Sliding cabinet doors save space and lessen the chance of spills when the boat rolls. There should be dual sinks deep enough for plates, a handy trash bin, and many storage bins and drawers. Another good idea is a fold-up sideboard, with fiddles to keep things from falling onto the sole. A fire extinguisher and the shut-off switch for the stove fuel must be within the cook's reach.

tional, but plastic that is not resistant to heat is no good. Metal should also be used to protect cabinetry above and behind the stove; even at some distance from the burners and oven, surfaces get very hot.

The Sink

The sink must be deep enough so that it won't spill even with a half load of dishwater. A depth of 8–10 inches will do. Many cooks like to have two sinks— one for washing dishes, the other for rinsing them. Using foot, hand, or pressure pumps, water can be readily accessible both from the boat's tanks and from the sea or lake. The drains need traps since sink waste is likely to give off unpleasant odors.

Sinks must be installed with care. They must be mounted high and as close to the centerline as possible so the drain never falls below the water level outside, which would cause a reverse flow of sea or lake water and require a pump to exhaust the sink. The reference must be the true water plane when the boat is floating; sometimes the designed or datum waterline (DWL) shown on the plans or indicated by the painted waterline is below the true plane.

The Stove

There are many stoves on the market. When buying a stove, look for the following features:

- Stainless-steel construction, which prevents rust
- An oven and, perhaps, a broiler
- An oven "can" or cavity constructed of dipped porcelainized enamel over steel, with rounded corners
- Removable top grates, for cleaning
- A sturdy, high fiddle rail around the burners to keep pots from falling over (removable clamp-on fiddles are also available)
- Sturdy gimbals positioned for good dynamic balance when the boat is rolling or sailing at severe angles of heel
- A lock on the oven door to keep casseroles from flying out in rough weather, and another lock to prevent gimballing when cooking at anchor

Cooking Fuels

Several stove fuels are available, each with its own strengths and weaknesses. Table 9-1 provides comparisons of their characteristics, including heat in BTUs and specific gravity. Let's look at them one by one.

Alcohol has the least hot flame of the five fuels and therefore cooks more slowly. Since it is not a gas, it does not come with a risk of explosion, but there is a chance that it may flare up and cause a small fire during or after the somewhat complicated priming and lighting procedure, when the liquid fuel is vaporized. (A new type of alcohol stove, using a large wick into which fuel is poured, requires no priming.) However, most alcohol fires can easily be doused with water.

Kerosene has the hottest flame and can be resupplied almost anywhere in the world. As a liquid, it requires a vaporizing priming procedure to be lit, and tends to smell bad to the point where crew members may be sick.

LPG (liquid petroleum gas) is often called "bottled gas." In BTU (British Thermal Unit) measurement, it is second after kerosene in flame heat. LPG is stored in liquid form and automatically vaporizes as it is released, so it can be lit like household stove fuel. Depending on where it is obtained, it can be pure propane, pure butane, or a mixture of propane and butane. Butane is sold only in warmer areas since it will not vaporize in cold weather; propane is always used in colder weather. LPG is economical, as it is widely available for filling metal cylinders ("bottles") that hold a good supply of BTUs. For boats, the cylinders usually are in 10-, 14-, or 20-pound sizes. The usual practice is to exchange an empty cylinder for a full one.

Table 9-1
COOKING FUELS

FUEL	SPECIFIC GRAVITY AS A VAPOR (AIR = 1.0)	BTUs* AS A VAPOR	BTUs PER LIQUID GALLON
Alcohol	1.11	765	64,643
Kerosene	2.90	3700	129,350
LPG propane	1.55	2343	91,044
LPG butane	2.07	3101	108,047
CNG (natural gas)	.56	1025	101,475 (vapor only)

*One BTU (British Thermal Unit) is the heat required to raise 1 pound of water 1 degree Fahrenheit. BTU data are in standard cubic feet at 14.7 pounds per square inch at 60 degrees Fahrenheit. Kerosene figures are approximate due to a wide range of available grades.

The big drawback to LPG is that when it combines with air it can be dangerous. Propane and butane are heavier than air. If they escape inside the hull, they may settle in the bilge and form an explosive mixture. Therefore, they must be stored and handled with care. Here are some rules of thumb:

1. Stow LPG bottles in a compartment that is completely isolated (airtight) from the hull's interior, and which automatically drains any loose liquid or gas overboard.
2. Install an electric-activated solenoid valve in the bottle stowage compartment. The valve's switch and warning light are located in the galley. Activating the switch allows the gas to flow to the stove, turning on the light. When the switch is turned off, or if the power is interrupted, the gas valve is automatically shut off at the tank, and the light goes out.
3. Install a flame-out safety shutoff in the oven and broiler and, if possible, on the top burners. While not generally available on U.S.-built stoves, this shutoff is found on European equipment.
4. Install a "sniffer"—a device that gives a warning if gas leaks into the bilge.

The marine atmosphere poses a problem with steel LPG cylinders, which must be carefully protected against rust and inspected periodically by qualified gas suppliers to ensure that they are sound. Aluminum LPG cylinders are an alternative, although some people consider them unsafe (for example, suppliers were not allowed to refill aluminum cylinders in England in 1979).

CNG (compressed natural gas) is a relative newcomer as a galley stove fuel. Like LPG, it is a gas. But unlike LPG, it is lighter than air; if it leaks, it rises and dissipates. Obviously, this safety factor is a great advantage. Though not as available worldwide as LPG, CNG can be obtained in major North American sailing centers. CNG is less economical, partly because the cost of exchanging cylinders is greater than with LPG, and partly because less CNG can be stored per cubic foot of cylinder capacity.

Refrigeration
Anybody who has done much cruising lately has discovered that ice is

increasingly expensive and difficult to find; neither is it any less awkward to handle. So some form of refrigeration is widely considered to be essential. Even small boats carry refrigeration in the form of portable boxes that are cooled at home before being carried aboard to be plugged into the boat's 12-volt system. During a short cruise, low temperatures can be maintained in these fridges without excessive battery consumption.

Two major considerations affect all fridge installations: how to move the heat out, and how to keep it out. In other words, the main issues with every type of refrigerator are how the cold is generated by a compressor and how the box is designed.

The choice is influenced by cost and the owner's habits. Except on a very big yacht, operating the refrigerator from a 110-volt AC system is impractical; large power supply is not continuous on the average sailboat, and charging at the dockside usually takes too much time unless the slip has shore power. So while a 110-volt compressor is relatively inexpensive and requires low maintenance (because it is totally sealed), it is not practical for most boats.

We are now left with refrigeration systems that are either driven by the boat's own electrical system or operated by a compressor from the engine or alternator. First, though, we should address the problem of the construction of the cabinet.

With any kind of operation, you must have an efficient box or cabinet. Design of a fridge cabinet is always a compromise between convenience, cost, and efficiency. By far the most important component is the insulation. There must be at least 4 inches of insulation on all sides, with a suitable vapor barrier (either aluminum or polyethylene sheet) installed on the warm side. An excellent method of installing insulation is to use freezer-grade polyurethane foam, sealing all voids with foaming caulk. A second choice is to use foamed-in-place insulation, which is less costly than polyurethane foam but has neither its consistency nor its homogeneity.

The type of door is an option worth thinking about. Many people believe that top openings are thermally more efficient, since the cold air does not pour out of them, but there are also many proponents of side-opening boxes, partly because opening them does not require rearranging food or other objects on the box top. Still, top openings don't dump food on the cabin sole when the boat heels, and if their doors are sectional, much of the counter space goes unimpeded.

Now let's look at ways to run the refrigerator. In many sailboats, operation of the compressor directly from the battery is a practical solution, so long as thermal efficiency can be made high enough and the boat's power supply is sufficient. Assuming that the box is properly insulated and is top-opening, a typical 5-cubic-food refrigerator (without a freezer) will draw about the same amount of power as one or two continuously burning cabin lights—2 to 4 amperes at 12 volts. A typical compressor system will run for 10–15 minutes per hour, drawing 16–18 amperes. These figures are about the same for all properly designed and installed self-sufficient systems, which can be used anywhere—underway or at the float—without any switching or other complications. To pay the freight, you will have to charge the batteries by running the engine 1–2 hours a day. The batteries themselves should be large—about 200 ampere hours each. With an electric refrigerator two banks of batteries are essential. Many cruising boats, especially in southern waters, have had excellent results with solar (more properly, "photo-voltaic") cells to make up the energy consumed by the refrigerator as well as to keep the batteries charged without running the engine.

There are two popular compressor systems that run off power other than the batteries. They are either directly engine-driven or electrically motor-driven, with power supplied by an engine-driven alternator.

Operating the compressor from the engine is a widely used method, with an electric clutch installed to stop the compressor when necessary. The alternator-driven system has a special alternator that generates the power for a 1½-horsepower, 120-volt DC motor. The compressor in both engine-driven systems is quite large—½ to 1½ tons—but only the engine alternator system may also be driven by shore current. Another advantage with the alternator-driven system is that the compressor speed is essentially independent of engine speed, as it is controlled by a special voltage regulator. With the direct engine-driven compressor, engine speeds are limited in both high and low ranges.

The direct engine-driven system has some other disadvantages, among them vibration, the need for large amounts of space, and various construction and mechanical problems. Long runs of pipe may be needed to reach from the engine to the fridge, and engine heat may limit cooling capacity of the compressor sitting near it. While the alternator-driven system does not have some of these problems, it has a few of its own. It is more complex, hence more expensive. And it uses 120 volts DC, which can be a lethal voltage around salt water.

Since in both systems the cooling occurs only when the engine is running, eutectic (holding) plates are needed to retain the cold. These plates take up some space in the cabinet. The battery-powered system does not require holding plates, since the cooling is available on demand. Each of these systems will use half as much power if water-cooled condensers are installed.

Besides battery-, engine-, and alternator-powered systems, a fourth system exists: thermoelectric or solid-state refrigeration. Its efficiency is roughly equivalent to that of the others, and, with the exception of a fan, there are no moving parts. But at the time of writing most thermoelectric devices are of insufficient capacity for a cabinet of the size needed by cruising boats. Nor is this type cost efficient in most cases.

Everything that we have said above applies to freezers as well as refrigerators. Preferably, separate holding plates with separate controls should be installed so that when the freezer is not needed it can stay warm and not waste engine time or battery capacity. If one set of plates is used for both, they are located in the freezer. The boxes are open to each other at the top and temperature-activated dampers located near the bottom control the amount of cold that flows from the freezer to the refrigerator.

Having discussed several options for refrigeration in this section, let's make some recommendations. While no one system is always to be preferred, the following characteristics constitute the best (not the least expensive) system for a cruising yacht.

- Alternator-driven compressor with water-cooled condensers
- Separate freezer and refrigerator controls
- Top-opening cabinet with *plenty* of insulation
- Holding plates with at least 18 hours' capacity

Buy a good system and have it installed and maintained by reputable technicians.

The Cabin Table

While it is not, strictly speaking, part of the galley, the cabin table is where the food ends up so it can be discussed here. The table must be firmly anchored and supported, preferably by vertical aluminum supports that run from the cabin sole to the overhead under the cabin top. It usually is not enough simply to bolt the table to the sole. Hinges for the folding table leaves must be strong and rust-

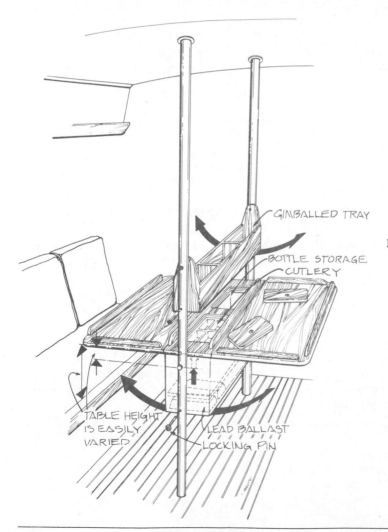

GIMBALLED TRAY

BOTTLE STORAGE
CUTLERY

TABLE HEIGHT
IS EASILY
VARIED

LEAD BALLAST
LOCKING PIN

Figure 9-4. If there are several holes for the pivot pins, a gimballed table may be raised or lowered to suit conditions and the clientele. There must be a locking pin to stop gimballing. In very rough weather, crew members may be content to eat off their laps and use the gimballed tray for condiments and drinks. The rods supporting the table must be strong and installed securely.

proof. Bins must be set into the center of the table to hold cutlery, napkins, seasonings, and bottles of wine (Figure 9-4).

While the table can be gimballed, many owners prefer to use stable tables with fiddles because gimbals can take up considerable room. If the table is not gimballed, an always-level place for condiments and cups of liquids can be provided by a long, swinging, high-sided shelf hung over the table on pivots on the vertical supports. In rough weather, the table itself is left folded up and crew members eat from their laps.

Stowage

Stowage can be either a convenience or a mess. When it is arranged poorly, it is the site of a constant battle between the inanimates that are wanted and the human hunters who want them. The key to good stowage is to follow the old adage: a place for everything and everything in its place. This means specialization.

Most people don't realize it, but except for variations in quantity the stowage requirements of different boats are about the same. All boats carry tools, cleaning compounds, and lubricants; food and eating utensils; pots, paper goods, and garbage; dry clothing and wet clothing; sails and boat-handling gear; and much, much more to meet the many human and sailing requirements. When shopping for a boat, or designing a new boat, make a list of all that needs to be stowed—the list in the previous sentence is a beginning—and then look at the boat to see if there are spaces and provisions for each item on the list.

Unfortunately, on only a few boats can you find several small drawers and lockers for specialized stowage of equipment. On most boats, builders seem to think it sufficient to provide relatively few large stowage spaces in the name of "flexibility" and "owner preference." Perhaps the cost of adding more drawers is a concern, but the return in greater convenience is certainly worth it.

While cavernous, undifferentiated lockers may seem to offer a lot of volume, much of it goes unused. If the locker is to leeward, everything seems to end up in a heap in the outboard bottom corner. You can be certain that what you need is at the bottom of the pile. If the locker is to windward, as soon as you open the door to begin your search everything spills out in your face and all over the cabin sole. As easily as things fall out, they restow with difficulty; shove a pair of pants or a can of beans back uphill, and you'll only jar loose a sweater or a box of pancake mix that has already been stowed.

What I'm saying is that two or three small lockers are superior to one enormous one. If there is no choice, you can improve the caverns by breaking them up with shelves that have adequate keeper bars or other restraints, with small bins, or with cloth stowage bags hanging on hooks. If may also help to add doors to provide easier access to the otherwise useless space too far outboard and down deep. If all else fails, block off the unusable outboard portion altogether rather than lose your clothes, food, or tools in it.

Galley Stowage

Most food is light enough to be stored in overhead lockers above the galley, although canned goods are best put low, in lockers near the cabin sole or even in the bilge (with restraints to prevent rolling). The doors on overhead lockers may be sliding or hinged at the bottom to prevent goods from falling out when the door is opened. Whichever doors you choose, they should be strong and have good automatic locks.

Some cabinets should be set aside specifically for soft goods like breadstuffs and cereal and for soaps, cleansers, and other items that might affect the taste of food. Rolls of paper towels make fine padding for eggs, which otherwise can be stowed either in the bilge or in waterproof containers, where they are packed with salt for long keeping.

Of course, some food will go in the icebox or refrigerator, where it may easily be lost. One good trick is to fasten a labeled string to each item before stowing it. Instead of feeling around for the cheese down at the bottom of a cold fridge, simply pull the string labeled "cheese" and up comes what you need.

Utensils that are lightweight and dull-edged can be kept near the counter in just about any drawer with a good automatic latch, but heavy pots and pans and sharp knives require special attention. Pots and frying pans should be kept under the stove or in a low, secure locker (a set of space-saving, rust-proof, nesting stainless-steel pots is an excellent investment). Most cutting and paring knives deserve their own drawer—preferably fairly low and with a secure latch so they won't be heaved across the cabin when the boat rolls sharply. Except in rough weather, you can stow the cook's favorite essential all-purpose cutting knife in a tight-fitting sheath secured to the counter.

A big stowage problem is presented by plates, cups, bowls, cutting boards, and other relatively bulky or fragile objects that are constantly in demand. While they must be secure, they must also be accessible. They may require a special overhead locker with built-in racks made of dowels, which should be off to the side of the stove so you needn't reach through the steam from the tea kettle to get to them.

Garbage presents its own stowage challenge. An increasing number of thoughtful sailors are no longer as callous as they once were about their environment. Instead of throwing overboard garbage and plastic stuff (some of which, like Styrofoam, is utterly indestructible), they stow it. For garbage disposal—or, more accurately, garbage retention—carry a large plastic basket in the galley, preferably at the foot of the companionway so it can be ventilated. Line the basket with a heavy trash bag, which, when filled, can be tied off and left in the dinghy or hanging on a hook in the sail locker to wait for the next trip ashore. At sea, the thoughtful crew throws only biodegradable garbage overboard, saving plastics (and reusing plastic garbage bags) to be disposed of properly at the end of the passage.

Special Clothes

Shore clothes should have their own locker so they are not wrinkled or dampened. The hangers should be high enough so that pants and skirts are well above the level of any bilge water. This locker should be louvered, for good ventilation. If you have any doubts about its watertightness, hang the clothes in a traveling bag or (in a pinch) pull a large plastic garbage bag over them.

Foul-weather suits are troublesome to stow in a hanging locker. If they have been dampened by salt water, they hardly ever dry. They are hard to hang up. And since they look alike, crew members are always making a mess of the hanging locker while searching for the gear. A better solution, first used (I think) by Dick Nye on *Carina,* is to replace the hanging locker with a number of cubbyholes. Each crew member has his or her own labeled cubby for foul-weather gear and boots.

Sails and Sail-handling Gear

For cruising, sails can be stowed either forward of the mast or aft alongside the cockpit (Figure 9-5). In modern boats there usually is no choice; with the advent of quarter berths, few boats have cockpit sail lockers any more. In smaller boats without good sail lockers forward, this means that sails must often be stowed under the V-berth, which is not a good trade-off since you must tear the forward cabin apart and disrupt sleepers whenever you need a new sail. A good alternative is to flake jibs in long, compact, sausage-shaped bags, which can be lashed on the cabin top or in the windward waterway beside the cockpit.

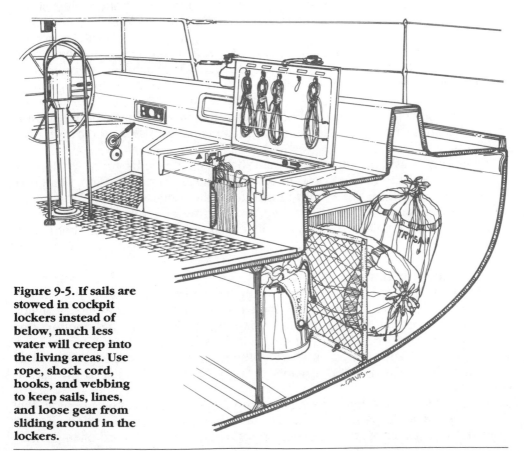

Figure 9-5. If sails are stowed in cockpit lockers instead of below, much less water will creep into the living areas. Use rope, shock cord, hooks, and webbing to keep sails, lines, and loose gear from sliding around in the lockers.

If you are fortunate enough to have a good old-fashioned sail locker either under the cockpit or forward, find some way to keep the sails from shifting to leeward and piling up on each other in a confusing heap. Bins, partitions, or a simple system of hooks and restraining lines all work well.

Sheets and other lines should be hung on hooks so that they stay coiled and are free to dry. One refinement is to restrain the lower reaches of the coils with lanyards to prevent annoying banging against the hull.

Pulley blocks, winch handles, shackles, spare line, tape, sail-repair tools and cloth, and other fittings and equipment are best carried in cloth bags made up to your specifications by your sailmaker or an awning maker. Don't make the bags too large or fittings will be lost in them. A good dimension is 15 by 20 inches. Use heavy, durable cloth and drawstrings. So that they can be easily identified in difficult conditions, code these bags with special color combinations or markings—for example, a triangle for blocks, a stripe for shackles, and a circle for winch handles.

Tools, Lubricants, and Spares

A practical way to stow tools is to mount a sturdy plastic (rust-proof) standard toolbox in a handy spot that is out of traffic—say, under the bottom step of the companionway ladder. Use cleats, bolts, and/or lashings to keep the box from sliding or spilling open during knockdowns. On larger boats, tools can be stowed in a shallow, wide, custom-built box. On my *Dora IV,* this box was mounted over the engine so the tools were warmed and dried with each engine operation. Perhaps, a store-bought toolbox could be located in the same position in a small boat.

Oil, grease, teak cleanser, and other potentially messy fluids can be stowed on a low shelf in a metal or plastic tray with 2-inch sides. Wedge the cans tightly with rags.

Bolts, nuts, washers, cotter pins, small shackles, light bulbs, fuses, small electrical spares, and the like are best stowed in transparent twist-top jars. I had bad luck with polyethylene boxes with hinged tops; the hinges kept breaking. Large engine spares, such as pumps and injectors, can be carefully sealed in clearly marked plastic bags. Stow them in the bilge, using restraints to keep them from rolling around.

The Navigation Station

Although Dick McCurdy and Tom Young have much to say about the navigation station in Chapter 14, we should look at it as a layout and stowage problem. In the general layout, provide enough space for a chart table and comfortable seat facing either forward or aft. If the table is as large as 36 by 28 inches, you will be able to open a rolled-up chart all the way and pin or tape it to the table without having to worry about maneuvering your parallel rules or protractor over folds.

A large shelf below the working surface will permit ready stowage of all the charts needed for a particular passage. All other charts can be rolled up and stowed on the cabin overhead, either under lengths of shock cord or in permanently mounted long tubes. For reference books, there should be a handy book case with retainers. For pencils, dividers, parallel rules, and other tools, provide a long, shallow tray above the table.

Howland B. Jones, Jr., and Avery Seaman contributed to the section on the galley.

CHAPTER 10

Ventilation

Thomas R. Young

The ventilation system of an offshore racing-cruising yacht is both a safety and a comfort device. Not only should the dodger, vents, hatches, and ports be able to rid the boat of noxious and flammable fumes, they must provide plenty of fresh air at a comfortable temperature and humidity to keep the cabin free of cooking, body, head, smoking, and other odors.

To control ventilation for varying conditions of heat, cold, rain, wind, waves, and spray requires considerable planning, a flexible system, and a thorough knowledge of some basic principles. In this chapter, we will look at the principles of air flow and ventilation, at different types of ventilation equipment, and at ways to use that equipment at sea and in port in fair weather and foul.

Ventilation Gear

Using carefully thought out combinations of equipment, basic natural ventilation arrangements have proven satisfactory for the wide variety of circumstances encountered on a boat. The crew must have a good understanding of how all these parts work together to form a ventilation *system*.

The central element in the system is the *main companionway*. When equipped with an adequate dodger, the companionway becomes a large, efficient inlet or exhaust device. With the wind aft, it is a huge air scoop; with the wind forward, it becomes a big funnel-shaped exhaust. In rough weather, the companionway may have to be closed off either partly (by installing one or more slats or boards while leaving the hatch open) or entirely (by installing all the slats and closing the hatch). Using a companionway slat that has louvers allows some air flow.

Another key part of the system is the *baffled cowl vent,* which keeps air flowing into the cabin while separating out most water. The most reliable baffled vent is the one known as the "Dorade" vent because it was first used by Olin and Rod Stephens on their famous yawl *Dorade* in the early 1930s. At the end of this chapter, Rod will add a few words about the proper construction, size, and placement of a Dorade vent. These vents should be removable, with their holes filled with screw-in deck plates. Other types of baffled vents have appeared over the years, most recently a one-piece cowl vent called the Dri-Vent, but for simplicity's sake I will call these vents either baffled or Dorade vents.

Besides these two main ingredients, the ventilation system includes *auxiliary devices.* Among them are unbaffled vents, mushroom vents, hatches, louvers, fans, and opening ports.

Ventilation Systems

Later in this chapter, we will have much more to say about the design and construction of these devices. But now we'll look at how they should be arranged on deck in a system.

Working together or alone, the companionway and vents provide air flow to vent engine compartments, cabins, galleys, heads, and lockers. The important thing to remember is that good ventilation depends on a good flow of air, and for air to flow below there must be a system of inlets and outlets handling the same amount of air—some facing into the wind to take air in, others facing downwind to exhaust the same amount of air out of the boat. Theoretically, if the dodger and the vents are all set to exhaust, no air can get in and there will be no ventilation. Conversely, if all vents are set to be inlets, no air can get out.

A typical 40-foot racer-cruiser would have the following ventilation equipment, as shown in Figure 10-1:

1. A main companionway with a dodger held up by shock cord.
2. Two Dorade vents located port and starboard, just abaft the mast and well inboard. A ⅛-inch or 3⁄16-inch line is tied through a hole near the top of each cowl and led forward to the deck to prevent jib sheets and other lines from fouling on the cowls.
3. A main cabin skylight opened either forward or aft for use in mild or moderate weather but dogged tight in rough weather. A dodger can be rigged for rough weather; if the dodger has a clear plastic panel, light will be let through to the cabin.
4. On the centerline of the after deck, a tall Dorade vent, perhaps on top of a lazarette hatch. The top of the cowl should be at least as high as the stern pulpit for unobstructed air flows.
5. A fore-and-aft opening hatch, protected by a dodger, on the foredeck to help air sweep through the forward part of the yacht. If weather permits, open the hatch forward. In rough weather, open it aft under the dodger.
6. A Dorade vent forward to ventilate the forward cabin or chain locker.

Not only does this combination provide plenty of circulation under way, it gives good ventilation when the boat is left unattended.

The top part of Figure 10-1 shows how these vents are arranged when the wind is forward of the beam. The main objective is to encourage flow toward the main companionway, the forward hatch, and the forward vent, where it is exhausted.

The bottom part of Figure 10-1 shows what to do when the wind is abaft the beam. Here, the main companionway, forward hatch, and forward vent work as intakes.

Galleys, Heads, and Lockers

The galley, head, and lockers require some auxiliary equipment of their own.

First, the galley presents several ventilation problems. The most important of these concerns the stove fuel, which, as has been stressed in detail in Chapter 9, can be potentially dangerous. Good ventilation can help. Except for compressed

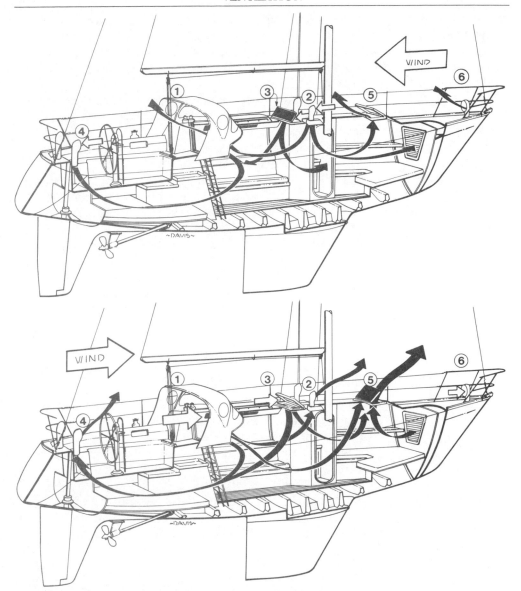

Figure 10-1. Depending on the wind direction, the companionway (1), hatches (3 & 5), and vents (2, 4, & 6) serve as either inlets or exhausts of fresh air. Since the companionway does much of the work, the dodger is a key ingredient in a good ventilation system.

natural gas (CNG), gas cooking fuels are heavier than air, which means that, in the case of gas escape through a leak or an unlit burner, the gas will settle in the bilge, where it may explode if a spark is set off nearby. Fortunately, the gas can usually be identified by sniffing the fumes through the human nose or an electronic device. The bilges must then be ventilated. This is best done by removing the floor boards or cabin sole or running the engine-compartment exhaust blower.

Another problem with bottled gas as a stove fuel is that, as it burns, it forms carbon dioxide and water vapor. Normally, all this does is increase the humidity in the galley, but if the ventilation is very bad or the burner is poorly designed, carbon monoxide may form.

In the case of an alcohol stove, the major ventilation problem is that, as a by-product of combustion, alcohol forms acetaldehyde, which has a bad smell and acts as a low-grade tear gas. Unlike gas, alcohol will not explode, but it will ignite. (In my own experience, fires and flare-ups are often caused after the flame is accidentally blown out. Pressurized liquid alcohol then runs out onto the burner or oven bottom, forming a pool ready to be ignited, either by a hot burner or by a crew member who tries to relight the stove without wiping up the alcohol.)

Obviously, then, both alcohol and bottled-gas cooking fuels require plenty of ventilation. So, too, do objectionable cooking odors and the heat rising from the stove in hot weather. An excellent way to vent the galley area is to place a fan or exhaust blower over the stove and direct it through the companionway or a small nearby vent. A new mushroom vent that would work well in the galley has a built-in solar-powered exhaust fan, which means that fumes and odors may be exhausted without having to rely on the ship's electricity. Sold by Nicro-Fico, this ingenious vent was nominated Best Product of 1984 by *Practical Sailor* magazine.

Like stove odors, air in the head should be exhausted. A Dorade vent can be used, but it can be an obstruction on deck. I prefer the solar vent described in the previous paragraph or a low mushroom type that exhausts by a combination of natural draft and suction created by wind passing over the dome. This type of vent has a screw knob for quick shutoff in very rough weather.

Lockers—whether for the anchor rode or for clothing—should have built-in louvers. The chain locker will need this auxiliary ventilation when the forward-most Dorade must be removed in rough weather. With hanging lockers, Dorades may be used, but I prefer relying on louvers in the doors. They will not let water onto your shore clothes in bad weather (in spite of all the theory, one well-aimed driving wave can make a Dorade vent act like a fire-hose nozzle), and, in any case, another Dorade means one more obstacle on deck, and one more deck plate to forget.

The Dodger

The dodger is often thought of solely as a device that keeps the cockpit dry when spray is flying, but it has another extremely valuable function. With the help of a good dodger, the typical main companionway is the main actor in the boat's ventilation system (Figure 10-2). When the wind is forward of the beam, it serves as a huge exhaust, removing as much air as all the hatches, vents, and other devices combined can take in. When the wind is aft, it scoops in great amounts of air that is exhausted through other devices. Obviously, then, the placement, design, and construction of the dodger are important. Of course, the dodger should be sturdily constructed and fit the boat. Leaks are not conducive to the well-being of cooks, navigators, and electronic devices. Some sailmakers

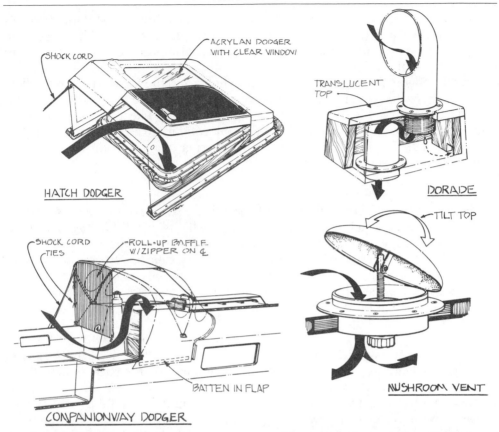

SHOCK CORD

ACRYLAN DODGER
WITH CLEAR WINDOW

TRANSLUCENT
TOP

HATCH DODGER

DORADE

TILT TOP

SHOCK CORD
TIES

ROLL-UP BAFFLE
W/ZIPPER ON ℄

BATTEN IN FLAP

MUSHROOM VENT

COMPANIONWAY DODGER

Figure 10-2. (Clockwise from upper left) If equipped with a small dodger, a hatch may be cracked open in rain and spray. The Dorade vent is the best source of ventilation in rough seas because it separates air from water. The mushroom or clamshell vent, low and unobtrusive, serves well over the engine, head, and galley. The companionway dodger keeps spray off the cockpit crew and also draws air into and out of the cabin; retractable baffle flaps on the side or back offer increased protection against spray.

specialize in dodgers; if you ask around, you'll quickly find out which manufacturers have the best reputations.

The dodger should run the full width of the cockpit and have enough overhang so that anybody sitting on the bridge deck is protected from spray. It should be held up with shock cord so it can be readily retracted to facilitate crew egress from the cabin, yet quickly raised by a single crew member. When it is pulled up, the dodger's after edge should slope forward from the companionway so that water drips onto the deck and not below (or onto the neck of anybody using the companionway). A baffle may also be installed across the top. The sides must be secure. It's a good idea to have special roll-down flaps that extend aft of the cabin. These flaps will prevent spray from splashing below when the companionway slats are installed but the hatch is left open to provide ventilation. The dodger should not be attached to the deck with snaps, which will lead to drips below.

Rather, its forward and side edges should be bolt ropes that are slid into grooves secured to the cabin top. If constructed with clear plastic panels, the dodger will let light below and allow the helmsman and cockpit crew to see forward with some clarity without have to stand up.

Small dodgers may also be rigged on skylights and the forward hatch to allow them to be cracked open in moderately rough seas. Like the main dodger, unless they have clear panels they may keep light out. Also like the companionway dodger, they should be installed with a bolt-rope-in-groove system, and they should be sturdily constructed, as they will take a beating from the sun, from feet, and from jib sheets.

Vent Design

As mentioned above, baffled cowl Dorade-type vents are the main source of fresh air in heavy weather, when portholes, skylights, small hatches, and even the companionway are closed, and when non-baffled vents will take on a considerable amount of water. Likewise, in heavy, relatively calm rainstorms, these vents may provide the only fresh air, since most other openings cannot be protected by dodgers or rain shields. Obviously, then, much depends on the cowl vents. The two factors that most determine the amount of air that can be sucked below are the cowl size and the wind strength.

To calculate how large the cowls should be, we must begin with the amount of fresh air that is actually needed below. According to the American Society of Heating, Refrigerating, and Air Conditioning Engineers, for each person there should be an air supply of at least 10 cubic feet per minute (CFM) and preferably 15 CFM. A vent's capacity can be readily determined using Table 10-1, which shows how much air can flow through holes of different sizes at varying wind speeds. The standard used to indicate vent size is the diameter of the deck plate. Vents are available in six sizes at 1-inch increments ranging from 3 to 8 inches. As Table 10-1 shows, a single vent of 3-inch and 4-inch deck-plate diameter provides marginal air flow in light winds, while vents that are 5 inches or larger are sufficient—at least for a singlehander.

Figuring how much ventilation is required on a singlehanded boat is rela-

Table 10-1
AIR FLOW THROUGH WELL-DESIGNED BAFFLED VENTS

VENT SIZE (INCHES)	INLET AREA (SQUARE INCHES)	WIND VELOCITY			
		4 KNOTS	8 KNOTS	12 KNOTS	16 KNOTS
3	28	8 CFM	18 CFM	29 CFM	42 CFM
4	50	12 CFM	29 CFM	50 CFM	73 CFM
5	78	21 CFM	49 CFM	80 CFM	112 CFM
6	113	35 CFM	74 CFM	117 CFM	162 CFM
7	154	52 CFM	107 CFM	160 CFM	222 CFM
8	201	70 CFM	144 CFM	220 CFM	310 CFM

Note: CFM is cubic feet per minute. A person requires 10–15 CFM. Vent size is the diameter of the deck plate. Inlet area is equivalent to an opening that is twice the vent size.

tively simple. Any combination that totals more than 15 CFM should do. But determining vent size and number for crewed yachts is a bit more complicated. Let's begin with the weather conditions, and especially the wind strength. As we have seen, there are two situations when the vents provide most or all of the fresh air: heavy weather and a rainstorm. In heavy weather at sea, we can assume that wind velocity will be greater than 16 knots. In a rainstorm, however, the wind often is much weaker—about 4 knots.

Our two examples are a 45-footer with an eight-person cruising crew and a twelve-person racing crew, and a 35-footer with a five-person crusing crew and a nine-person racing crew. Assuming that everybody is below (which is not unlikely in these two conditions), the *minimum* requirements are shown in Table 10-2.

In making these calculations, I have made three assumptions. First, in the 16-knot case, I have assumed that the main companionway is closed and that, there-

Table 10-2
VENTILATION REQUIREMENTS FOR A 45-FOOTER AND A 35-FOOTER

45-FOOTER

(A) 8-person cruising crew: 8 × 15 CFM = 120 CFM required

16 knots	4 knots
2–4" inlets = 146 CFM	2–6" aft of mast = 70 CFM
1–6" exhaust = 162 CFM	1–7" aft = 52 CFM
	TOTAL = 122 CFM

(B) 12-person racing crew: 12 × 15 CFM = 180 CFM required

16 knots	4 knots
3–4" inlets = 219 CFM	1–4" at bow = 12 CFM
1–7" exhaust = 222 CFM	2–7" aft of mast = 104 CFM
	1–8" aft = 70 CFM
	TOTAL = 182 CFM

35-FOOTER

(A) 5-person cruising crew: 5 × 15 CFM = 75 CFM required

16 knots	4 knots
2–3" inlets = 84 CFM	2–4" aft of mast = 24 CFM
1–5" exhaust = 112 CFM	1–7" aft = 52 CFM
	TOTAL = 76 CFM

(B) 9-person racing crew: 9 × 15 CFM = 135 CFM required

16 knots	4 knots
2–4" inlets = 146 CFM	2–6" aft of mast = 70 CFM
1–6" exhaust = 162 CFM	1–8" aft = 70 CFM
	TOTAL = 140 CFM

Note: In 16 knots (the left-hand column), when vents must provide all the inlet and exhaust, the capacity of each vent or combination of vents must exceed the crew's CFM requirement. In 4 knots (the right-hand column), when the companionway is assumed to be open, the *total capacity* must exceed the requirement. The best practice would be to design the boat's ventilation system for the most extreme requirement, which is a racing crew in 4 knots of wind.

fore, baffled vents must provide both inlet and exhaust capabilities. Second, in the 4-knot example, I have assumed that the main companionway, protected by a dodger, can be opened slightly to provide exhaust so that all the vents are used for intake (a 2-inch opening in a 24-inch-wide companionway will pass as much air as two or three 8-inch baffled vents). In other words, at 16 knots the baffled vents must handle 15 CFM of inlet air per person as well as 15 CFM of exhaust air per person. At 4 knots, all the baffled vents handle inlet air only, and exhaust air is handled by the companionway. My third assumption is that the best arrangement is with one vent forward, two vents just aft of the mast, and one vent on the centerline near the after pulpit.

At the end of this chapter, Rod Stephens will say more about the design and construction of baffled vents. There he offers a simple formula for determining the optimum total area of intakes.

Total intake area in square inches = beam × waterline length.

Using this formula, we see that a typical 45-footer with a beam of 12.5 feet and a waterline length of 34 feet should have a total inlet area of 425 square inches ($12.5 \times 34 = 425$). Applying this total to Table 10-1, we see that three 4-inch vents and one 7-inch vent will satisfy this requirement. This was also my recommendation for a 45-footer sailing in 16 knots with a large crew.

Hatches and Other Auxiliary Vents

While the main companionway and the baffled vents are the boat's primary source of ventilation, there are several other devices that can provide air below. Of these, perhaps the most helpful are amidships and forward hatches. When equipped with good gaskets and dogs, these hatches can act both as skylights and as vents (and, in the case of the forward hatch, as a passageway for crew, sails, and gear). Preferably, the hatch should have hinges fore and aft so it can be opened in either direction to be used as either an intake or an exhaust.

A hatch should have a tight-fitting dog at each corner to cinch it down, as well as some device that allows it to be opened and shut from both on deck and below. The hatch sides should be straight (with no flare) and should be close to the deck when the hatch is closed so that lines won't catch under them. Be sure everybody on board knows how to tighten the dogs properly, with equal pressure on each dog; otherwise, the hatch will be left partially closed and will drip water onto somebody's bunk—almost certainly yours. Since gaskets can dry out and lose their give with age, they should be replaced periodically; carry extra gasket material in case of emergency. If the hatch is equipped with a dodger, fitted into grooves forward and on the sides, the aft side can be left slightly open in rain and light spray.

Hatches can be damaged easily if used improperly. When closing a hatch, be sure that a sheet, sail stop, or other object is not caught under the lip or in the hinge at the dog. In particular, the corners of forward hatches can easily snag a jib sheet during a tack or jibe. A sheet under great strain may bend up a hatch corner, which will leave a gap. If that happens and you're far from a chandlery or machine shop ashore, all you can do is dog or wire the corner down as tightly as possible before covering the gap with layers of tape, cloth, and plastic. Still, it's much better if that accident doesn't occur in the first place, so make sure that all forward hatches are dogged closed (or left all the way open) before tacking. If there's any chance that a hatch corner will hook a sheet even when the hatch is closed, install a guard at the corners.

If a hinge breaks, you may be able to wire the hatch shut. To do this, first drill small holes in the aluminum top and bottom frames; a hand drill should be sufficient. Then make several passes with small wire between the holes. Finally, tighten the wire with a Spanish windlass: insert a screw or stainless-steel cotter pin in the wire loops and turn it as far as it will go before tying it off. While you won't be able to open the hatch, at least you can be assured that it won't leak badly.

A crew member who falls partly or completely through an open hatch may be badly injured. Therefore, everybody on deck must be informed whenever a hatch is left open. A loose sail must never be left over an open hatch, and all hatches must be tightly closed before anchoring or before reefing, furling, or changing sails—in fact, before any crew member distracted by a sail-handling or boat-handling job can accidently stumble into an opening.

Besides the hatches, there are several other types of auxiliary vents. One is a small unbaffled cowl or clam-shell vent, which, since it can take water, should be used in protected areas for specialized purposes—for example, near the cockpit to ventilate the engine compartment (Figure 10-3).

An air scoop that funnels air into the forward hatch not only ventilates the forward cabin but keeps air moving throughout the entire boat in only a small amount of wind. For an air scoop to work best, it should face forward and work in conjunction with the main companionway with the dodger raised; one will be an inlet and the other will be an exhaust.

Portholes can provide good cross ventilation and, when equipped with rain shields, may be left open in light rain or spray. However, heavy vertical rain will splash off the deck and into an open port. Like hatches, they require good gaskets and dogs, and must be dogged down with care so they do not snag sheets.

Electric fans greatly improve comfort below; only air-conditioning works better. Small, inexpensive 12-volt, 5½-inch-diameter rubber-bladed fans are rated to circulate air at 250 CFM. When located in the galley, main saloon, and sleeping quarters, these fans can provide considerable relief in hot, humid weather.

It bears repeating that good ventilation of lockers can be provided by louvered doors, as long as the lockers are not too crowded and their contents are not wet. To avoid mildew, keep all wet gear in its own lockers, away from dry gear. Louvers also provide an exhaust when set into companionway slat.

A type of specialized vent that, while not used for air circulation, should be given careful attention is an overflow vent for fuel and water tanks. For obvious reasons, the fuel-tank vent must exit overboard, preferably in a place where fuel stains are not too noticeable.

Condensation, Odors, and Screens

Condensation occurs on surfaces colder than the air's dew point. When the

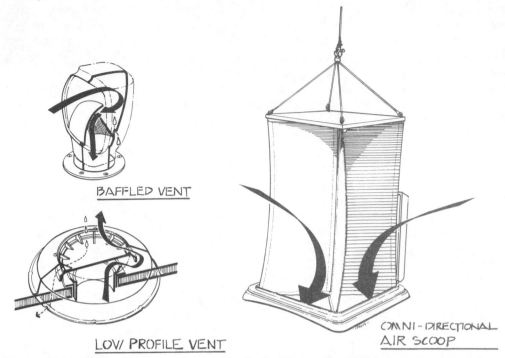

BAFFLED VENT

LOW PROFILE VENT

OMNI-DIRECTIONAL AIR SCOOP

Figure 10-3. (Clockwise from upper left) The baffled vent, while not as efficient as the Dorade, can work well in drier parts of the deck. The omni-directional air scoop redirects wind from any direction into the cabin through hatches. The low-profile vent does not stub toes or bark shins, and can pull in a sufficient amount of air to ventilate small lockers or the head (one type has an automatic fan).

boat is in use, it may appear on the inside of the hull on a spring day when the water is colder than the air or a fall night when the air is cooled to below the water temperature. Condensation can also appear at any season when a boat has been left unoccupied at anchor or a mooring; she is so buttoned up that the stagnant air inside becomes much warmer than the water. The solution is to make sure that the cabin is properly ventilated with baffled vents and louvered slats in the companionway.

Lockers and other storage areas may be dampened by condensation long before the rest of the hull. It helps to pack gear loosely to encourage free air to circulate. Good insulation can be a benefit, too, because it keeps engine noise and heat from the living area, and prevents heat from passing through the hull and deck—outward in a cold climate and inward in a hot one. Metal hulls will pass heat more readily than wooden or fiberglass hulls, and dark hulls will pass heat more readily than light-colored ones.

Noxious and unpleasant odors have been given some attention already in our discussion of galley and head ventilation. Another kind of bad smell can be created by the human body, which, while it won't get dirty during an offshore passage, can perspire. Since ultraviolet rays from the sun will kill body-odor bacteria, you can improve the atmosphere below by hanging your smelly clothes in the sun when the chance arises.

Since screens reduce ventilation by about 50 percent, anybody cruising in a hot, buggy area will have to make a sacrifice. Many people can get by with sprays and lotions and a screen located in the companionway only (it may help to spray the screen with bug repellent). Other people, however, need screens everywhere. For some reason, bugs do not seem to want to swarm down a vent cowl; perhaps that's because there's no light in the vent to attract them.

Safety

So far, we have been talking primarily about how good ventilation improves the crew's on-board comfort. Now we will address safety concerns. U.S. Coast Guard regulations concerning ventilation are provided in detail in the American Boat and Yacht Council (ABYC) manual *Safety Standards for Small Craft,* Sections H2, H24, and H32.

The ventilation of the engine compartment is necessary to remove flammable gases and heat. For this reason, I strongly recommend the use of diesel engines and fuel. Gasoline is particularly hazardous and extreme precautions are necessary to be certain that *all* gasoline fumes are removed before starting the engine. Because of this danger, the Coast Guard has certain specific regulations about the ventilation of boats with gasoline engines and enclosed gasoline fuel tanks. These rules, and regulations concerning ventilation of diesels, are listed in Coast Guard publications and are summarized in *Piloting, Seamanship, & Small Boat Handling* ("Chapman's") and *The Annapolis Book of Seamanship*. If you have any doubts about the legality or safety of your engine ventilation system, request a courtesy inspection by your local Coast Guard Auxiliary.

When running, engines act as their own exhaust fans by taking in air from the engine compartment and blowing it out through the engine exhaust system. Still, while requirements for ventilation for diesel engines are much less stringent than those for gasoline engines, it's a good idea to have a system that includes a blower and two large natural-draft vents leading from the deck to the engine compartment through clam-shell vents and large-diameter vent tubing. One vent will serve as intake, the other will serve as exhaust.

Cabin Heaters

It is not safe to use open-flame cabin heaters whose combustion discharges into the cabin. There are several reasons for this recommendation. First, the time when they are used—cold weather—is also the time when ventilation is reduced by shutting the companionway and hatches. Second, their flames produce increased humidity, undesirable levels of carbon dioxide, and possibly carbon monoxide. Alcohol heaters, like alcohol stoves, also turn out smelly, tear-forming acetaldehyde. Cabin heaters, then, should exhaust through their own independent flues or chimneys.

But even chimneys may be dangerous. A chimney works only if the hot gas inside is sufficiently lighter than the surrounding air to provide suction, which creates an upward draft. However, this will not happen if the surrounding air in the boat's cabin is itself under suction. When air is being pulled out by the companionway dodger or by cowl vents that have been aimed downwind, the chimney will actually work in reverse and force smoke and fumes *into* the cabin instead of out of it. In anticipation of this dangerous situation, some heaters are equipped with exhaust blowers. However, by adjusting the inlets and closing the outlets in the ventilation system, the crew can usually put the cabin under slight positive pressure and make the chimney work properly.

In the solution to this last danger, which has proved fatal to too many crews, we see once again the importance of a thorough understanding of the principles of ventilation (Figure 10-4).

A Note on the Dorade Vent

It is generally agreed that there is no difficulty getting air *out* of the boat. There are numerous ways to get rid of air even in adverse conditions. A companionway with a dodger, opening into a sheltered area such as a cockpit, makes an excellent exhaust outlet. So does a forward hatch whose after side is propped open 25 or 20 degrees under a tight dodger that allows no openings at the forward corners.

But in rough weather, the key to good ventilation is getting air *in* without water. A lazarette hatch raised to a 35-degree angle provides a very effective forced intake for the after part of the boat, assuming that air passages exist through the bulkheads under the cockpit. However, when the hatches must be closed,

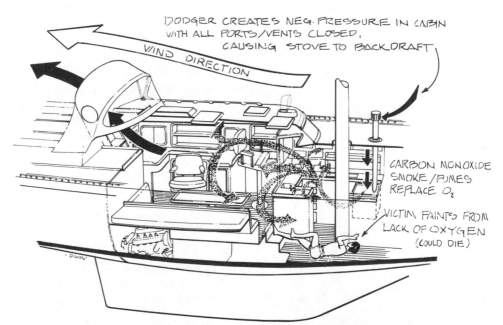

Figure 10-4. Ports, hatches, and vents must be left open when an open-flame cabin heater is in use. Otherwise smoke will be sucked into the cabin and possibly kill crew members.

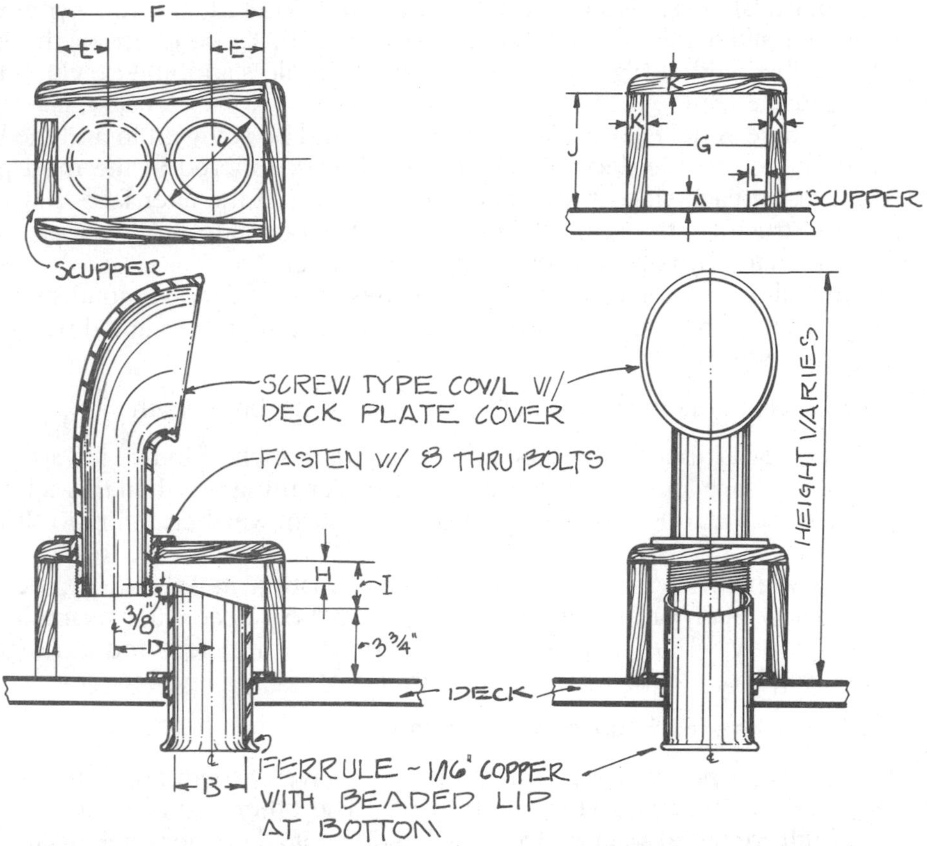

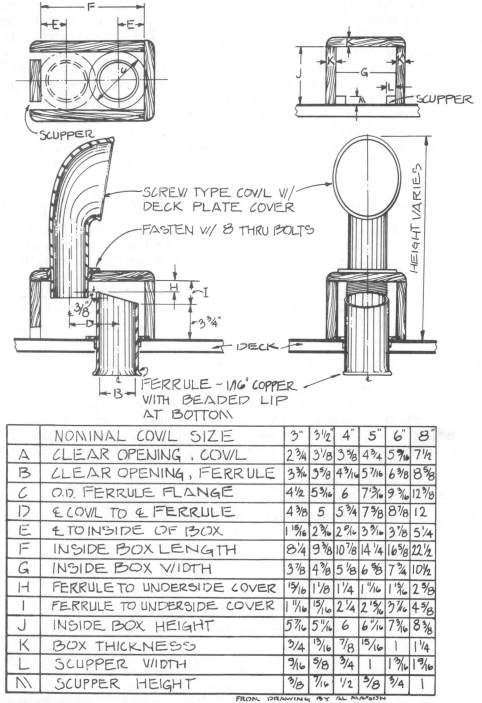

	NOMINAL COWL SIZE	3"	3 1/2"	4"	5"	6"	8"
A	CLEAR OPENING, COWL	2 3/4	3 1/8	3 5/8	4 3/4	5 9/16	7 1/2
B	CLEAR OPENING, FERRULE	3 3/16	3 5/8	4 3/16	5 7/16	6 3/8	8 5/8
C	O.D. FERRULE FLANGE	4 1/2	5 3/16	6	7 13/16	9 3/16	12 3/8
D	℄ COWL TO ℄ FERRULE	4 3/8	5	5 3/4	7 5/8	8 7/8	12
E	℄ TO INSIDE OF BOX	1 15/16	2 3/16	2 9/16	3 5/16	3 7/8	5 1/4
F	INSIDE BOX LENGTH	8 1/4	9 3/8	10 7/8	14 1/4	16 5/8	22 1/2
G	INSIDE BOX WIDTH	3 7/8	4 3/8	5 1/8	6 5/8	7 3/4	10 1/2
H	FERRULE TO UNDERSIDE COVER	15/16	1 1/8	1 1/4	1 11/16	1 15/16	2 5/8
I	FERRULE TO UNDERSIDE COVER	1 11/16	15/16	2 1/4	2 15/16	3 7/16	4 5/8
J	INSIDE BOX HEIGHT	5 7/16	5 11/16	6	6 11/16	7 3/16	8 3/8
K	BOX THICKNESS	3/4	13/16	7/8	15/16	1	1 1/4
L	SCUPPER WIDTH	9/16	5/8	3/4	1	1 3/16	1 9/16
M	SCUPPER HEIGHT	3/8	7/16	1/2	5/8	3/4	1

FROM DRAWING BY AL MASON

Figure 10-5. Dorade vent construction details. Dorades should be as close to the centerline as possible to prevent their being flooded with water in rough seas.

the most practical device is a well-designed and well-located "Dorade"-type vent, which traps water while allowing air to pass through. To be effective, the vent must be sizable, with a big box, large scuppers, ample standpipe height, and a high cowl intake.

On a Dorade vent (Figure 10-5), the cowl should be screwed in and the box should be bolted to the deck. The box should be scuppered in the most protected place, on each side of the *after* face. However, if the after face is against some deck structure, the scuppers must be in the box sides; in that case, they must be protected by flaps to prevent ingress of water.

As a guideline, the total area in square inches of Dorade cowl mouths should at least equal the product of the boat's maximum beam and designed waterline length (both in feet):

Total intake area in square inches = beam × waterline length.

In other words, there should be at least 1 square inch of intake for approximately every square foot of area to be ventilated. Anything less than this 1:1 ratio is unsatisfactory for rough weather offshore. For warm weather, the ratio should exceed 1.5:1.

Starting with this figure, and using the information in Table 10-1, we can determine how many and what kinds of vents any boat needs. For example, Ed Greeff's 48-foot yawl *Puffin* has a maximum beam of 12.5 feet and a designed waterline length of 33.5 feet. Using the formula:

12.5 × 33.5 = 418.75 square inches of area.

Puffin is equipped with seven Dorade vents. Five of them are 6-inch vents, each with a mouth area of 113 square inches. The other two are 4-inch vents, whose mouth area is 50 square inches each. Adding it all up, her total intake area is 665 square inches, which is 1.6 times the product of her beam and waterline length—an ample ratio for warm-weather sailing, as experience has proved.

The location of the Dorade is extremely important. It must be as near the centerline as possible—off center no more than 60 percent of the distance from the centerline to the deck edge. Any farther outboard, and the vent risks being flooded with water.

The note on the Dorade vent was written by Roderick Stephens, Jr.

PART III

SPARS, RIGGING, AND SAILS

CHAPTER 11

The Sail Plan, Spars, and Standing Rigging

Roderick Stephens, Jr., and Mitchell C. Gibbons-Neff

O ur goal in this chapter—the first of three on rigging and sails—is to describe the design and construction of proper rigs for cruising boats. We will be discussing everything from the right sail plan for your boat to the proper way to use a cotter pin. Along the way, we will survey good gear for the job. While we find much new gear that is helpful, new is not necessarily better, and we will be looking at all equipment with a critical seaman's eye for strength, reliability, and simplicity.

Sail Plans

While the sloop or cutter rig is the logical sail plan for any boat smaller than about 45 feet in waterline length, and while most modern cruising boats have a masthead foretriangle, other rigs are attractive for cruising boats as long as the owner knows their limitations in offshore conditions.

Sloop, Cutter, Split, and Cat Rigs

It used to be that a single-masted rig on a medium- to large-size boat was considered too much for the normal small cruising crew, but even the 45-foot limit that we have just suggested may not apply because of the power of today's efficient and dependable sail-handling devices, such as roller-furling sails and powerful winches.

The choice in single-masted, mainsail and jib rigs lies between the sloop and the cutter. There always has been confusion as to their definitions, so before proceeding further, we should distinguish between the two. In this discussion, when we say "sloop" we mean a single-masted sailing yacht with only one stay (the headstay) for a single jib. By "cutter" we mean a yacht that can carry two jibs. One jib is set on the headstay, which runs to the stem, and the other is set on a forestay (often called an "inner forestay"), which runs to the foredeck. The advantage of the sloop is simplicity, with only two sails—a mainsail and genoa jib—and little standing and running rigging to go wrong. The advantage of the cutter is flexibility and ease of handling—mainsail and two relatively small headsails, a forestaysail and an outer jib.

Split rigs (the yawl and ketch) were developed and became popular in offshore yachts in the 1930s mainly because they carried smaller sails than a cutter or sloop. That was important in those days because of widespread lack of faith in cotton sails, wooden spars, linen sheets, small winches, and weak wire halyards and standing rigging. With great improvements in the strength and dependability of materials, those concerns no longer apply for most boats.

On the other hand, the split rig has several advantages. First, it offers greater flexibility for sail reduction, allowing a combination of headsail and mizzen ("jib and jigger") in fresh or strong winds. Another tremendous advantage, which unfortunately in considerably obscured by today's over-reliance on auxiliary power, is that the mizzen aids steering control when maneuvering under sail at low speeds in tight places. By trimming the mizzen to swing the bow to windward or backing it to pull the bow off, the crew can make the boat turn surprisingly sharply even with very little way on. A mizzen can also be a good riding sail to keep a boat lying head to wind when moored or anchored. Finally, the mizzen-mast provides support for two valuable objects: a radar device and an awning for the helmsman.

The traditional cat rig, with only a big mainsail on a sturdy mast, was improved in the 1970s and 1980s in a way that makes it attractive for many daysailors. Modern cat ketches and cat boats, many with wishbone rigs that make sail-handling easier and the sails more efficient, are extremely simple. Yet, while this makes a daysailing sailor's life more easy, it is not an advantage for offshore sailing, where you need to be able to set several different combinations of sails in order to make the boat balance properly under storm conditions.

The schooner rig is an anachronism, but it makes pretty pictures. If you love a schooner, you will not care what opinions other people express about it.

Masthead and Fractional Rigs

Except, of course, for the cat rig (which does not carry a jib), all the rigs that we have discussed offer a choice between fractional and masthead arrangements for the headstay and jib halyard. In the masthead rig, the headstay runs from the stem all the way to the top of the mast. In the fractional rig, the headstay runs partway up—about 84 percent of the mast height is a good compromise. Until recently, the masthead rig was by far the most popular. This has been because, of the two, it is the least complicated, not requiring running backstays (since the permanent backstay counters the headstay). A more significant reason for its popularity has been that rating rules for racing have tended to encourage large jibs and small mainsails, and, as we know, trends in the design of racing boats all too often influence cruising boat design (Figure 11-1).

Yet the fractional rig is making a comeback, which we welcome because there are several good reasons for carrying it:

■ *Ease of rigging*. The largest and most powerful sail is the mainsail, not the jib. Therefore, the sails that must be put on and taken off—the jibs—are much smaller and easier to handle and stow on the fractional-rigged yacht. This means that you can bend on the largest sail at the beginning of the season and keep it permanently rigged on the boom until decommissioning.

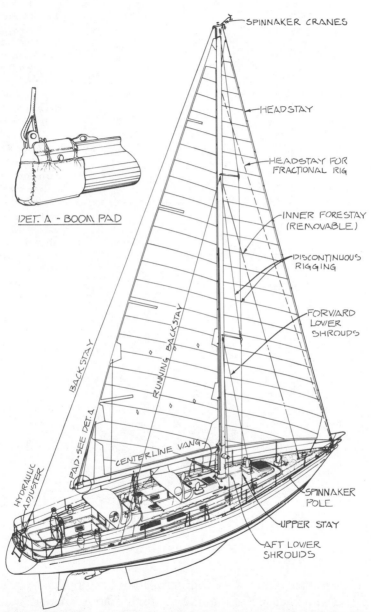

DET. A - BOOM PAD

SPINNAKER CRANES

HEADSTAY

HEADSTAY FOR FRACTIONAL RIG

INNER FORESTAY (REMOVABLE)

DISCONTINUOUS RIGGING

FORWARD LOWER SHROUDS

BACKSTAY

RUNNING BACKSTAY

PAD - SEE DET. A

CENTERLINE VANG

HYDRAULIC ADJUSTER

SPINNAKER POLE

UPPER STAY

AFT LOWER SHROUDS

Figure 11-1. This setup for an offshore boat shows both masthead and fractional rigs, each of which has its advantages. Note the padded boom end (Detail A), the removable inner forestay (countered by a running backstay), and the crane for the spinnaker halyard. Unlike today's racing boats, this boat has both forward and aft lower shrouds to keep the lower part of the mast from bending. Discontinuous shrouds fatigue less than full-length stays. A backstay hydraulic adjuster is useful if the boat will do some racing; it must be installed and handled with care.

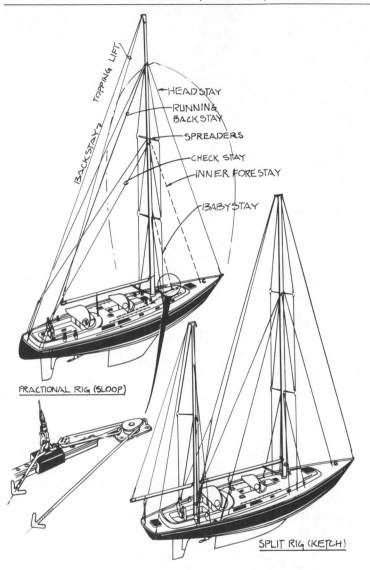

Figure 11-2. (Top) While it requires plenty of fore-and-aft support from running backstays (and, in smaller boats, swept-back spreaders), the modern fractional rig can be excellent for cruising. The detail drawing shows a way to rig a babystay on deck so it can be adjusted and pulled out of the way. **(Bottom)** The split rig (either yawl or ketch) used to be the standard cruising rig. Two of its advantages are that the mizzen aids steering and the boat may be sailed under two small sails (mizzen and jib) in rough weather.

TOPPING LIFT

BACKSTAY

HEADSTAY

RUNNING BACKSTAY

SPREADERS

CHECK STAY

INNER FORESTAY

BABYSTAY

FRACTIONAL RIG (SLOOP)

SPLIT RIG (KETCH)

- *Ease of handling.* When shortening sail, you usually depower the largest sail first, and it is easier to reef the mainsail than to change headsails.
- *Smaller spinnakers.* Besides smaller jibs, the fractional rig also carries smaller spinnakers than the masthead rig because the hoist is lower. Spinnakers that are set relatively low on the mast are easier to control in fresh winds than larger spinnakers set from the masthead.
- *Lower cost.* Since fewer headsail changes are required, the boat can have a smaller inventory of jibs.

Of course, like everything else, the fractional rig has some disadvantages to go with its advantages. The primary disadvantage is that, except on very small boats with swept-back spreaders, running backstays must be rigged to keep the headstay relatively straight and the mast in column (not bending in its middle section, which can lead to a dismasting). The running backstays must be of adequate strength, with a good purchase, leading to the after deck from the hounds. Unless the mast is properly sized and supported, you may damage or lose it if the running backstays are not properly handled during tacks and jibes and in rough seas, when the mast may pump back and forth violently. A word of caution: if the crew is not well trained, a runner may be allowed to drape behind a spreader, which it may pull out when a strain is taken on the whip as the boat tacks or jibes.

Forestays and Babystays

Regardless of her rig, any boat heading offshore should carry a forestay (inner forestay) for setting a small storm forestaysail in storm conditions. This stay runs from partway down the mast to the foredeck, where the stay fitting must be strongly backed up (usually with a support in the forward cabin). There should be a strong halyard to hoist the sails using this stay.

This rig is important because, in very rough weather, you want to carry storm sails as close to the mast as possible in order to facilitate their handling and to keep the boat well balanced. Carrying a storm jib out on the bow can cause lee helm. This inner forestay should be opposed by special running backstays, often called "checkstays," to keep the mast straight and in column when the storm forestaysail is set in very rough conditions.

Other than the inner forestay, there is another kind of stay running forward of the mast inside the headstay. This is the so-called "babystay," which provides fore-and-aft support for the lower mast when there are no forward lower shrouds, as is often the case in modern boats (Figure 11-2). Both it and the forestay should be adjustable as well as removable, to facilitate tacking and jibing the spinnaker pole. (We prefer forward lowers; a good seaman naturally favors forward lower shrouds because they never have to be disconnected.) Many attachment and adjustment systems have been used on these stays. The simplest is a sturdy turnbuckle attached to the deck with the proper-sized trigger-type snap shackle (Figure 11-3), which does not rely on a pin for security (Sparcraft makes an excellent shackle of this type). Another good system utilizes a Hyfield lever, which, however, can pinch fingers and catch sheets.

If quick adjustment of the babystay is important, you can rig a hydraulic adjuster, but that is too complicated as well as too slow. An excellent alternative that allows both quick adjustment and fast removal is to secure the bottom of the stay with a Sparcraft-type shackle to a reinforced roller slide on a strong track on the foredeck. The slide is adjusted with a block and tackle led aft to the cockpit: to tighten the babystay, pull the slide forward; to loosen it, pull the slide aft. A great benefit of this system is that to remove the babystay before tacking, so the jib sheets don't hang up, you needn't go out on a wet, pitching foredeck in the middle of the night. However, this system also has its disadvantages. First, the

Figure 11-3. The trigger-type snap shackle (left) is the best one to use when the load is great, for example, on the bottom of the babystay. A fid may be needed to open it. On many boats, the trigger-type shackle is rigged on spinnaker sheets, halyards, and the jib tack. The old-fashioned pin-type shackle is more subject to failure under extreme loads.

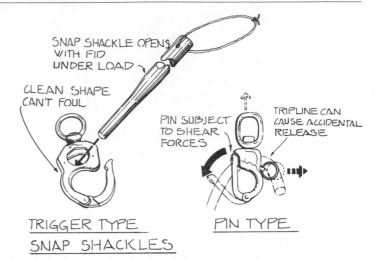

SNAP SHACKLE OPENS WITH FID UNDER LOAD

CLEAN SHAPE CAN'T FOUL

PIN SUBJECT TO SHEAR FORCES

TRIPLINE CAN CAUSE ACCIDENTAL RELEASE

TRIGGER TYPE

PIN TYPE

SNAP SHACKLES

track may take up valuable foredeck area where you might want to install a hatch or an anchor windlass. Second, since stay tension is adjusted without the crew member sighting up the mast or even feeling the stay itself, it may lead to maladjustment. When pulling the track forward, instead of simply providing safe fore-and-aft support for the mast, you may be bending it excessively.

Spars

With modern materials and engineering, great advances have been made in the strength, efficiency, dependability, and ease of maintenance of spars. Yet a responsible skipper must not simply put faith in the work and judgment of the boat-yard rigger. If the mast comes down or the boom snaps in the middle of the night, it's the skipper and crew whose lives are in jeopardy, not the rigger asleep in bed ashore.

Spar design and construction are now less complicated than before. The general acceptance of aluminum alloy for masts, booms, and spinnaker poles has provided a large number of available sections. No longer must an owner and builder undergo the expense and delay of waiting for special extrusion dies or a custom-built wooden spar. When it is available, anodizing is an excellent finish for a spar because it extends the life of the spar and reduces corrosion. Several very durable paint systems—among them Awlgrip and Imron polyurethane paints—work well when anodizing is not available.

Masts

Some recent trends in masts have not been at all worthwhile for cruising or dual-purpose boats. Designers and builders of pure racing boats have produced some masts of extremely small diameter, which make very little windage and can be easily bent to shape the mainsail. Compared with the sturdier masts, not only are these masts smaller in section and bendier fore and aft, but they require elaborate athwartships support systems that include triple and quadruple pairs of spreaders and complicated sets of shrouds. *In no way are these high-perfor-*

mance masts adequate for today's typical offshore cruising or racing boat. They are sensitive, complicated, fine-tuned, and unforgiving structures that require high operator expertise and considerable maintenance. A simple single-spreader rig (for boats smaller than about 30 feet on the waterline) or double-spreader rig (for larger boats) on a sturdy, relatively inflexible aluminum mast will suffice on any offshore boat, regardless of what your racing-oriented sailmaker may say.

Another unhealthy trend, found in many smaller crusing boats, is the mast stepped on deck. This is an attempt by designers and marketers to remove the "unsightly" mast from the interior, and to save some construction costs. With a deck-stepped mast, if a shroud that terminates on deck breaks or is disconnected, the whole mast will topple over. A proper seagoing yacht must have her mast stepped through the deck and onto a well-engineered mast step that is structurally supported by the keel. In the event of a dismasting, there will almost always be a stump of spar left to carry sail. As an additional safety factor, there must be a transverse bolt in the step to restrain the stump from jumping out and holing the hull or damaging the interior and crew.

An old complaint about keel-stepped masts is that there are leaks around the partners. A good neoprene mast boot will solve this problem. One of the best developments in yacht construction, a mast boot is a length of inner tubing that is secured tightly onto the mast and deck with a mechanical device—usually a hose clamp—to seal off the gap between the mast and partners (Figure 11-4). The rubber will deteriorate in the sun unless it is shielded with a canvas or Dacron outer boot.

Booms

The boom's structure is fairly simple. It usually is a stiff aluminum extrusion, as there is no advantage in having the boom bend. The main danger is from a low boom due to a low-clewed mainsail. With the short booms of the modern masthead-rigged boat, the end of a low boom swept across the cockpit at head height with lethal force every time the boat is tacked or jibed. Any sharp corners on the extrusion must be rounded off. A soft pad secured to the end will minimize damage to a human head when the head's owner forgets where the boom end is located (see Figure 11-1).

In Chapter 13, we'll have much to say about booms when we talk about sheet, vang, and reefing systems.

Figure 11-4. A secure mast boot is needed to keep the partners from leaking. The arrangement shown here works well.

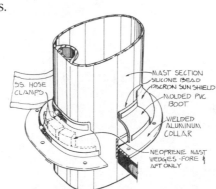

MAST SECTION
SILICONE BEAD
DACRON SUN SHIELD
MOLDED PVC BOOT
WELDED ALUMINUM COLLAR
NEOPRENE MAST WEDGES -FORE & AFT ONLY
SS. HOSE CLAMPS

Spinnaker Poles and Reaching Struts

Typically, a spinnaker pole is an anodized or painted aluminum tube with cast or forged end fittings that are attached with screws (not welds). The end fittings should be the same diameter as the tube; otherwise, the tube may require tapering, which will reduce the pole's strength unless the spar manufacturer strengthens the taper with solid aluminum adapters.

Reaching struts (also called "jockey poles") were developed to reduce the tension on the spinnaker after guy when the boat is close reaching under spinnaker. The inboard end of the strut is attached to a padeye on the side of the mast. The strut stands out athwartships so that its outboard end, which contains a sheave, holds the after guy out so that the angle between the guy and the pole is increased. This decreases the loadings and stretch, and facilitates keeping the pole off the headstay, whose luff-feeding system might otherwise be dented. In addition, the strut prevents the after guy from chafing on lifelines and stanchions.

Provide chafing material (leather works well) on spinnaker poles and reaching struts where they might make contact with standing rigging.

Standing Rigging

In this section, we will look at the stays, terminals, turnbuckles, cotter pins, and other equipment that keeps the rig aloft, paying special attention to maintenance problems.

Stay Materials and Terminals

The choice today for stay material is between 1×19 stainless-steel wire and solid stainless-steel rods. Rod stretches less than wire but is considerably more expensive (partly because it requires special terminal fittings). The low stretchability of rod allows the mast to stand straight under great side loads—say, when carrying a genoa jib in a fresh breeze—with less initial tension taken with turnbuckles or hydraulic backstay rams. The first place where you should consider using rod is in the upper shrouds, where it is especially advantageous if you increase loads by shortening the spreaders in order to allow the jib to be trimmed closer. However, while undeniably valuable for racing, rod rigging is not so important for cruising, where 1×19 wire is the best choice. It stretches less than the 7×19 wire rope used in halyards, but provides just a little elasticity to take the shock out of peak loading—for example, when the boat smashes through a wave.

Both types of standing rigging can be rigged in either continuous or discontinuous sections. In continuous rigging, the stay runs in one length from the mast over the spreader or spreaders to the chain plate on deck. In discontinuous rigging, each partial section between the spreaders, the mast, and/or the deck has one relatively short length of rod or wire that terminates at a tang or turnbuckle. Well-engineered discontinuous rigging reduces fatigue at spreader ends and keeps masts straighter over a wide range of sail loadings.

Obviously, a stay is only as strong as its connection with the mast, spreader, or deck, where terminals in the rod and wire are secured to turnbuckles or tangs. The ends of rod stays usually are threaded so they can fit into turnbuckles on deck and aloft. With wire, several possibilities exist. The best wire terminals are the swaged ones known as "Tru-Lock." The swaging should match the wire exactly. Make sure that both are in *either* metric *or* English dimensions, and not one of each; otherwise there will be a mismatch. Swaging equipment should never be used with too much pressure or too rapidly, and must not be used for terminal and wire diameters greater than what the swaging machine was designed to handle. A good routine is to test sample assemblies of each size of wire and terminal that you are working with. These swaged terminals should be inspected periodically. If there is any sign of a longitudinal crack (a possibility under the great pressure of swaging), or if the swaging is out of alignment with its stay, the swaging should be replaced immediately. Water may seep between the terminal and the wire and cause corrosion. To keep water out, plug the top of the terminal with sealant.

Where a swaging machine is not available—say, on board during a passage—a more expensive but otherwise suitable mechanical device can be used to make a terminal. This device is known as a Norseman or Stalock fitting. Because both work under the "Mexican handcuff" principle (the more tension is applied, the greater is the holding strength), there is less initial pressure than on a Tru-Lock swaging, and therefore these fittings appear to have a longer life. This type of mechanical fitting is also easier to inspect than a Tru-Lock terminal. As with swagings, make sure that the fitting and the wire match exactly.

One popular kind of terminal that does not belong offshore is the so-called "tee" terminal—a T-shaped fitting that is inserted into either the mast or a small fitting on the mast. Originally developed for dinghy spars, the Tee terminal migrated into larger boats. But tests and experience prove that it is unseamanlike because there is excessive friction at the attachment point, and it does not allow adequate toggling action, which means that there is too much flexing in the wire rod. Obviously, flexing will severely weaken any wire. It is best to use a time-tested swage or Norseman-type fitting that is attached by a clevis pin to stainless-steel tangs secured to the mast.

Before heading off on a long trip, swage a terminal on the end of a length of spare wire long enough to replace any piece of standing rigging on the boat. If there is more than one wire size (which is usually the case), make one spare for each size. Take along Norseman-type fittings for the other ends, plus wire cutters and a hacksaw to trim off the excess wire.

Turnbuckles and Toggles

Turnbuckles, which the British call "rigging screws," are the normal gear for tensioning stays, although hydraulic rams may be used on backstays and, on racing boats, on inner forestays and babystays. They are best constructed of forged or machined bronze, which provides a good strong grip between the barrels and threads, as well as a soft surface that serves as a self-lubricant to facilitate adjustment.

This strong recommendation contradicts the new popularity of stainless-steel and chromed bronze turnbuckles. Stainless steel should be avoided because the close tolerance on threads makes the turnbuckles very susceptible to "galling,"

Figure 11-5. The best turnbuckle is the bronze, open-body type. The cotter pins should be the right size and length and installed with care. The best lubricant is anhydrous lanolin. Toggles must always be rigged on stays and should be as short as possible.

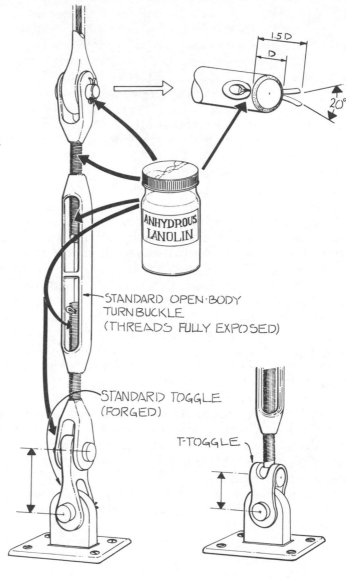

1.5 D

D

20°

ANHYDROUS LANOLIN

STANDARD OPEN·BODY TURNBUCKLE (THREADS FULLY EXPOSED)

STANDARD TOGGLE (FORGED)

T-TOGGLE

or cross-threading, which leads to freeze-ups. Navtec has overcome this problem by using a bronze turnbuckle screw threaded into stainless-steel ends. Chromed bronze turnbuckles may look better, but they cost more than similar-size all-bronze turnbuckles. More important, the chroming weakens the critical threaded area. If you desire chromed turnbuckles, install the next size larger than the recommended bronze fittings (Figure 11-5).

Besides bronze materials, we urge use of the open-barrel design, as furnished for years by Merriman, Lewmar, and other manufacturers, which allows you to see if a sufficient amount of thread has been wound up. Because there is no way to inspect the threads in closed-barrel, or tubular, turnbuckles, they are most inappropriate.

Be quite careful when you assemble turnbuckles and other threaded rigging. It is vital to maintain meticulous cleanliness to keep grit and bits of rag or tape away from the threads, which might become galled or corroded and jam, inviting further damage when you apply excess torque to try to free them. Lubricate turnbuckles with anhydrous lanolin at least annually. By the way, it's a good policy to lubricate all rigging pins with lanolin to facilitate extracting them in case of emergency.

Rigging turnbuckles on rod rigging can be a problem. Earlier rod rigging utilized threaded ends (with right-hand threads at one end and left-hand threads at the other end) that were wound into terminals, which were then attached to chain plates, toggles, spreader ends, or mast tangs. In effect, this entire section of rod and its end fitting worked like a giant turnbuckle. This was a great idea— except that it was discovered that rod rigging likes to unwind itself. Unlike the more stretchy wire, which rebounds when the load comes off and so remains fairly tight when on the leeward side, rod shrouds hang slack when they are unloaded. The motion of a boat pitching into a seaway provides a very strong rotating moment in the stay that can back off a locking nut or even sheer off a cotter pin. This problem has been solved by a system developed by Navtec, which allows the stay to rotate without backing off the threads.

Regardless of which type of standing rigging you use, be sure that each end is drilled out for cotter pins; the hole will also help you determine how much thread has been wound up. It is also *absolutely essential* that all lower ends, on deck, be fitted with toggles, which provide for angular movement to allow the terminals and turnbuckles to swing and stay aligned with the stays. Without toggles, fatigue and eventually fracture in the wire or rod will occur. Aloft, toggles are required only on the headstay and forestay in order to compensate for the side movement of the stay caused by the jib.

Toggles compensate for temporary misalignment, not the permanent misalignment of chain plates and stays (which should be corrected structurally). They should be as short as possible, to minimize eccentric loading and twist, and they should fit snugly on chain plates, with the help of washers or shims if necessary, so that they are centered properly for optimum load distribution. Apply a thin coating of anhydrous lanolin to the pins to keep the toggles from freezing up and becoming misaligned.

Toggles should be either forged, machined, or welded. Cast toggles have been proved unreliable.

Cotter Pins

Cotter pins remain the best all-round fitting for securing all parts of the standing rigging. The only reason many people dislike them is that they don't know how to rig them properly and they fail. There's a right and a wrong way to install a straight cotter pin. Here's the right way:

1. The pin should be big enough for the job. If the only pin that will fit seems flimsy, drill out the hole. This is safe since the hole is at the very end of the fitting. Table 11-1 gives proper sizes. The hole should be just larger than the cotter pin, and slightly countersunk on each side to facilitate the pin's entry. Stainless-steel pins are recommended; they have a higher sheer strength than bronze pins.
2. The pin should be the right length. Excluding its head, it should be 1½ times the diameter of the piece that it is securing. See Table 11-1 for recommended lengths.
3. Round off sharp edges with a file after the pin has been cut to length.
4. Install the pin properly. *Do not* simply stick it in and spread it 180 degrees: that greatly weakens the pin and makes quick removal in an emergency impossible. If you are dismasted, the fastest way to clear away rigging is to pull the turnbuckle cotter pins and drive out the clevis pins; modern stays are too tough to be cut with wire cutters. Instead, spread the pin *no more* than 20 degrees—10 degrees on each side. In a turnbuckle, the pin should be turned so the two legs are one above the other; that way, they will block the turnbuckle barrel at the same time.
5. Pad and protect the pin (and protect objects from it), first, by applying some silicone sealer to it and, second, by applying two or three turns of rigging tape.

Table 11-1
COTTER PIN SIZES

DIAMETER OF FITTING OR THREADED SECTION (INCH)	COTTER PIN DIAMETER (INCH)	COTTER PIN LENGTH (EX-HEAD) (INCH)
¼	3/32	3/8
3/8	1/8	9/16
½	5/32	3/4
3/4	3/16	1⅛
1	7/32	1½

Recently, cotter "rings" have become popular. Our opinion about them is simply stated: if you have a cotter ring, immediately replace it with a cotter pin. Experience has proven, first, that rings will distort easily and fall out when subjected to chafing and, second, that they are impossible to remove or install when the boat is pitching or rolling in a seaway.

On large turnbuckles, in place of cotter pins you can use machine screws threaded into the cotter-pin holes.

Some types of turnbuckles have compression lock nuts above and below the barrel. These nuts are most insecure under the inevitable tension and twisting and should not be used.

Hydraulic Adjusters

Many cruisers may consider a hydraulic adjuster an unnecessary complication, but if you wish to do some racing, and if you use the adjuster carefully, a hydraulic backstay can be a good piece of gear to have on a cruising boat because it will work faster than a turnbuckle. While hydraulic cylinders are used on racing boats on the permanent backstay and babystay (to straighten the headstay and bend the mast), on the boom vang, and (on larger boats) on the outhaul and reefs, if a cruising boat is going to have a hydraulic adjuster it should be limited to the permanent backstay. When the boat is sailing to windward, the cylinder is pumped up to tighten the backstay and straighten the headstay in order to flatten the jib and improve upwind performance. Off the wind, bleed off some pressure to let the stay sag off a bit and put more draft in the jib.

The most important rule is never overtension the adjuster. It should not be pumped up to more than one-third of the rigging's breaking strength (a figure that can be provided by the boat's builder or designer). Competitive racing crews disregard this rule at their own risk, often pumping the adjuster up to one-half or even three-quarters of the rigging strength. If you want to keep the mast in the boat (and the boat in one piece under the mast), don't follow their example. Ask the boat's builder or designer for the rigging's breaking strength, divide it by 3, and mark the result on the adjuster's pressure gauge. Most high-quality adjusters have a relief valve that protects the rig and boat from overzealous crews. Make sure the valve is operable and set to release when the tension has reached one-third of the stay's breaking strength.

Even when you follow this rule, you may be putting too much stress on your rigging when you sail in rough seas, since the moment of the whipping mast will be added to the hydraulic adjuster's load. Therefore, in rough water ease off the adjuster. (This has the added virtue of straightening the mast and minimizing the chances of its coming out of column.)

If for some reason you use more than one hydraulic adjuster, each should be connected to its own independent pump and reservoir. Otherwise, all the adjusters will fail if something goes wrong with the system.

Lubricants and Tapes

We would like to end with a word or two about the best lubricants and tapes to use on board to maintain your rigging properly. There are many marine-oriented lubricants on the market, and all seem to work, although some are lighter and therefore wear off more quickly than others. The important fact to remember is that, if the system has movement, you must *lubricate it often.* However, one piece of gear that must never be lubricated is the set of brake bands used to keep a reel halyard winch from backing off.

The best permanent-type lubricant for turnbuckles, clevis pins, and many other items is anhydrous lanolin, a product like thick grease that is available in small tins from most drugstores. Apply it with your fingers or a tongue depressor. Different types of Teflon also are effective for high-load jobs, where light oil may quickly wash or wear off.

Every well-found yacht should have an adequate supply of rigging tape. While many tapes for the marine market are available, industrial tapes—for example, duct tape and electrician's tape—certainly seem to be adequate for all jobs at a fraction of the expense of special marine products. The best way to pad the points of cotter-pin legs or other small, sharp objects is to apply a gob of silicone sealant.

In the next chapter, we will look at running rigging—the halyards, sheets, and other gear that control the sails hung on the standing rigging—and then in Chapter 13 we'll conclude this section with a discussion of the sails any cruising boat should carry.

CHAPTER 12

Running Rigging

Roderick Stephens, Jr., and Mitchell C. Gibbons-Neff

E normous advances have been made over the years in the area of running rigging. Durable, low-stretch synthetic materials, strong blocks, and powerful winches mean that there is much less elasticity—and therefore much higher efficiency—when carrying sail. However, these improvements do not eliminate seamen's responsibility for knowing their boats' systems of rigging, and for being careful not to push so hard that major damage to the hull and rig is risked. In this chapter we will look at many of those systems and their components, emphasizing some new developments of interest to all cruising sailors.

Rope Materials and Construction

The transition from natural fibers (Manila hemp, cotton, and linen) to synthetics (Dacron, nylon, and Kevlar) has provided a great increase in strength along with control of elasticity and elimination of rot. For the cruising sailor, one important result of the development of high-strength/low-stretch rope is that rope is now a very desirable alternative to wire in halyards, and we strongly recommend using it there in place of flexible 7 × 19 stainless-steel or galvanized wire rope, which is the traditional material for halyards.

The combination of the rope's material and its construction determines its characteristics and use on board a cruising yacht. For minimum elasticity—which is demanded in sheets and halyards—the best combination often is Dacron in a cored, braided arrangement. Here, the main body of the rope is a core made up of low-stretch longitudinal fibers. This core is surrounded by a braided cover that keeps the rope from twisting when under load. However, this type of rope is not the best for docking lines, anchor rodes, or other cables where chafing occurs. Once the braided cover is chafed, the rope quickly loses its integrity. The best rope for these applications is old-fashioned three-stranded nylon, which resists chafing better than braid. And, since it is more elastic than Dacron, nylon suffers minimum damage from shock loading, which is typical when anchoring or docking.

The best type of rope for sheets and most halyards in cruising boats (as well as in many racing boats) is one called Gleistein Cup Sheet, a rope that was developed in Germany and is marketed by Sampson. Its low stretch makes it a desirable substitute for Dacron, and unlike Kevlar (discussed below) it does not demand extra-large sheaves. Compared with wire, Cup Sheet is both more resistant to fatigue and easier to handle. And with it there is no need for the difficult and expensive wire-to-rope splice. The only place where Cup Sheet is not desirable is in the spinnaker halyard, where some stretch is worth having in order to absorb the heavy shocks that are imposed as the spinnaker fills and collapses. The best material for this halyard is braided Dacron, which stretches just enough to be a good shock absorber.

The diameter of any rope is primarily dictated by the expected maximum loading that the line will face, and rope manufacturers specify safe loads for the various diameters in which their products are made and sold. Another consideration affecting diameter is handling characteristics; you may wish to rig a large-diameter mainsheet not because of its strength but because it allows the crew to trim sails without suffering cut hands.

Kevlar

A further development in rope materials is now under way. This is an extremely low-stretch material called Kevlar, which can be formulated to stretch even less than 7×19 wire rope. At the same time, it is lighter than wire rope. The main problem with Kevlar is that it is severely weakened when it takes a sharp turn or rubs against another surface. Since even a knot or a normal-size sheave can cause failure, it must have special terminals and must lead over extra-large sheaves (Table 12-1). It is also extremely expensive. Lines made of this material are currently found almost exclusively on Grand Prix racing yachts, but once Kevlar's vulnerability to chafing and fatigue is solved, it may well find its way aboard many cruising boats for use in sheets and halyards.

The Buntline Hitch

Halyards and sheets should be tied, not spliced, into shackles and other fittings. With a knot, the line can be easily turned end for end to avoid loading on a worn or damaged area (and to avoid having to purchase another expensive sheet or halyard). And, unlike a splice, a knot will not jamb in sheaves and spinnaker pole end fittings.

The buntline hitch is the best knot to use on halyards, guys, and other lines that do not have to be tied and untied frequently (Figure 12-1). As strong as a splice, this knot has one advantage over the more commonly used bowline in that, by slipping along the standing part, it is reduced in size when under load— a valuable feature when you require maximum hoist in a halyard. Because it also tightens under load, the buntline hitch often must be undone using a spike.

The bowline, which is more easily untied, remains the best knot for tying sheets into jib clews and for other applications that require relatively quick release.

Halyards

Halyards can be, and have been, arranged in many different ways, some better than others. One trend in deck layout has been toward leading all halyards aft from the mast to winches near the cockpit. For racing, this keeps the weight aft and low, and for shorthanded cruising it allows a single crew member in the cockpit to handle the halyards and sheets in one place.

However, there are disadvantages to this arrangement. First, it clutters up the deck with halyards and winches. Second, it fills the cockpit with line. Third, the

Table 12-1
MINIMUM SHEAVE DIAMETERS

Dacron braid and Cup Sheet: 6 times the rope's diameter
Kevlar rope: 16 times the rope's diameter
7 × 19 stainless-steel wire rope: 20 times the rope's diameter
7 × 19 galvanized wire rope: 16 times the rope's diameter

turning blocks at the base of the mast increase friction on the halyards; if the halyard leads straight down to a winch on the mast, one person can usually haul it up hand over hand part or most of the way before grinding up the remainder with a winch. And fourth (a major problem for shorthanded crews), it moves the crew member far from the foredeck and the problems that often occur there when sails are hoisted or doused.

Another modern trend—one that is probably more constructive—is that of rigging internal halyards. From the sheave down almost to the winch, the halyard is led inside the mast. This arrangement has the major advantages of cutting

Figure 12-1. The buntline hitch is an excellent knot for tying guys, halyards, and reefing lines (as shown here), although it can be hard to undo.

INCORRECT
UNLESS MAIN FOOT IS IN A GROOVE

CORRECT
BUNTLINE HITCH ILLUSTRATED
BOWLINE ON A BIGHT IS ALSO OK.

windage, nighttime slatting, and the chances of an external wrap by one-half, but unless the halyards are led properly inside the spar there may be a foul-up. It's a good idea to have the sparmaker make up a clear sketch showing how internal lines should be led to clear each other and fittings, such as spreaders, tangs, and fastenings.

The exit for an internal halyard should provide a fair lead to the winch or turning block. When internal halyards first became popular, it was believed that they should exit the mast above the winch through special sheaves. Today, we know that it's sufficient to lead them out through a simple oval slot. To keep wire halyards from digging into the mast, place a small stainless-steel strip under the slot, and replace it when worn. In order to strengthen the mast, all exits should be kept well clear both of the partners and of each other (Figure 12-2).

Multiple Halyards

The simplicity of the internal halyard system, coupled with a concern for backups and the vogue of double-grooved headstays for changing jibs, has led to provisions for multiple jib and spinnaker halyards so that a new sail may be hoisted without dousing the old one. As we will mention in more detail in Chapter 13, this system has both advantages and disadvantages. In one extremely popular arrangement that was originally developed for racing boats, there are three wire halyards forward of the mast: a center halyard for the jib and two 'wing" halyards that can be used either for jibs or for spinnakers, since there are fairing strips on either side of the sheaves.

While probably efficient over the short run (assuming that the fairing strips are rounded to a sufficiently large radius), this system is not a good one for cruisers. This is partially due to the ease of wrapping halyards around themselves and the headstay. But the main objection to this system is that, with it, there usually is too much chafing on the wing halyards; a windward halyard carrying the spinnaker inevitably rubs over the headstay.

Since this can happen with other halyard systems as well, spinnakers are best set on braided Dacron rope halyards led through large blocks hung on struts on the forward side of the mast that are called "cranes." The rope offers some give under the enormous shock load of a collapsing spinnaker, and the cranes keep the halyards well clear of the headstay (Figure 12-3).

Halyard Length

A major concern with wire halyards is that, when the sails are raised, there must be enough wire available to take at least three turns on the winch; otherwise the wire-to-rope splice (which is relatively weak) will be forced to take much of the load. This means that main halyards must have plenty of extra wire so that turns can be taken when the mainsail is at full hoist, you'll have a problem finding a place for the awkward coils of that extra wire.

Because the luffs of the jibs in the average inventory are usually of different lengths, getting a minimum of three turns of wire jib halyard on the winch can be a problem as you run through the headsail inventory. The best solution is to secure wire pendants (lengths of 7×19 wire, often called "pennants") into the

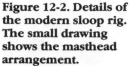

Figure 12-2. Details of the modern sloop rig. The small drawing shows the masthead arrangement.

(1) Tang for removable inner forestay, with staysail halyard sheave.

(2) Shock cord to prevent chafing between main boom topping lift and mainsail.

(3) Spinnaker pole topping lift sheave.

(4) Removable inner forestay.

(5) Spinnaker halyard.

(6) Reefing lines (may be led with messengers).

(7) Winch and cleats for reefing lines.

(8) Topping lift tail leading to cleat.

(9) Main halyard winch.

(10) Jib halyard winch.

(11) Staysail halyard winch.

(12) Centerline boom vang with 4:1 purchase, leading to cockpit winch.

(13) Jib sheet.

(14) Main sheet and winch.

(15) Outboard track for jib sheet.

(16) Foot block to lead jib sheet to winch.

(17) Inboard track for jib sheet (used mainly when racing).

(18) "Lazy" (not in use) jib sheet.

(19) Wire tack pendant to raise the jib foot above waves.

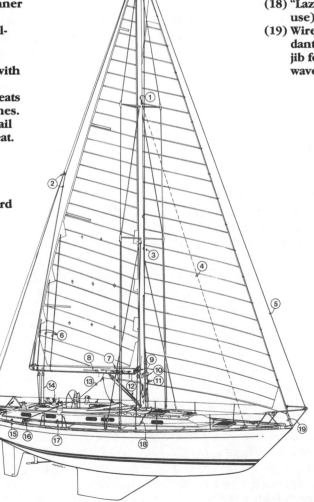

heads of the jibs so that the halyard shackle will always be at approximately the same height (usually the height of the head of the largest jib) no matter which headsail is set. This head pendant should be short enough so the sail can be pulled up on a tack pendant at least 5 percent the length of the headstay in order to lift the foot of a low-cut sail out of the water when reaching. Alternatively, if you shackle (not splice) the pendant to the sail, it can be shifted to the tack in order to raise the foot of the sail.

This complication is an excellent reason for rope halyards. If you do use rope, cut the halyards several feet too long when they are originally rigged and, each year, either trim the worn parts at the ends or turn them end for end to put the load in a new place. (Another good reason for rope that must be mentioned is that, when the boat is moored, rope—unlike wire—does not clatter against the mast and chip away at the paint.)

Halyard Maintenance

All lines used in running rigging should receive frequent inspection on deck. This is easy with sheets, but not so simple with halyards and lines led inside the boom, such as a reefing line, which must be removed using a messenger line. Messengers should be ⅛-inch or 3⁄16-inch braided nylon lines at least twice the length of the mast. A Flemish eye—a small loop of light line seized to the rope's bitter end—should be put in the end of every halyard and internally led line to allow attachment of a messenger so you can pull and inspect the entire line from time to time (Figure 12-4). (Some skippers are so concerned about chafing and clatter aloft that they rig messengers and remove all halyards not currently in use.) Carry at least three good messengers, but keep them out of the ditty bag, where they're sure to be found and cut up by crew members looking for a lanyard for their knife or eyeglasses.

While the messenger is pulled into the sheave, the halyard is pulled out. Do this slowly so you have time to examine the halyard for wear, and determine the source of any chafing on the mast, boom, or any fittings so you can make changes in the rigging.

With internally led halyards has come abrasion from sharp edges on built-in sheaves and from line-against-line friction inside the mast. If there is chafing on a spinnaker halyard, it often occurs where the halyard crosses the headstay if a crane has not been rigged to hold the block above the stay. Any sign of deterioration in halyards or reefing lines should lead, first, to replacement of the line (although rope can be end-for-ended to remove the bad section from a loaded to an unloaded location), and second, to a careful inspection of the sheaves and the routing inside and outside the spar.

If inspection shows that a wire halyard has "meat hooks" (broken wires), trim them with wire cutters or rub them off with the back of your knife, but replace the halyard quickly. Any wire halyard should be replaced as soon as possible if it has developed meat hooks, opened up, or become brittle with corrosion. If a halyard is kinked or worn at turning points, you may trim off a few inches of wire or rope and then resecure the shackle with a splice, knot, or Nico-Press. Another problem with wire halyards is that they gradually pick up oil and dirt,

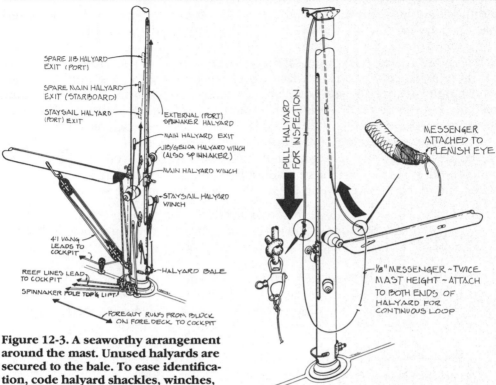

SPARE JIB HALYARD
EXIT (PORT)

SPARE MAIN HALYARD
EXIT (STARBOARD)

STAYSAIL HALYARD
(PORT) EXIT

EXTERNAL (PORT)
SPINNAKER HALYARD

MAIN HALYARD EXIT

JIB/GENOA HALYARD WINCH
(ALSO SPINNAKER)

MAIN HALYARD WINCH

STAYSAIL HALYARD
WINCH

4:1 VANG
LEADS TO
COCKPIT

REEF LINES LEAD
TO COCKPIT

SPINNAKER POLE TOPG LIFT

HALYARD BALE

FOREGUY RUNS FROM BLOCK
ON FORE DECK TO COCKPIT

PULL HALYARD
FOR INSPECTION

MESSENGER
ATTACHED TO
FLEMISH EYE

⅛" MESSENGER ~TWICE
MAST HEIGHT ~ATTACH
TO BOTH ENDS OF
HALYARD FOR
CONTINUOUS LOOP

Figure 12-3. A seaworthy arrangement around the mast. Unused halyards are secured to the bale. To ease identification, code halyard shackles, winches, and mast exit holes with tape of various colors. A small tackle is rigged to raise and lower the slide for the spinnaker pole's inboard end.

Figure 12-4. Use a light messenger line, secured to a Flemish eye, to pull and replace halyards and reefing lines.

which quickly spread to the sails. Wipe them down periodically with clean rags (and wipe off the shrouds and mast, too).

A common problem with rope halyards and sheets (especially braided ones) is that they kink badly during frequent coiling. To get kinks out, drag the halyard or the rope tail overboard behind the boat when you're sailing fast. For obvious reasons, this is not good practice when you're under power.

Halyard Replacement

There are many ways to lose a halyard; often, somebody with cold hands simply drops the shackle while hooking it to the jib, and a shipmate, who thinks that all is well, pulls it up the mast. There should be a backup halyard ready for use. It's a good idea to have at least a spare main halyard sheave and a block for an external-jib / spinnaker halyard. You needn't rig permanent backup halyards: simply run messengers and be sure to carry a spare halyard for each sheave in your sail locker. That way, the backup can be rigged without having to go aloft—

a difficult and possibly dangerous job except when done in a small, landlocked harbor. Later on you can retrieve the lost halyard or replace a broken one.

A halyard may break because it is too weak for the job, because it chafes through, or because somebody carelessly overtensions it. Therefore, plan ahead for the time when you must replace a broken halyard. It is most important that mast fittings—especially spreaders and shroud tangs—be arranged so that internal halyards can be easily replaced. On larger masts with several sets of spreaders and tangs, a removable plate should be installed close to each main obstruction so that the proper routing of halyards can be checked visually.

To replace a broken halyard, you'll need a very light messenger line attached at one end to a lead weight small enough to pass over the sheave and at the other end to the Flemish eye in the new halyard. Here are the steps:

1. Heel the boat to the side that the halyard will be coming down. For example, if the mastbuilder's drawing showing halyard routing indicates that the halyard you are replacing runs down the port side of the mast, heel the boat to port.
2. Pull the other halyards tight and secure them to the other side (starboard in this case).
3. Send a crew member aloft in a bosun's chair. This person feeds the messenger down into the mast, while somebody on deck holds a loop of stiff wire—a coathanger will do—through the exit slot to snag the messenger.
4. Once the messenger is retrieved, extract it from the slot and pull the halyard down as the person aloft feeds it into the sheave.

The Luff Gauge

For best performance, one halyard that must be hoisted to a point and stay there is the main halyard, whose shackle should not be allowed to slip below the black band (except, of course, in light air and when reefed). An excellent way to make sure that the mainsail is always at full hoist is to rig a gauge wire, described in Chapter 13.

Sheets

Frequent inspection is simpler with sheets than with halyards because sheets are on deck. On the other hand, since sheets are always visible, many crews tend to take them for granted. To guarantee that they are examined, it's a good practice to remove all but the sheets led to boomed sails (such as the mainsail and mizzen) after use. Any chafe is bound to be noticed during coiling. If you're lucky, it will be near the ends and you can either turn the sheet end for end or cut the chafed spot off—a good reason for being generous with the length of sheets. But if you have committed the two mistakes of not leading the sheet properly and not inspecting it while it's under load, you may be stuck with a bad spot in the middle. If so, instead of one long sheet you now have two short ones.

So if you want to save the considerable expense of having to replace a long sheet, rig sheets with care. Lead them around stanchions, the boom, and other chafing points with blocks. If rubbing is unavoidable, protect them with some chafe guard—a length of leather or split hose or heavy plastic tubing. Tie the guard to the line itself, not to the stanchion or other abraider.

Sheet Systems

On a boomed sail—a mainsail, a mizzen, or a boomed jib—the number of blocks and the size of the sheet will depend on the availability of winches and the size of the sail. The greater the pull, the more parts may be used. However, virtually irrespective of the size of the boat, jib sheets on nonboomed sails should be of a single part; adding a part by shackling a block or blocks into the clew creates unacceptable danger to the crew during a tack, and the blocks themselves will be quickly demolished as they strike the mast or babystay.

One extremely bad practice is to fit a wire pendant between the main boom and the upper block in the mainsheet purchase. The intention here is to reduce windage and shorten the mainsheet, thereby reducing stretch. However, the effect is to endanger the crew with a wildly flying block at about face height whenever there is any slack in the sheet during a tack or jibe. This is an increasingly high price to pay for a very slight increase in efficiency.

Gear on the Boom

The boom vang and boom topping lift can be rigged in a variety of ways, but since each affects the other, they should be thought of as part of a single system. They both come into play when the reefing gear is used.

One important piece of boom gear is rarely installed: a pad for the boom end, which, in modern-day boats, usually sweeps right across the middle of the cockpit at little more than the height of a tall person.

Boom Vang

There is nothing at all new in using a line to hold the boom out and down when sailing downwind; preventers and vangs (also called "kickers") have been with us for a long time. But recently, bigger boats have picked up something that originated with very small ones: a boom vang led permanently to the aft face of the mast that does not require adjustment when the main sheet is trimmed or eased. Called the "centerline vang" because it is rigged permanently to the boat's centerline, this vang can be a tackle or a rigid rod adjusted by either a tackle or a hydraulic pump. Of the two, the tackle is preferred because it has some built-in elasticity and is less complicated.

The centerline vang has several special features. First, it imposes large bending and compressive loads on the boom, so the gooseneck must be very strong; you should check with the designer or builder before installing this piece of equipment. Second, it does not hold the boom outboard, so a preventer should be rigged when running and reaching. A good preventer is made of relatively light, stretchy nylon line led from the foredeck to the end of the boom so that, if and when the boat rolls the boom heavily into the water, the boom can come inboard; this relieves some of the load on it.

One valuable safety feature is to make sure that the crew can let off the vang and preventer from near the center of the cockpit. Another is to make sure that the vang has some built-in shock absorber to minimize the effects of the load that occurs when the boat is jibed in heavy winds, for if there is no give in the vang, something may break—it could be the vang, the gooseneck, the mainsail's headboard, or even the boom. A block-and-tackle vang has some automatic give because it contains rope; a rigid hydraulic vang should be eased off slightly before a jibe.

A rigid vang should be double-acting, which means that it holds the boom both up and down (Figure 12-5). If the vang is reliable, you may be able to dispense with the topping lift (which we'll discuss in a moment). The very best rigid vangs have compression springs or compressed-air reservoirs that absorb sharp downward forces—for example, when the mainsheet is trimmed hard but the vang is not adjusted, or when the main halyard or headboard fails.

Topping Lift

If you don't have a totally reliable double-acting vang to keep the boom up, you must carry a wire topping lift on the main boom of any boat that isn't so small that you don't really care if its boom falls on your head. Even when the mainsail is set, never disconnect the topping lift unless there is a very strong strut to support the boom in case the main or halyard or headboard fails.

A poor way to rig a topping lift is to run it from the end of the boom to and through a spare halyard sheave or other block aloft and then down the mast. That's bad not only because of the inevitable chafing but also because of the motion in the lift, which is slack and whipping about when the boat is sailing, will quickly fatigue the wire at the masthead block. The only seamanlike arrangement is to secure one end to the masthead (using a toggle or shackle to allow free movement) and attach the other end to the end of the boom with a short tackle. In the main part, use plastic-coated 7×19 wire rope; in the tackle, use nylon line so there is some shock absorber when the sheet is trimmed hard and the tackle is not eased out (and that will occur frequently).

To minimize chafing, it is extremely important to keep the topping lift clear of the mainsail. Here are three ways (of many) to keep the lift off the sail:

- Attach a length of shock cord to the topping lift with a snap hook or shackle (preferably one that will not snag the sail), then lead the shock cord to the windward upper shroud. Tighten the shock cord to pull the lift to windward. Disadvantage: the shock cord must be moved to the other side whenever the boat is tacked or jibed.
- Secure one end of a length of shock cord to the lift, and lead it through a block secured about two-thirds of the way up the permanent backstay and down to the deck or stern pulpit. To adjust the tension on the lift, lengthen or shorten the shock cord. Disadvantage: the shock cord wears rapidly and is difficult to replace when underway.
- Have a pair of sheaves mounted back to back, with one over the permanent backstay and the other over the lift. As the mainsail is eased and trimmed, the sheaves will slide up and down, keeping the lift off the sail.

Figure 12-5. On this double–acting vang, the spring-loaded rod keeps the boom up so that the topping lift can be eliminated, and the tackle pulls the boom down.

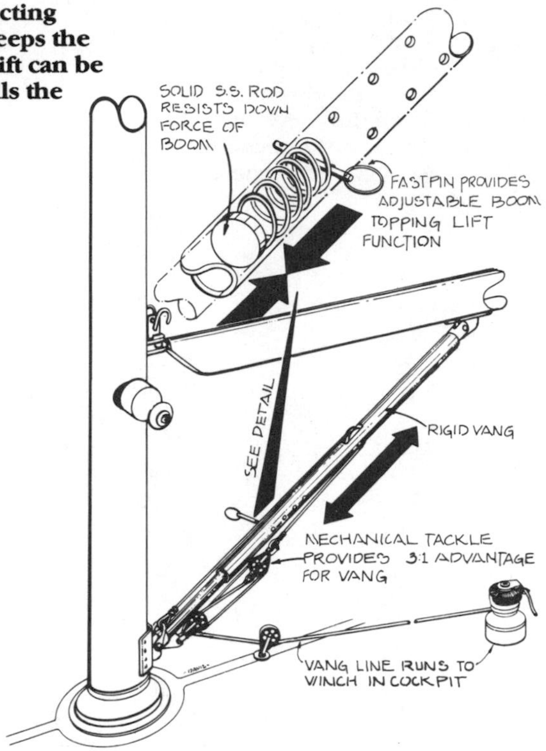

SOLID S.S. ROD RESISTS DOWN FORCE OF BOOM

FAST PIN PROVIDES ADJUSTABLE BOOM TOPPING LIFT FUNCTION

SEE DETAIL

RIGID VANG

MECHANICAL TACKLE PROVIDES 3:1 ADVANTAGE FOR VANG

VANG LINE RUNS TO WINCH IN COCKPIT

Disadvantage: wear and tear, plus noise, as the sheaves ride up and down the backstay.

Of the three, the first is the simplest to rig.

Outhaul

Though it is adjusted infrequently on cruising boats flying modern, low-stretch synthetic sails, the outhaul does deserve attention. It should be strong and its tackle should be both accessible and readily adjustable in moderate to fresh winds, when pulling the clew out can considerably flatten the sail. From time to time, check that the outhaul wire leading from the end of the boom is not fatiguing where it runs over the block.

Reefing Gear

Many boats had roller reefing 20 or 30 years ago, but today almost everybody has shifted over to tied-in "slab" or "jiffy" reefing. When shorter booms and very stable, strong synthetic sailcloth, full pressure can be put on the sail as soon as the leech and luff cringles are secured to the boom, without having to wait to tie up individual reef points.

Light braided nylon messengers should be rigged through the leech cringles so that at least two relatively deep reefs can be tied in without having to lower

Figure 12-6. A good boom-end arrangement, showing the topping lift and messengers for leading reefing lines. Note the small eyes and rotten twine (string) that keep the messenger lines secure to the leech until needed; otherwise, the messengers may tangle in the topping lift.

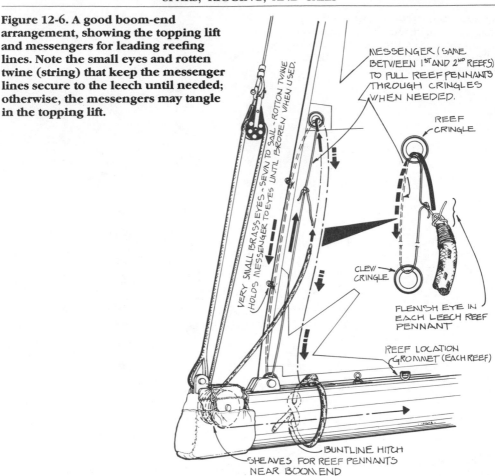

MESSENGER (SAME BETWEEN 1ST AND 2ND REEFS) TO PULL REEF PENNANTS THROUGH CRINGLES WHEN NEEDED.

REEF CRINGLE

VERY SMALL BRASS EYES - SEWN TO SAIL - ROTTEN TWINE (HOLDS MESSENGER TO EYES UNTIL BROKEN WHEN USED.)

CLEW CRINGLE

FLEMISH EYE IN EACH LEECH REEF PENNANT

REEF LOCATION GROMMET (EACH REEF)

BUNTLINE HITCH

SHEAVES FOR REEF PENNANTS NEAR BOOM END

the mainsail to lead the reefing lines. The messengers are often led in continuous loops, one for each reef: the first reefing line between the clew and the first cringle: the second between the first and second cringles; and the third between the second and third cringles. A short length of line is left hanging free from each loop to tie into the Flemish eye in the end of the reefing line, which is then pulled up through the upper cringle and down to the boom to be secured with a buntline hitch or a bowline (Figure 12-6).

The conventional arrangement for the reefing lines used to be to lead them outside the boom through cheek blocks, up and through the leech cringles, and then down to padeyes on the other side of the boom. This system presents problems. First of all, the sail may be hauled into the cheek blocks and torn. And second, the cheek blocks and padeyes may have to be moved when you buy a new mainsail with reefs at a different level. These problems do not appear in the asymmetric arrangement seen on most modern boats, in which the reefing lines are led through the boom, out its end to the leech cringles, and then straight down to the boom, where they are tied around the boom through reef location grommets in the mainsail foot. When tightened, the line should bisect the angle between the foot and leech at the cringle. Always add a backup lashing securing the cringle to the boom.

Reefing lines take a heavy strain in rough weather, and chafing is a constant threat. An important aid in performing preventive maintenance is a large opening at each end of the boom to allow you to see what is going on inside and to facilitate reeving reefing lines using a "snake." This is a length of 1 × 19 stainless-steel wire that is about 1 foot longer than the boom, with a tight serving on each end and a small, neat eye in one end. To lead a new reefing line, first lead the messenger through the boom-end block and secure it to the eye of the snake. Then push the snake through the boom to the gooseneck. Once the messenger is rove, tie it into the Flemish eye on the end of the new reefing line and pull the new line through. (To permit turning the line end for end when it is worn, put an eye in each end of the reefing line.)

At the gooseneck end of the boom, the luff cringles are generally looped over stainless-steel hooks, one on each side. These hooks can be made quite small and light if instead of installing bulky cringles the sailmaker fastens D-rings to the sail to be secured under the hooks.

In the next chapter, we'll look at roller-furling and roller-reefing systems.

Fittings

Now we will look at some recent developments in gear used for sail handling and other important purposes. First, however, let's say a word or two about the size of sheaves.

Sheaves and Foot Blocks

The diameter of the sheave over which hemp or wire rope passes should not be too small, for otherwise the rope will make too sharp a turn and be fatigued. In wire, fatiguing leads quickly to meat hooks—jagged ends of broken wires— which can tear up the hands of even the toughest sailors. In rope, fatiguing leads to fractures. Table 12-1 shows optimum ratios between rope diameter and sheave diameter for different types of ropes.

As to construction, sheaves for hemp rope are not a problem, but sheaves for wire rope running rigging must be given special consideration. The best sheaves for wire are made of bronze or aluminum, with smooth bushings to help them rotate. Tough plastics such as Delron and Celcon will also serve satisfactorily. On the other hand, nylon and Teflon sheaves are too soft for wire and will crack under a heavy load, and Tufnol—made of what appears to be cloth impregnanted with plastic under high pressure—will delaminate under loading and the abrasion of wire. Sheaves for wire rope must be scored with a groove that provides a close fit.

Foot blocks—heavy sheaves that turn the sheet 180 degrees back to the winch— should be used on jib sheets. Not only do they guarantee that the sheet reaches the winch at the right angle, but by being in line with the main force of the sheet they facilitate moving the jib lead forward or aft. Foot blocks also reduce loads on the location pins on the jib-sheet cars on deck tracks.

Lock-offs and Cleats

A jammer called a "lock-off" (or "sheet stopper") is a good device that was first developed for racing and has undergone continued development until its usefulness became obvious to cruisers, too (Figure 12-7). It consists of a fairlead with a slightly rough surface on one side and, on the other side, a cam that the sailor engages with a short lever in order to squeeze the line and hold it; to let the line go, just disengage the lever. Using a lock-off forward of a winch frees the winch that has been holding the line for other uses. This means that one winch can serve several needs. The beneficial side effect is that the boat can carry fewer winches.

Compared with other types of securing devices, the lock-off has several other distinct advantages as well. Unlike the traditional horn cleat, the lock-off allows the line to be secured when under strain; unlike the Clam Cleat (Figure 12-8), it allows the line to be released when under heavy load without having to first trim it an inch or two farther; and unlike the Clam Cleat it works only when you want it to, so it does not accidentally grab the line. On the other hand, a good lock-off usually is more expensive than one of these other cleats, and may take up more room as well.

Perhaps the best use for a lock-off is for securing leech reefing lines. In the past, these might have been led to a small winch on the boom, which was awkward and slow to use. An improvement is to lead the line through a lock-off in the boom just aft of the gooseneck, around a sheave, and down to a powerful halyard or sheet winch on the mast or deck. After the line has been taken down, the lock-off is engaged and the winch is free for other duties. Another good use for a lock-off—one that most people don't think about—is on the spinnaker halyard to keep it from getting away while being hauled up. Once the sail is fully hoisted and secured, the lock-off should be disengaged.

Figure 12-7. A lock-off secures the line when the lever is pulled. It is installed forward of the winch.

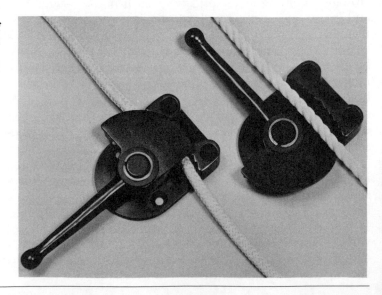

Figure 12-8. Clam Cleats (shown here for the jib sheet and traveler control) are simple to use: simply drop the line into the cleat. But they have been known to accidentally secure lines that should not be cleated—for example, the sheet being eased out during a tack. (John Rousmaniere)

Lock-offs are often used on foot blocks to jam a genoa sheet temporarily while the winch is used to take a strain on another sheet. Unfortunately, this does not work well at high loads, and the sheet often slips because the sheave rotates. For a lock-off to be really effective, it must work against a fixed surface that is specifically shaped to generate friction without damaging the rope.

Winches

Winches have gotten larger, more complex, and more powerful—not to mention more expensive. Today, virtually all sheets and halyards are organized with a view to leading to a winch, sometimes through a lock-off. Due to weight and cost considerations, many yachts are being outfitted with aluminum winches. However, that is not a good idea: the combination of aluminum drums, stainless and bronze internal mechanism, and, for ocean sailors, salt water will create maintenance problems that may shorten the winch's life.

One expensive option with many winches is a self-tailing capability. This can be extremely helpful to the shorthanded cruising boat as well as to the crowded racing boat because it allows a single sailor to crank in a sheet or halyard with both arms, with nobody else needed to take in the slack. The self-tailer acts as a cleat, but since the loaded line can be unwrapped by water running along the deck a regular cleat should be furnished for each self-tailer and always used for security.

An option seen on some large cruising boats is a winch powered by electricity or hydraulics. While they will surely become more efficient and less expensive in the future, these winches should always be installed with an eye to the failure of the power supply, and there should always be a manual backup.

Another type of winch, one that used to be quite popular, is the reel halyard winch. We're glad that fewer boats are carrying them, because they are extremely dangerous. While offering a shortcut of working like a self-tailing winch as they reel up a wire halyard, reel halyard winches come with a considerable price.

Since the drum must turn to let the wire out, many people make the mistake of trying to control the speed of the sail being lowered by inserting and holding the winch handle. All too often, the handle spins wildly and fractures arms, noses, and even skulls.

A sheet, halyard, or other line should approach the winch drum in a plane that is at least 10 degrees below the perpendicular from the bottom of the working part of the drum. This arrangement will help prevent overrides and bad turns.

Steering and Centerboard Gear

While not, strictly speaking, running rigging, the steering and centerboard controls use some of the same kinds of equipment that the sails use, so can be discussed in this section.

Steering Gear

The usual gear for connecting the steering wheel to the rudder is a system combining chain and wire rope (called cable in this context). A backup system should be carried aboard. Make sure the center of the spare chain is marked to match the kingspoke position on the wheel, and that you have the correct tools and that there is sufficient space around the system so you can quickly install the spare assembly in case the first one fails. To make replacement easier, it's a good idea not to use swagings and other preapplied terminals on the wire. Instead, carry wire clamps of the required size; after installing these clamps, carefully tape and tightly serve the terminal to improve the clamp's holding power. Inspect the steering gear at least every 100 hours of sailing, checking for slackness, misalignment, and chafing. A squirt of a light machine oil or Teflon spray should prevent any squeaks in the sheaves and bearings.

As with halyard sheaves, the sheaves for the cable should be oversize—at least 16 times the wire's diameter—and scored for precise alignment. Guards must be closely fitted on the sheaves to prevent the cable from dropping off when the system is slack.

Centerboard Gear

Unballasted centerboards with negative buoyancy are raised and lowered with centerboard pendants, which should be made of sturdy nylon or Dacron rope, since wire can corrode. The best arrangement for the pendant is a two-part tackle with the standing end dead-ended under a waterproof cap and gasket above the boat's loaded waterline, where it is accessible from the cabin. The pendant runs from there, through a single sheave with guards on the side of the centerboard, and then to a winch on deck. A reel-type winch can be used to spool up the excess line. The line should be long enough so there are at least two turns on the winch when the board is fully lowered.

It should not be hard to inspect and replace the pendant while the boat is in the water. The end of the pendant should have a Flemish eye to take a messenger. When the board is fully lowered, attach a messenger to the end at the waterproof cap and pull the pendant from above until it is entirely removed from the system. If it is worn, make another one (remembering to make a Flemish eye), disconnect the bitter end of the old one, and make the switch.

Now that we've looked carefully at the boat's rigging—both standing and running—in Chapter 13 we'll survey the requirements for sails.

Sails for Cruising

Roderick Stephens, Jr., and Mitchell C. Gibbons-Neff

Having discussed some recent developments and improvements in running rigging, let's now turn to the sails themselves. In this chapter, we'll look at the many considerations that go into the selection of a cruising boat's sail inventory.

We'd like to begin with some advice about choosing a sailmaker. That choice may not be easy in this day of dozens, if not hundreds, of sailmaking firms. Unless you place a large order for a well-known racing boat, you may not get the service from some sailmakers that you would like. If you consider yourself an average customer, go with the sailmaker who has the most experience in building sails for boats that are like your boat and who you think will best serve your special needs. In many cases, that means someone who is located near your home port who knows your local conditions and can provide prompt personal service.

Sail Fabrics

The area of greatest recent development in sailing gear is that of sails, where Mylar and Kevlar have revolutionized the design and construction of mainsails and jibs for racing boats. Sails constructed of these two fabrics stretch much less than Dacron sails and are much lighter as well.

Unfortunately, Mylar and Kevlar have other, less attractive characteristics that make them a bad choice for the inventory of any offshore yacht. First, sails constructed of these new fabrics cost very much more than Dacron sails. Second, because they are quite stiff and slippery, sails constructed of them are difficult to stow and furl; mainsails must be carefully flaked on the boom, and jibs must be flaked in long, somewhat unmanageable folds. Third, these fabrics chafe easily, which means that they have a short life even in moderate conditions. The crew must be extremely careful to keep the topping lift, reefing lines, stays, lifelines, and loose halyards well clear of a Kevlar or Mylar mainsail or jib.

For all these reasons, we cannot recommend Kevlar and Mylar for cruising or offshore use. Dacron is much to be preferred for the mainsail and all jibs. However, in the not-too-distant future sailcloth manufacturers and sailmakers may be able to overcome these problems, and cruising sailors may well be able to enjoy the advantages of the two fabrics without having to contend with the disadvantages. Therefore, we will be talking here only about Dacron and nylon sails, which created a revolution of their own when they were introduced back in the 1950s.

Handling and Stowage

Before looking at specific applications, we should stress the importance of protecting sails from the sun and dirt when they're not being used. The greatest threat to a sail's longevity is the sun's ultraviolet rays, which break down the synthetic fibers. Therefore, whenever a sail is not being used, cover or bag it.

Sails that are easy to handle generally will be stowed more frequently than ones that are difficult to handle, and ease of handling is related to the characteristics of the cloth used in the sail. Dacron sailcloth is now available in a wide variety of weights, textures, and cuts. The first two options have the greatest effect on sailhandling. Generally speaking, heavy, stiff fabrics stretch less than light, soft ones and are preferred for good performance; any sails constructed of them hold their shape in a variety of conditions. On the other hand, a cruising sailor wants sails that are easy to furl and fold, even if this means a sacrifice of speed. Most sailmakers are naturally concerned about optimum performance for racing, and, unless you keep your needs and goals firmly in mind when ordering sails, you may find that you have less ease of handling than you want and more performance than you need.

Furled mainsails and other boomed sails must be religiously protected with sail covers of the right size. Covers keep sails clean in harbor, but more important they keep the sun off them. The easiest and neatest covers do not wrap around the forward side of the mast but, rather, end at the sail's headboard and gooseneck with a couple of restraining ties. After being secured at the boom end, the cover is draped over the sail and tied down and adjusted with shock cord leading through a series of hooks.

Jibs should be flaked, folded, and put away in sailbags. If necessary, they may be stowed when wet and then dried later. Don't simply stuff them in: the package will be so bulky that you won't be able to get it below through the hatch. If the bag is too small or does not function properly, it won't be used, and before long your jib will fall apart because it's seen too much sun. We recommend using the long sausage-shaped "turtle" bag, which allows two people to bag and stow a jib relatively quickly and with little bulk. The weak point on this type of bag is the zipper used to close it up; have your sailmaker inspect turtles annually and, if necessary, replace damaged zippers.

Besides having to fight stiff sailcloth and inadequate bags, another reason why people often do not stow jibs below is that there's no decent stowage out of the way of the living area. It's no fun trying to live with sailbags, dry or wet. Allow for plenty of stowage space in cockpit lockers or sail bins forward.

Halyard Marks

Almost all sails are made with stretchy rope luffs, which encourage accurate, easy sail shaping. As the wind freshens and the cloth stretches, tighten the halyard to stretch the luff and pull the draft forward so it is about halfway back from the luff; as the wind lightens, ease it to let the draft back aft. However, the combination of stretchy luff and masthead foretriangle can lead to pulling the jib and main halyard shackles into the sheaves, which damages both the sheave and the halyard. So that you'll know when the maximum hoist has been reached, it's good practice to put marks on the halyards to compare against a gauge on the mast. The arrangement may also be used to indicate optimum halyard tension for different sails and conditions.

Don't use tape to make marks; it will slip. Rope can be marked with an indelible pen. A wire rope halyard is best marked with a length of single-strand copper bell wire tucked through alternate strands in the wire halyard. An excellent way to prevent overhoisting the mainsail or mizzen is to rig and use a luff gauge wire. This is a light stainless-steel wire running from the forward corner of the headboard down through the luff seam, exiting the sail about 2 feet above the tack to terminate in an eye, which is attached to the tack with some shock cord. When the sail is hoisted to the black band, about 1 foot of this wire should be exposed, with its end next to a preestablished reference mark on the mast. If the sail is overhoisted, the wire end will be above the mark; if underhoisted, it will be below the mark (Figure 13-1).

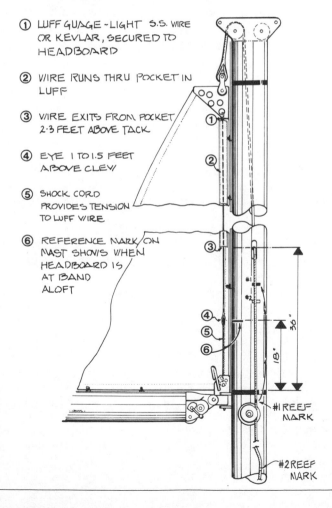

① LUFF GUAGE - LIGHT S.S. WIRE OR KEVLAR, SECURED TO HEADBOARD

② WIRE RUNS THRU POCKET IN LUFF

③ WIRE EXITS FROM POCKET 2·3 FEET ABOVE TACK

④ EYE 1 TO 1.5 FEET ABOVE CLEW

⑤ SHOCK CORD PROVIDES TENSION TO LUFF WIRE

⑥ REFERENCE MARK ON MAST SHOWS WHEN HEADBOARD IS AT BAND ALOFT

#1 REEF MARK

#2 REEF MARK

Figure 13-1. The best way to determine whether the mainsail is fully hoisted is to rig a wire gauge in the luff. Halyards should be marked at full-hoist and reefed positions.

Make these marks carefully; one that is located inaccurately or that slides up and down the halyard is worse than no mark at all. You might be able to site the marks on the halyards and mast by looking aloft through binoculars, but it's usually safer to haul somebody up the mast on a spare halyard when the sails are raised and have him or her call down when the mainsail headboard is right at the black band or the jib halyard shackle is just short of the sheave. While you're at it, tie in the reefs and mark the main halyard for each reef.

The Danger of Luff-fed Sails

Many developments in sails have been directed primarily at the racing sailor. Unfortunately, some of them do not benefit cruising sailors. One of these is the way that jibs are attached to the headstay.

In the early 1970s, hardware manufacturers came up with a system that, by dispensing with sail hanks, improved aerodynamic flow around the jib. With this system, instead of hanking the jib onto the wire or rod headstay and then hoisting it, the crew feeds the top of the sail's rope luff into a groove (either integral with a rod stay or installed over it), and the remainder of the luff is automatically pulled into the groove as the sail is hoisted. After a while, this system was altered to allow the installation of two luff grooves on the stay so that the crew could change jibs without having to sail bald-headed for a while: while the sail to be replaced still flies off one groove and one halyard, the new jib is hoisted in the second groove on another halyard and trimmed to a sheet of its own. Once the new sail is hoisted and trimmed properly, the old sail is doused on deck, either to leeward or to windward of the newly hoisted jib.

Obviously, this double-grooved headstay system is a major advantage in races, where the minutes that are lost during a "bald-headed" sail change (when the old sail is doused before the new one is hoisted) might never be made up. Yet, while good for short races with a large, well-trained crew, this is a bad rig for shorthanded cruising and for sailing offshore. There are several major problems with this system:

1. Somebody must always go forward to the bow to pull the sail down (and, sometimes, when the jib is being hoisted, to feed the luff into the groove). That is bad seamanship in rough weather.
2. Even in smooth water, a second crew member must handle the halyard, thereby making what could be a singlehanded job with a hank system into a multihanded one.
3. More serious, because it is unsecured everywhere but at the tack, clew, and head, the sail may easily be washed overboard when it is on deck, either before or after lowering. Often, somebody must go forward to sit on the doused sail, which at best is a waste of manpower and time that nobody should have to put up with in a sudden squall. At worst it is a risk to life.

Therefore, the most seamanlike jib system for cruising is the traditional bronze sailhank hooked over a rod or 1 × 19 wire headstay (Figure 13-2). Bronze is the best material for a hank because, being relatively soft, it will not damage the stay on which it is used.

Figure 13-2. For cruising, a hanked-on sail is much safer than one fed into a grooved stay since the hanks keep the sail on deck when it is doused. To prevent outer jibs from ripping on the staysail's hanks during tacks, have the sailmaker sew protective patches over the hanks.

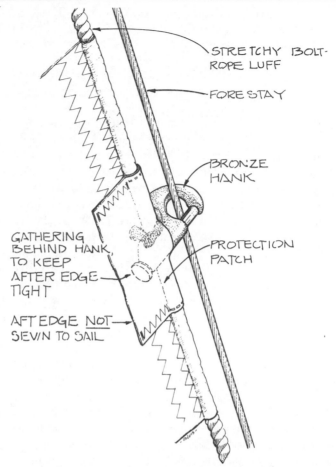

STRETCHY BOLT-ROPE LUFF

FORE STAY

BRONZE HANK

PROTECTION PATCH

GATHERING BEHIND HANK, TO KEEP AFTER EDGE TIGHT

AFT EDGE NOT SEWN TO SAIL

When dousing the sail with this system, just let go the halyard and sheet. The sail should drop at least halfway on its own. The clew may drag in the water, but because the sail is attached all up and down the luff, as long as the sheets are well eased it will not catch water like a sea anchor (or, more to the point, like a loose luff-fed jib). In order to get the sail all the way down without having to crawl forward on a pitching foredeck, some shorthanded crews rig rope downhauls from the jib's head down to a block at the tack and then aft to the mast or cockpit.

Mainsail Systems

A similar luff-feeding system is now used on many racing mainsails—and with much the same risk for cruising sailors. When a luff-fed mainsail is lowered, it tends to fly over all the boat, if not overboard, and it may take the entire crew to get it properly flaked and secure on the boom.

Instead of this system, the mainsail luffs of all cruising and offshore boats should be attached to the mast with sturdy plastic or metal slides that feed into a slot or track on the after side of the spar. That way, the whole luff remains secured to the mast whether the sail is up or down. These slides (and similar ones on the mainsail's foot) should be secured to the sail with seizings or heavily sewn sail stop material rather than shackles, which can open up when the sail flogs.

Recommended Inventories

At the beginning of Chapter 11, we described the various rigs in use today—the cutter, sloop, yawl, ketch, schooner, and cat configurations—as well as the masthead and fractional setups for the foretriangle. The rig that we favor for offshore cruising is the double-headsail cutter. Not only are its two relatively small headsails lighter and easier to handle than one large genoa jib, but with the cutter's high-cut jib topsail there is no big, low-cut sail draped to leeward threatening to scoop up the bow wave and block the crew's view to leeward. Another advantage of a high-cut headsail is that it can be easily wung out on a spinnaker pole when running before the wind (Figure 13-3).

For cruising under the cutter rig, we recommend a small, versatile sail inventory: a proper mainsail, a large light jib topsail, a small heavy jib topsail, a forestaysail, a storm trysail, and a storm staysail. With this inventory, you can handle just about every condition. For light winds, a large light Dacron reacher-drifter jib will be a good addition. On smaller vessels with ample crew power, a poleless nylon cruising spinnaker—set like a genoa except that it is not hanked to the headstay—can be added to complete the inventory.

A cruising mainsail should have two reefs, with each reef equal to about 25 percent of the sail's total area. With the second reef tied in, the mainsail area is halved. The next step would be to set the storm trysail, whose area should be about one-half that of the double-reefed mainsail, or about 25 percent that of the entire mainsail. The sailmaker should cut the mainsail's luff curve fairly straight so that extreme mast bend is not needed to obtain an efficient shape. The roach should be moderate, less than that on a racing mainsail, in order to reduce loading on the battens. The batten pockets should be strong, and have ties or some other provision for securing the battens—it is not enough to push the batten down against elastic and slide it under a flap.

A problem with the double-headsail rig is that when the boat is being tacked the jib top risks being torn by sail hanks as it sweeps across the luff of the staysail. To protect the sail, you can have the sailmaker sew a protective patch over each staysail hank. These patches fit tightly when the staysail halyard and luff are tight, but when the halyard is eased they can be opened (Figure 13-2).

The inventory for a single-headsail sloop will be smaller than that on a cutter because there is no provision for a staysail. The largest jib might be about the size of an IOR Number 2 genoa, but with a higher clew and shorter luff (to keep the foot out of the water and facilitate lifting the tack in rough weather). If there is a cringle in the leach about 7 feet above the deck, the sail can be reefed to about the size of a Number 3 jib simply by moving the jib sheet. When the genoa is reefed, lead the sheet way aft, and lift the tack slightly on a pendant. Tie up the foot of the sail, but be alert to foul-ups when changing tacks. To complete the cruising sloop's inventory, carry a Number 3 jib (perhaps reefable as well) and a small working jib, plus of course storm sails.

Figure 13-3. A good cruising inventory for a cutter. Note the absence of a low-cut genoa, which obscures visibility to leeward, scoops up the bow wave, and is hard to handle.

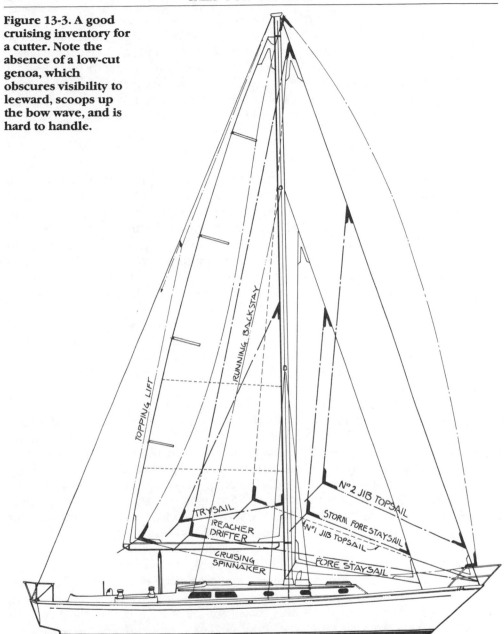

TOPPING LIFT

RUNNING BACKSTAY

N° 2 JIB TOPSAIL

TRYSAIL

STORM FORE STAYSAIL

REACHER DRIFTER

N°1 JIB TOPSAIL

CRUISING SPINNAKER

FORE STAYSAIL

If you carry a low-cut genoa jib, make sure there is some way to pull the foot out of the bow wave when reaching. Have the sailmaker install a strongly reinforced grommet about one-third of the way aft of the tack. When spray begins to fly into the sail when you're reaching, hook the spinnaker topping lift or an unused halyard into the grommet and pull the foot up. Or raise the sail above the deck with a tack pendant equal to at least 5 percent of the luff length (if the sail has a short head pendant, remove it from the head and install it on the tack).

For double-headed and single-headed yawls and ketches, the inventories that we have recommended for the cutter and sloop are sufficient, with, of course, the addition of a reefable mizzen. For reaching in light and moderate wind, you might carry a large light nylon mizzen staysail; there must be a running backstay to support the mizzenmast when the staysail is set.

Storm Sails

For some reason—perhaps because the storm jib and trysail are seldom needed—many if not most of today's inventories are devoid of true storm sails. This lack of owner foresight must be a symptom of owner ignorance. For an offshore yacht, the storm trysail and storm jib should be the sails that are first ordered and best cared for. These are the only sails that can get the boat where she's headed in any wind stronger than a drifter. They are the cruising sailor's best possible insurance policy, and their absence or neglect has played a prominent part in difficulties in serious storms. No matter how rarely they are needed, all hands should know how to set and trim them.

The boat's designer should be able to tell the owner how big the storm sails should be, since their size is related to the boat's stability. They should be more than just one step down in area from the heavy-weather configuration of a deep reef and small jib. As we said earlier, the storm trysail should be about 25 percent the area of the full mainsail.

On most boats, the storm trysail is set on the mainsail luff track, onto which the trysail luff slides are inserted through a small gate. That is a bad rig. In order that it be clear of the luff of the doused mainsail stacked on the gooseneck, the switch for the gate must usually be so high that even tall crew members must strain to reach it. In another system, which is only slightly better, a low track for the trysail feeds into the regular luff track through a switch, which, unfortunately, never seems to operate smoothly. The best arrangement, and the only one worth considering on a large boat, is to rig a separate track from the deck the full luff length of the trysail (Figure 13-4). The trysail slides can be rigged on this track well in advance of heavy weather and the sail left in its bag, ready to be hoisted.

Ideally, the storm jib should be fitted with hanks and set on the forestay—not the outer headstay—in order to bring the sail plan's center of effort aft near the mast. With this arrangement, undesirable lee helm is not generated by a jib flying way out on the bow. With the storm trysail set fairly far forward, the two sails will be near each other and the boat should balance well and steer easily.

Roller Furlers

After the grooved headstay was developed in the early 1970s, it was adapted for use in roller-furling systems, which have since become extremely popular. Each manufacturer's system is undergoing constant development and has its advantages and disadvantages, so anybody considering installing one should do thorough research. Since these systems can malfunction, the most seamanlike

Figure 13-4. A good arrangement for storm sails, with the trysail set on its own track and the storm jib set on the forestay. The trysail should be about 25 percent the size of the mainsail, and the storm jib much smaller than the regular forestaysail.

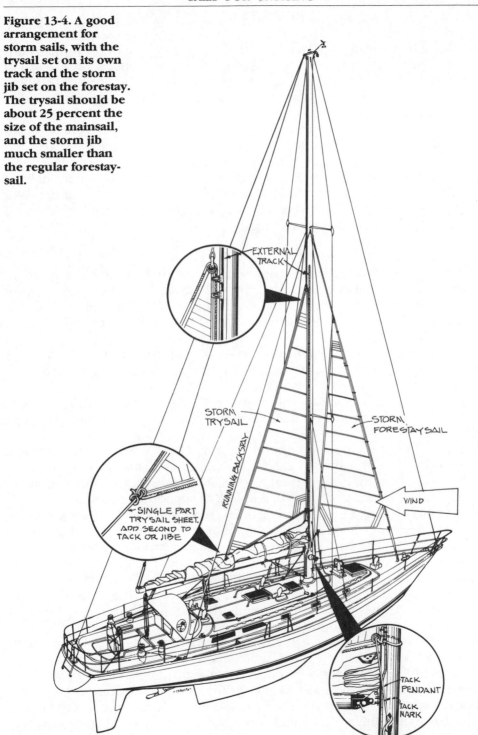

EXTERNAL TRACK

STORM TRYSAIL

STORM FORESTAY SAIL

RUNNING BACKSTAY

WIND

← SINGLE PART TRYSAIL SHEET. ADD SECOND TO TACK OR JIBE

TACK PENDANT

TACK MARK

arrangement is to have a forestay on which you can hank a staysail as a backup should the furler fail.

One problem area for the typical roller-furling system appears with a short-luffed jib. Usually, a pendant must be rigged between the furler's top swivel and the sail's head in order to position the swivel near the halyard sheave. This pendant creates an angle between the swivel and the jib halyard sheave, which prevents the swivel from turning with the stay and causing the halyard to wrap around the stay. Eventually, either the halyard breaks or the stay is twisted and kinked. The solution is to raise the jib with a foot pendant so that the swivel and the head alike are positioned near the halyard sheave.

Another common difficulty is that crew members sometimes leave unused jib or spinnaker halyards near the stay, and the halyards are wrapped up when the sail is furled or unfurled. Eventually, the stay will twist. Obviously, then, all unused halyards must be kept at the mast.

Mainsail Stowage

As for stowage of the mainsail, many people still use the traditional, inexpensive, and very seamanlike system of lazyjacks. These are light lines running from aloft on the mast to two or three spots on the boom. When the sail is dropped, it is automatically contained in the bights of the lines and so kept off the deck and out of the crew's way until they have time to do a proper furl.

More recently, four new and more complicated mainsail stowage devices have been developed: vertical stowage in a zippered pouch aft of the mast; vertical rolling up on a rod extrusion in the mast; vertical rolling up on a rod extrusion aft of the mast; and horizontal rolling up in the boom. As with jib roller-furlers, they have their pluses and their minuses, and you should consider them carefully before buying.

With the zipper arrangement the mainsail luff is attached to the mast with slides, which means that the sail can be lowered, raised, and reefed. However, like the two vertical rolling-up arrangements, it does not permit the mainsail to carry battens, so the sail loses area due to lack of support in its roach.

The vertical rolling-up systems add some weight aloft, so if they are being retrofitted, the owner should ask the naval architect how they will affect the boat's stability. Ballast may have to be added. Another problem with them is that shortening sail deeply pulls the clew far forward onto unsupported sections of the boom, which might bend or break. In that situation, it's better to sheet the clew directly to the rail, as you would with a storm trysail. The system that rolls the sail up inside the mast has the unique disadvantage of being quite noisy when the boat is beam to the wind (say when lying in a marina slip), since the open slot in the aft side of the mast acts like a huge blowhole on a flute to create an annoying low whistle.

Systems like these are being introduced on the marketplace every year. Some are better than others, and most have bugs that must be ironed out over time. Anybody thinking of buying and installing one should make sure that the manufacturer has thoroughly tested it and should try it out under a variety of conditions.

Spinnaker Systems

Despite the development of poleless cruising spinnakers, many cruising crews will want to carry traditional spinnakers when running in light and moderate winds. Unfortunately, large masthead spinnakers and their long poles can be hard to handle.

Some interesting spinnaker stowage systems have appeared. Called by several names—"snuffers," "squeezers," "sleeves," etc.—they work by pulling a large sock up and down over the spinnaker to set and douse it. This means that the sail is well under control when it is hoisted and lowered. Obviously, this is a great advantage and can be recommended for shorthanded sailing. Another labor-saving device is to stow the spinnaker pole vertically on the mast track, pulling the inboard end far up the mast when the pole is not in use. The only disadvantages of this system are weight and windage aloft.

If your boat does not have a special retrieving system, you can make dousing easier if you always rig two sheets on each clew—one led aft for use as the sheet, and the other led fairly far forward (to the rail at approximately the point of widest beam) for use either as the after guy or as the sheet when dousing the sail, since it pulls the sail safely into the lee of the mainsail.

PART IV

AUXILIARY EQUIPMENT

CHAPTER 14

Navigation, Weather, Radio, and Sailing Instruments

Richard C. McCurdy and Thomas R. Young

To a high degree, a boat's instrumentation ought to reflect the owner's philosophy and objectives—that is, the instruments ought to match what the owner wants to do with the boat, and how he or she wants to go about doing it.

For example, some owners may want to go to sea in order to "get away from it all" on their own, using only the classic combination of compass, sextant, clock, lead line, and barometer to help them cross an ocean. That is a superb thing to do, and elaborate instrumentation (satnav, Loran, and so on) probably would detract from the experience. At the other end of the spectrum, there are skippers who want to or have to keep in touch with the world, or who like to analyze weather using all available data, or who are determined to squeeze out the last possible drop of performance. For them, a remarkable array of sophisticated instrumentation is now available. Fortunately, in the electronics area, performance is increasing while size, power demand, and cost are decreasing.

There are many choices for the skipper to make while assembling a group of instruments to do the job at a level of cost, power consumption, weight, and space utilization that he or she can tolerate. Our purpose in this chapter is to provide basic information about various devices and their uses in order to assist skippers in this task. We will cover gear as traditional and simple as the magnetic compass and as modern and complex as satellite navigation systems. After surveying the varieties of instruments that are available for different tasks—navigating, communicating, weather forecasting, and measuring boat performance—we will suggest several packages of instruments for different types of cruising. While instruction on how to use all these various instruments is outside the scope of this book, we will make some suggestions about operation and setup, after taking a look at the requirements for a good navigator's station.

Navigation-Pilotage Gear

This group includes the following equipment: magnetic compasses (both fixed and hand-bearing); binoculars; sextant; clock; water-depth indicator; speed indicator; distance-run indicator; and electronic devices including radio direction finder (RDF), Loran-C, Decca, Omega, and satnav. To this list we might add some

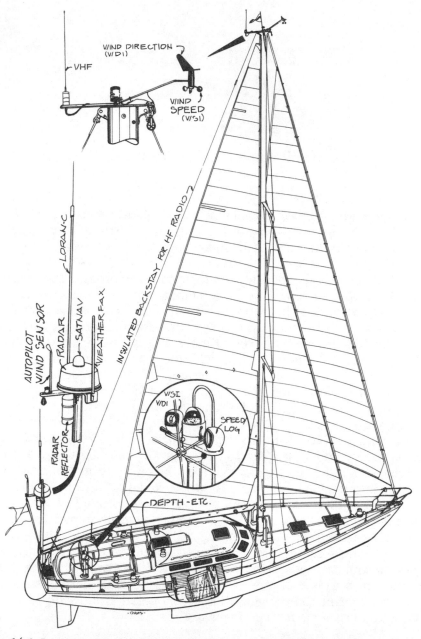

Figure 14-1. Instruments may be arranged aloft and on deck in various ways depending on the owner's preferences. This illustration shows some options. The authors prefer to install wind and speed dials on the aft face of the cabin trunk rather than on the binnacle so they can be seen from the helm without the steerer's having to refocus his or her eyes after looking at the jib. Finding room for a yacht club burgee near masthead instruments can be a problem.

other superb instruments, namely, one's eyes, ears, and even feelings and hunches.

In dealing with this gear, realize that all navigational systems are subject to troubles ranging from degradation to total failure. It is a fact that any or all of this equipment can go awry, sometimes subtly and at the most awkward times. Thus there are advantages in having redundant gear aboard to provide both a backup should one system fail and a warning of possible trouble should the two systems disagree. For example, Loran-C usually is extremely reliable within a given, charted range, at the edge of which it can provide inaccurate positions; anybody cruising to a destination near the limits of the range should know how to do celestial navigation and may want to carry Omega or satnav (Figure 14-1).

Compasses

The main compasses—there must be at least one good spare—should be high in quality. With wheel steering, it is hard to beat a large-diameter magnetic compass mounted on a binnacle on the centerline. With either a wheel or a tiller, a pair of compasses mounted port and starboard offer good visibility for a helmsman steering from the side as well as redundancy and a backup. If the boat has a navigation station below, another good compass should be mounted there; when installed in a remountable bracket, this compass can be taken on deck should the main steering compass be damaged.

A hand-bearing compass is excellent for taking bearings. The best one is the small "hockey-puck" type, which is both handy and accurate. After experimenting with various positions for taking bearings, choose the one that offers the minimum of deviation and the greatest accuracy and comfort.

Be alert to deviation. Compensation magnets in compasses and binnacles are helpful but not always a blessing, as their effect can vary with the angle of heel, so it is important to put together a reliable deviation table for each compass for various headings not only when the boat is upright but also when she is heeling. Heeling error can be minimized by mounting a vertical magnet directly above or below the compass. An offshore navigator should know how to use the shadow pin on the compass, or a shadow pelorus, to check deviation when at sea. If a pelorus is carried for this purpose, there should be a deck mounting for the device. A digital compass is usually installed along with advanced computerized performance-measuring gear, since it speaks the language that computers speak.

Binoculars

A pair of binoculars should be mounted where they are both accessible and out of the weather. For good night vision, 7×50 binoculars are the answer as they pick up more light than 7×35 binoculars. Carry a spare.

Celestial Navigation Equipment

The sextant and related gear are basic for open ocean work, and can be surprisingly handy on-soundings as well. The main drawback of the sextant is that, for a reliable, complete fix, it requires reasonably clear weather and some length of time to take a sufficient number of sights, and the sun and / or stars are not always there when and where you want them to be. However, this instrument (along with a timepiece and the necessary tables) provides a reliable navigation system that is completely independent of the boat's electrical system. Sextant navigation can be the primary system, or it can either back up or be a check on electronic navigation.

A top-grade sextant is expensive, but this high cost can pay off in accuracy and reliability. Less expensive sextants will also work, though with reduced accuracy, either as a backup to the primary sextant or, where economy is a real objective, as the main instrument. Regardless of the quality of the sextant, a good sight requires an accomplished operator, so whatever class of sextant you use, practice with it in various sea conditions in order to determine probable errors.

Calculators and Timepieces

Almanac and sight-reduction tables are available in book form and, better yet, in hand calculators. Calculators with these tables in their memory can be God-sends to navigators, particularly when crews are small and the time available for sights and calculations is limited. Their convenience will surely increase the number of sextant shots that are taken. Like all electronic instruments, these calculators can fail from time to time, so the regular printed tables should be carried, just in case.

A crystal digital watch, cheap but highly accurate, is another blessing of modern technology. Each boat should carry at least three digital timepieces for backup. As accuracy doesn't seem to be a function of price to any important degree, there is no virtue in spending a lot of money on them. If you want to dress up the boat, carry a classic chronometer and check it (and the watches) against radio time signals, which can now be received anywhere in the world. Another kind of watch worth having aboard is a stopwatch, which many navigators prefer to use when taking the time during sights and which can be very useful when "running out your time" in poor visibility.

Depth-sounding Equipment

To determine depth, there is nothing wrong with the classic lead line except the limited depth it can sound and its inconvenience: it can be awkward to use, and the boat must often be slowed. However, the lead line is a good backup to electronic sounders.

These electronic sonic sounders automatically sound to great depths regardless of the boat's speed and, if properly installed, provide readouts for both the helmsman and the navigator. Most sounders show only the present depth under the boat. One step up in capability (and price) is the recording depth sounder, which shows depths over time. Where the bottom has character—for example, a gradual rise as you approach a coastline—a recording sounder's trace can be matched with depths shown on the chart in order to provide an accurate track of the boat's course and progress independent of the ones shown by dead-reckoning pilotage and electronic navigation devices. This can be a great help when approaching an unfamiliar shore in fog, when the crew may be too busy to watch a non-recording sounder steadily.

The basic instrument should be a non-recording sounder readable on deck and at the navigator's station, and a recording instrument should be carried for special situations and redundancy. If the recording sounder has a substantial depth range (say, 200 fathoms), the other instrument can have less range. When both sounders are running simultaneously, they may interfere with each other unless they operate on different frequencies.

Speed and Distance Meters

The backbone of dead reckoning—the basic skill of all passage-making—is knowledge of the boat's speed and distance covered over a known course. The compass gives the course, and a speedometer and log give the distance. The electronic speedometer and log are very useful instruments for pilotage and navigation, replacing the traditional taffrail log, which can be carried as a backup on a long voyage. Therefore, the speedometer ought to be one of the first instruments chosen.

The choice is a broad one, as the modern electronic speedometer can be quite sophisticated. While the standard inexpensive digital instrument shows speed to a tenth of a knot, for racing and performance cruising there are speedometers whose readings can be expanded to detect and display minute changes in speed—a great help while trimming sails—and which can be tied into computers to indicate optimum performance for given conditions (we will say more about this capability in the section on performance instruments).

The transducers for these instruments are generally small paddlewheels or propellers. Of the two types, the former is preferred as it is less likely to pick up weeds. Both types may be difficult to calibrate, and must be pulled out and cleaned frequently. These problems do not exist with a new type of transducer that measures the boat's speed by sending sound waves through the water.

The transducer should be located on the centerline about one-third of the way from the keel to the forward end of the waterline. If it is necessary to mount transducers off the centerline, install one on each side and connect them to a switch that automatically shuts off the windward one and connects the leeward one. Time spent in calibrating the speedometer will pay off handsomely in accurate dead reckoning as well as in reliable measurement of boat performance.

Radio Direction Finder

The radio direction finder (RDF) has probably been used for more years, by more mariners, than any other modern electronic navigation system. While it is not as accurate as the other devices, it is a useful and relatively inexpensive instrument that is most helpful in areas where visibility is often bad, and when the more costly Loran-type systems or radar either are not carried or are not effective. The RDF operates by sensing the bearing toward a radio transmitter, which works on a frequency below the broadcast band and, typically, is installed as an adjunct to a lighthouse. While the RDF can be used to determine a line of position (LOP) and, using two or more LOPs, to fix an approximate position, it is often most effective for homing in on a destination near a transmitter. The effective range of some transmitters may be as large as 200 miles.

The type of RDF that is easiest to use consists of an antenna and a small magnetic compass in a hand-held package. This unit may contain its own radio receiver or be connected to a fixed radio below. Using this system, the navigator stands on deck or in the companionway, aims the antenna, listens for the transmitter's Morse code signal through earphones, and, when the signal is inaudible ("null"), reads the bearing right off the compass. With this system, there is no need to take into account the boat's precise heading, which is necessary when the RDF is fixed below in the cabin.

Be aware that RDF bearings are affected by many factors that change from time to time. RDF fixes should not be regarded as precise; they give *approximate* positions. With this understanding, a navigator will find the RDF quite a useful tool. Among the influences on the accuracy of a radio bearing are the boat's hull (if it is metal), rigging, lifelines, sails (if they are wet), and angle of heel. The loop of the wire lifelines should be broken by using a rope lashing to attach them to one of the pulpits.

Just as with steering and hand-bearing compasses, the compass in the RDF will have deviations at various headings and angles of heel, so a deviation table should be made up. This is not difficult to do:

1. Select a secure, comfortable position (or positions) where the navigator will stand or sit while taking bearings. Often this is a standing position in the main companionway with the body well braced and the bearing instrument held above the level of the lifelines.
2. Calculate and chart the boat's location, or better, locate the boat so the RDF beacon is in sight.
3. With the navigator handling the instrument in the selected position (or positions), "swing the boat" by taking bearings on one or two RDF stations, preferably at several heel angles.
4. Compare the bearings with the ones charted or seen from your known location. The differences are the deviations.

The most elaborate direction finders work automatically. Called automatic direction finders (ADFs), they require a special antenna at the top of the mast so are best suited for larger boats. Recently, another innovative type of RDF has appeared. Operating at very high frequencies and using a special antenna, this system may prove to have a unique use for homing in on other vessels in distress situations.

Omni

This is an aircraft-type RDF system, using transmitters generally located at or near airports. While Omni is very accurate, it has disadvantages and is used little today. Since it operates at very high frequencies, its range is limited to line-of-sight distances (generally less than about 50 miles). Omni is relatively expensive and requires a special antenna and a coaxial cable running aloft.

Radar

Until recently a big-ship instrument, radar is now available in small, relatively inexpensive packages that make the system extremely attractive for cruising boats.

Figure 14-2. A radar readout screen shows nearby objects and weather with considerable accuracy. On many cruising boats, a screen is located on deck where the steerer can see it.

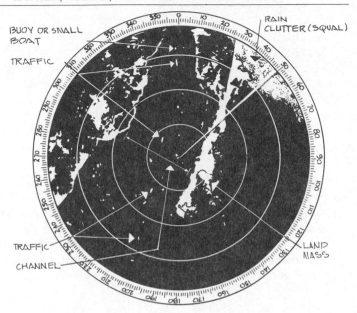

A closed-dome, 2-foot-diameter antenna will give adequate range for sailboat use, and can be mounted on a mast or, failing that, on a post standing up from the deck. In 1986, a reliable unit satisfactory for sailboat use could be purchased for about $2000, or less than the cost of a sophisticated Loran-C unit. And, unlike Loran, radar can be used anywhere worldwide and is not very susceptible to outside interference.

Radar works by emitting radio pulses at ultra-high frequencies, sweeping the horizon with its beam and showing on a screen the echoes that come back. A properly functioning radar instrument will mark the exact distance and bearing to any reflecting object in the line of sight of its antenna (Figure 14-2). Using these data, and without having to do any extra work with charts or other instruments, the crew can usually locate the shoreline and buoys (many of which have large radar reflectors or transmitters), as well as track the progress of nearby ships and squalls. In effect, radar provides a pair of "eyes" that see for miles around the boat in all types of visibility. If the readout screen can be located where the helmsman can see it from the wheel or tiller, the system provides instant short-range pilotage and collision avoidance capability for shorthanded crews.

Radar does have some limitations. While darkness and fog pose no problem, heavy rain and breaking waves ("sea clutter") significantly degrade returns and target identification. And it is not effective when the boat is heeling more than about 20 degrees, unless the antenna is installed on a self-leveling mount.

Hand-held sets, affectionately known as "belly radars," are available for skippers who do not wish to carry a full radar instrument. There is no screen with this device; echoes are indicated by audible tones in earphones, with the pitch varying with the proximity of the reflecting object.

Loran-C

Loran-C is an extremely accurate system for fixing position that operates by receiving signals from several widely spaced transmitters on land and very precisely comparing the difference in arrival time of the signals. It is an outgrowth of the old Loran-A, the main differences being that Loran-C is more accurate, automated, and computerized (there is a continuous automatic fix) and has a lower operating frequency, and therefore gives wider coverage and range and less trouble with sky waves. With improved circuitry and the increased volume of production, the price of Loran-C sets has been dropping quickly until the most simple ones are competitive with RDFs.

Modern Loran-C systems have a very impressive bag of tricks, not the least of which, for the sailor, being their ability to calculate speed and course over the bottom; by comparing these data with the compass course and speedometer readout, the navigator can readily determine the current's set and drift. Many instruments also can be programmed to indicate the course and distance to a turning mark or destination. If this information is displayed on a repeater in the cockpit, the helmsman can steer the exact course without the navigator's having to give directions from the cabin.

Loran-C has drawbacks. First, it is not a worldwide system, and there are many cruising areas where it cannot be used (Decca, a system similar to but not compatible with Loran-C, is used in Europe). Loran's accuracy quickly degenerates near the limits of its coverage. However, the area of its reliable coverage is quite extensive in heavily used sailing areas in North America, where it is truly a navigational workhorse.

The second drawback is that, being a complex computerized electrical system, Loran-C is subject to failure in many ways. Since it is quite inexpensive for its navigational value, many boats carry a second set as a backup.

Third, various kinds of electronic "noises" will interfere with Loran signals, which are relatively weak as received. Sets contain filters to tune this interference out; some filters are better than others. While some interference comes from other radio signals, much troublesome noise can be generated in the boat itself, for example, by fluorescent lights. At the end of this chapter, we will describe some ways to reduce on-board noise. A professional electronics technician will be able to provide some good advice on improving reception.

Omega

Roughly similar to Loran-C in the way it determines a boat's position, Omega has greater range since it operates at still lower frequencies. Its advantage is that it has worldwide coverage, whereas Loran has only regional coverage. The disadvantage of Omega is that, for its data to be meaningful, the boat's approximate position must be known when the instrument is started. The instrument is then left running. If it is restarted, another updated approximate position must be known. Loran, on the other hand, is accurate whether or not the navigator knows the boat's approximate position; if a Loran-C set is turned off and then back on, it still gives a fix once it has warmed up. This drawback with Omega is not serious so long as the navigator keeps up a good dead-reckoning plot or is able to get other fixes.

Omega is excellent for long-distance work. But for coastwise navigation or racing, Loran-C and Decca, which are more accurate than Omega, are the best choices.

Satellite Navigation

Called "satnav" or "navsat," this system is based on signals that are received from one or more of a set of special-purpose satellites. Using these signals, the computer in the instrument calculates the position. Satnav fixes usually are quite accurate. The drawback with the system is that for various reasons the fixes are not continuous. Depending on the boat's geographical position, an hour or more may elapse between fixes, during which time the machine calculates and displays dead-reckoning positions based on the boat's progress since the last fix. These dead-reckoning positions may be inaccurate in areas of currents, and the navigator must be careful to keep track of the between-fix displays.

Satnav is fine for offshore cruising. In areas where Loran-C is only marginally effective but still usable, satnav can be used to provide periodic checks on continuous Loran positions when more frequent positions are required.

The Global Positioning System (GPS), sometimes called "Navstar," is a new satellite navigation system under development. When it is fully installed around 1990—and if it is made available for general use—Navstar will advance yacht navigation in a major way because it will provide continuous, highly accurate fixes from more than one dozen satellites. Commercial firms are developing Navstar receivers. If the system comes into general use, the price of the receivers could be most attractive.

EPIRB

While not a receiver, the emergency position-indicating radio beacon (EPIRB) should be mentioned in this section. It is a portable, buoyant, very-high-frequency (VHF) transmitter for emergencies only, sending out signals that can be identified for homing in on the distressed vessel by aircraft, satellites, and U.S. Coast Guard stations. Type A and Type B EPIRBs operate on distress channels monitored by aircraft; Type A is for commercial boats and Type B is generally for yachts. The Type C EPIRB operates on VHF emergency channels 15 and 16, and is intended for use near shore.

These devices should be stowed or mounted where they are quickly accessible. One may be kept in the emergency bag that is prepared to be thrown into the life raft when the crew abandons ship.

Weather and Communications Instruments

This group includes the barometer, wind speed and direction indicators, temperature and humidity indicators, the weather facsimile machine, and various radios, including single-sideband, VHF-FM, the general-purpose communications receiver, and ham.

In addition to these devices, the stored knowledge available in a modest shelf of well-chosen technical and instructional books, while hardly to be classed as "instruments," will sooner or later provide a lot of comfort at sea. In this library there should be at least an elementary text on meteorology. Read it in good weather rather than in distress. It will help any sailor get the most out of available weather data and, in particular, help him or her to make local predictions based on weather forecasts for large areas.

The Barometer

This is the classic instrument for understanding and predicting local weather. While any decent barometer will serve, if the real import of weather gyrations is to be made clear, frequent readings must be made and written down. Because this routine may be difficult to keep up, it is likely not to be followed. Since Murphy's Law is always in effect at sea, the time when it is not done will be just when it *should* be done.

The solution to this problem of following barometer fluctuations over a period of time is to carry a recording barometer, which traces, on graph paper, an hour-to-hour history of barometer readings for a week. Once in a while, a recording barometer is worth its weight in gold. Since about an ounce of gold (about $350) will purchase one of these instruments, it's a good deal.

Relative Wind Speed and Direction

Wind-measuring instruments are useful for weather evaluation and prediction, and they are essential for maximizing boat performance. If you know the apparent wind speed and the relative wind direction, you can estimate the true wind speed and direction, which will help you determine the location of nearby weather systems. Knowing the wind speed will help when the crew makes decisions about which sails or reefs to carry; in a gradually building wind, the numbers on the wind-speed indicator will be a more accurate indicator of a rising gale than the "feel" of a crew distracted by other jobs. At night, the wind-direction indicator can be a great help to a helmsman who is unable to see the jib luff when sailing to windward or the spinnaker when sailing off the wind.

The simplest devices are a small hand-held anemometer and a masthead wind arrow, which may be all you need for cruising. But if you are concerned about performance, you should consider installing an electronic speed / direction unit at the top of the mast, with a clear readout in the cockpit and, perhaps, in the navigator's station. For best accuracy, mount the unit on a 3- to 4-foot wand (longer for masthead rigs and larger boats) projecting forward and upward at about 30 degrees from the tip of the mast. Calibration of this instrument is important to its accuracy. In the next section we will say some more about this instrument in terms of boat performance.

Air and Water Temperature

Sometimes the air and water temperatures are important considerations when predicting weather and navigating. They are excellent indicators of arriving fronts and fog and of the presence of strong tropical currents (the 80-plus degrees of the Gulf Stream is the best example). While simple hand thermometers held in the air or in a container of seawater, such as the toilet, are satisfactory, a better but more elaborate method is to place one sensor way down in the hull to measure water temperature and another on deck to measure air temperature, and lead their cables to a single dial in the navigator's station. Using a switch, the navigator can read one temperature and then the other. (While you're at it, install a third sensor in the refrigerator.)

Related to these instruments are devices for predicting fog. The classic ones are the hygrometer and the sling psychrometer, which give the temperatures of wet and dry bulb thermometers. Those figures are then entered into a table to determine the dew point—the air temperature at which fog will occur. A compact humidity indicator may also be helpful. All these devices are simple, handy to use, inexpensive, and very helpful when doing intensive weather work both at sea and alongshore.

Radio

While there is no disputing the value of weather information collected by the instruments mentioned above, as well as by the mariner's own observations, the quality of the whole exercise will be greatly enhanced by weather reports received from the outside world. This information comes by radio in various ways, transmitted by stations around the world. These stations and their frequencies are listed in a government publication *Worldwide Marine Weather Broadcasts,* available from:

> Superintendent of Documents
> U.S. Government Printing Office
> Washington, D.C. 20402

The quality of the results from a radio weather broadcast can depend on the crew's knowledge as well as on the type of radio instrument that is used. The same is true of the other use of radio—communications. Here we will introduce the topic with a look at the utility of several types of instruments. At the end of the chapter, we will discuss installation, antennas, and grounds, and describe a way to reduce static.

Very-high-frequency FM radio (VHF-FM) provides reception of weather forecasts as well as two-way communications within the relatively small range of approximately 50 miles. The VHF transceivers on the market today are quite small and inexpensive, and very capable. By all odds the best type to install is the "synthesized" instrument that provides communication on all channels plus the weather channels that, in the United States, receive continuous National Weather Service broadcasts. This type is immune from the bothersome, costly crystal changes that were necessary with early models to provide coverage of many channels.

When installing VHF, remember that since the signals travel by line of sight, the higher the antenna is mounted, the longer is the instrument's range. Don't be impressed by claims for "high-gain" antennas, for while an argument can be made for their use on boats that remain upright, like powerboats, they do not work well when a boat is heeled.

A VHF transceiver is quickly out of range of weather stations when a boat heads offshore, and soon after that medium-frequency commercial stations become increasingly hard to pick up. The basic deep-sea instrument for picking up weather broadcasts and communicating is the *high-frequency (HF) single-sideband radio-telephone (SSB)*. An SSB is expensive and may remain so due to some built-in costs: its system is complex and its frequency tolerance must be very tight. One alternative to SSB is direct satellite communication, but it is not yet on the horizon for modest-sized boats.

If two-way communication is not important, or if the crew wants to receive more elaborate weather information than that provided by SSB (as well as news and music on the AM broadcast band, which is not available on SSB), a versatile type of radio called a *communications receiver* offers excellent service. In their best form, these are HF receivers with many special features that allow them to receive both voice and code transmissions, even in unfavorable conditions. Besides variety and compactness, the hallmark of these receivers is their clear reception, due, first, to their tuning accuracy and, second, to controls that allow the operator to select the bandwidth—music requires a lot of bandwidth, voice somewhat less, and code least of all. In simplified form (for example, with the line of small Sony synthesized receivers), these controls include a two-position bandwidth switch labeled "music" and "news" and a mode switch labeled "normal" and "SSB," which allows fine tuning with a thumbwheel.

Verbal weather forecasts are worth receiving, especially since the advent of the weather satellite system. However, verbal marine forecasts generally cover large areas of ocean with a rather broad brush. For more localized information, which will allow the crew to make and interpret weather maps on board, the best source is data sent via Morse code over special channels that can be received over the communications receiver. Unfortunately, the code is sent at a fast rate; if nobody on board can read it, the message can be recorded on a tape recorder and played back at a slower speed. Decoding machines are also available from ham radio suppliers.

With a *weather facsimile machine* on board, there is no need to draw your own weather maps. These machines receive radio-transmitted data and convert the information into maps that, supplemented by voice broadcasts, can enable a crew to practice weather analysis to the full extent of their interpretive ability. While much of the information sent over "weatherfax" stations is of interest mainly to aircraft pilots, some of it can help sailors. For example, there are maps that show sea state. The machine itself should be driven by a high-quality receiver, such as a good communications receiver (some facsimile machines have built-in receivers). The decision whether to carry a facsimile machine has to be based on a balance between the cost, which is appreciable, and a realistic judgment as to the value of the data that it will provide.

Another method of long-distance communicating is the *amateur or ham radio*. A special Federal Communications Commission license is needed to operate a ham instrument, but the effort of studying for the license may well be worthwhile for an offshore sailor, since this is a very effective means of communication. Ham has four big advantages. First, the transmitter can, if desired, be operated at a higher power than marine-band transmitters, and has at least as long a range. Second, a sailing ham can make telephone calls by "patching into" shore ham stations, thereby bypassing crowded marine telephone stations (by law, the call cannot be used for business and various other specified purposes). Third, a ham installation is less expensive than marine SSB installations. And fourth, it is versatile; the latest generation of ham radio transceivers can function as high-quality, general-coverage communications receivers, thereby serving many of the purposes served by the other instruments that we have already mentioned.

Although ham radio has been used for successful distress calls on many occasions, it should not be regarded as a substitute for a marine SSB, since nearby commercial vessels will not be carrying ham radios, and the Coast Guard does not continuously monitor ham frequencies, as it does with SSB and VHF. However, by arranging radio appointments at a given time and frequency, a sailing ham operator can set up a system by which friends ashore or on other vessels can follow the boat's progress and be aware of developments, good or bad. There are also volunteer "marine nets" that operate on certain frequencies by common usage; their members are delighted to help yachtsmen.

One limitation for cruising sailors is that a vessel generally may not operate on ham bands within the territorial waters of a country that is not her country of registry, unless she is licensed in that country. This means that, for all practical purposes, ham radio is used by sailors only on the high seas in the waters of the country of registry.

Anybody wishing more information on ham radio activities should contact the American Radio Relay League (Newington, CT 06111), which offers publications and support for amateur radio operators.

Boat Performance Instruments

In this group are devices that can help the crew evaluate and improve the boat's speed and pointing ability. While these instruments have been developed for racing boats, they can also be valuable when cruising. We have already discussed some of them. They are the boat speed, distance run, and relative wind speed and direction devices that provide the raw data that are fed into more advanced devices that keep a dead-reckoning plot, calculate the true wind speed and direction, or analyze boat performance. In addition, a boat may carry a computer to help the navigator and skipper make decisions based on many variables.

Raw Data

Instruments that measure and display relative wind speed and direction were discussed in the previous section. Besides helping with weather evaluation, they are essential for analysis of boat performance, since they provide raw data for the performance instruments and the computer (if there is one). Therefore, they must be calibrated carefully.

Besides basic wind and boat speed data, the heel angle is another type of raw data used in these calculations. It is measured by an inclinometer that yields an electrical readout, which helps calculate leeway and improves the accuracy of the boat and wind speed devices by correcting for heel.

Calculation and Analysis of Raw Data

Special performance instruments, into which the relative boat and wind speed and direction are fed, automatically calculate various performance indicators. Two of these are true wind speed in knots and true wind direction in magnetic degrees, which otherwise could only be estimated. The instruments obtain these results by performing vector calculations using a built-in electronic compass. The results are displayed to the cockpit and, in some boats, to the navigation station. This is not information that concerns only racing crews; any cruising skipper would want to know the true wind speed when deciding which jib to change down to or how many reefs to take in.

The same data and calculations are used to determine velocity made good (VMG), which is the progress made directly toward an upwind or downwind destination when sailing to windward or off the wind. For example, when the boat is sailing close-hauled, the VMG helps the helmsman determine whether footing off a couple of degrees is more (or less) effective than pointing up a little closer into the wind. If the VMG drops but the true wind speed stays the same, the helmsman should try a different tactic.

Performance instruments that include an electronic compass can perform dead-reckoning pilotage with a high degree of accuracy. Although navigating by Loran-C is now more common than assiduously keeping a good dead-reckoning plot, it's well to have a dead-reckoning position for backup. This is especially true when running near the limits of Loran coverage, since an accurate, automatic dead-reckoning system can detect the moment when the Loran begins to go awry. When the two positions diverge, the navigator should carefully examine the Loran displays and the log, where all Loran readouts should be recorded in areas of questionable reception. The amount of Loran error is usually in 10-microsecond increments, which can usually be spotted during an inspection.

Some performance instruments are able to determine local current set and drift by comparing the dead-reckoning fix (the position relative to the water) with the Loran fix (the position relative to the bottom). Important for racing tactics, this information can also be very valuable for safe passage in constricted, tide-swept waters in poor visibility. Carrying performance analysis further, instruments can be programmed with the so-called "polar curves" of the boat. These are graphs that show how fast the boat will sail at various angles to the wind in various wind speeds (Figure 14-3). The basic polar curves can be derived from the Velocity Prediction Program (VPP) developed for the International Measurement System or from any full source of performance data, including the crew's own detailed records of the boat's behavior. On a cruising passage, the polar curves can be used in conjunction with readouts from the true wind speed and direction indicators to help find the proper sail combinations for future legs, or to figure estimated times of arrival at destinations or turning points. When racing, the crew will use the curves as performance benchmarks so they get the most out of the boat.

Nowadays, it is fairly common to include a programmable calculator or portable computer as part of the gear on a racing yacht. These machines can be hooked up to the other instruments and used to monitor, record, display, and

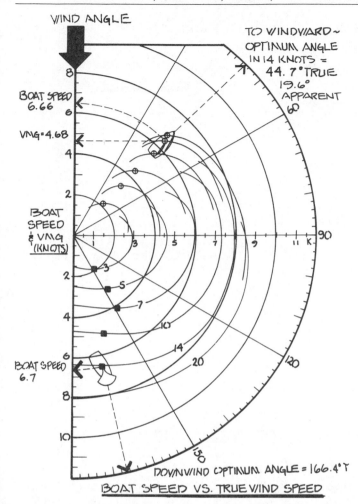

WIND ANGLE

TO WINDWARD~
OPTIMUM ANGLE
IN 14 KNOTS =
44.7° TRUE
19.6°
APPARENT
60

BOAT SPEED
6.66

VMG=4.68

BOAT
SPEED
& VMG
(KNOTS)

90

BOAT SPEED
6.7

DOWNWIND OPTIMUM ANGLE = 166.4°T

BOAT SPEED VS. TRUE WIND SPEED

Figure 14-3. Polar curves are graphs that show how fast a boat will sail at various angles to the wind at various true wind speeds. Performance instruments may be programmed with this information to aid on-the-spot analysis.

(if desired) print out information on the performance of the boat, together with other data such as wind direction and current. In conjunction with polar curves, computers can help the navigator determine the best course to take when various combinations of wind and current are available. Some computers have even been programmed to monitor wind, boat speed, and position data while the navigator is sleeping—and then to wake the navigator if the situation demands attention.

Obviously, performance instruments are not for everyone. Installations require considerable study and planning, and demand more than the average amount of maintenance and operator skill. Whenever you use any instrument of this sort, keep in mind that the output is most accurate and reliable when, and only when, the calibrations of the basic data-producing instruments—the relative boat speed and wind speed and direction devices—are as good as they can be made.

Table 14-1
SPARTAN INSTRUMENT PACKAGES

Spartan Group A: Coastwise and Bay Sailing

Instruments	Capability
Main compass	Dead reckoning and piloting
Hand-bearing compass	
Electronic speedometer/log	
Sonic depth sounder	
Binoculars	
VHF-FM radio	Short-range radio for weather and communications

Cost, $1000–$1500

Spartan Group B: Offshore Sailing

Instruments	Capability
Main compass	Oceangoing; no dependence on ship's power
Hand-bearing compass	
Sextant	
Navigation tables	
3 quartz watches	
Taffrail log/speedometer	
Lead line	
Portable all-band radio	
Barometer	
EPIRB	
Binoculars	

Cost, $1500–$2000, including $500 for a sextant

Instrument Packages

In Tables 14-1 and 2 we describe some representative packages of instruments for various sorts of boat use at various levels of expenditure. Table 14-1 includes "Spartan" packages; these instruments offer a minimum of complication, expense, and power drainage. Table 14-2 recommends instrument "upgrades," which offer greater accuracy and sophistication (as well as more maintenance problems and increased demands on the owner's bank balance and the navigator's skills). Obviously, many of these choices involve questions of opinion or taste, but we hope that they will trigger thoughts in the minds of prospective boat owners about their needs and priorities concerning electronics and other instruments.

Two basic questions must be addressed by any owner contemplating the purchase of instruments:

Question 1. Will the boat usually stay close enough to landmarks so she can get along without long-range navigation, weather, and radio equipment? (The owner or potential owner should know whether he or she will be sailing mainly on soundings or mainly offshore.)

Table 14-2
UPGRADES FOR SPARTAN INSTRUMENT PACKAGES

Upgrade 1

Instruments	Capability
RDF	More navigation accuracy
Radar	Increased safety near shore and shipping lanes
Add VHF and sonic depth sounder if upgrading Spartan Group B	

$2500–$3700

Upgrade 2

Instruments	Capability
Loran-C or Decca	Accurate coastwise and offshore navigation within signal range
SSB	Long-range weather and communications
Wind speed and direction	Improved weather evaluation and sailing performance
Through-hull thermometer	Navigation and weather evaluation aid

Cost, $3500–$5000

Upgrade 3

Instruments	Capability
Satnav	Worldwide navigation, radio reception, and weather evaluation
Communications receiver	
Weather facsimile machine	
Recording barometer	
Computerized performance system	Sophisticated racing package

Cost, $15,000 and up

Note: Costs in Tables 14-1 and 14-2 are approximate 1986 average prices, installation extra. Owner installation is possible on many instruments, and discount prices may be available. Tom Closs, Jr., helped in the preparation of these recommendations.

If the answer is *yes,* Package A in Table 14-1 provides a Spartan instrument list for coastwise and bay sailing. If more electronics are desired and can be afforded, Upgrade 1 in Table 14-2 offers a somewhat more elaborate coastal cruising inventory. Upgrade 2 is for a boat that may go offshore from time to time.

However, if *no* is the answer, Package B in Table 14-1 is a Spartan list for a boat that will often be sailing out of sight of land. Unlike Package A, it includes no instrument that is dependent on ship's power. Package A combined with Upgrades 1 and 2 in Table 14-2 offers more sophistication. Upgrade 3 offers transoceanic capability with or without the performance package for racing.

Question 2. Does the boat require performance instrumentation? (If the boat is going to engage in reasonably serious racing, the owner should know and admit it before making a list of instrument needs.)

If the owner answers *yes,* and the racing is done near shore, Package A with all or part of Upgrades 1, 2, and 3 might be on the shopping list. Package B with upgrades as desired applies if the racing is offshore.

On the other hand, if *no* racing is planned, the recommendations under Question 1 can be followed, thereby saving some money.

The Navigation Station

Accurate navigation and piloting require a good work space. On a minimally instrumented boat, all the navigator needs are a flat surface on which to lay out the charts and a place to stow them. The main cabin table and a bunk under the mattress will do fine. However, a regular navigation station is needed on boats with several instruments so that the indicators are clustered in a location where they can be seen by the navigator while he or she is seated at the table or standing by. Radios can be located behind or to one side of the seated navigator, who should be able to wear the earphones while working at the table.

Location and Design

The navigation station is best located so it is protected from rain and spray coming down the companionway, yet where the navigator can communicate with the crew in the cockpit. The working surface should be stoutly constructed and large enough to hold at least a chart folded in thirds, and preferably an unfolded chart. Below the surface, there should be a shelf or drawer for stowage of several charts. In larger boats, a second area for bulk chart stowage can be nearby; otherwise, stowage can be under the cushion in the navigator's bunk (Figure 14-4).

If the boat will be on long passages and is big enough, the station should have a comfortable, well-constructed seat. Inevitably, the boat will approach a landfall in rough conditions, poor visibility, and tricky currents, all combining to make dead reckoning both difficult and time consuming. In these situations, the overworked navigator gets little rest and so requires all the support possible. Ideally, the navigator should be able to brace him- or herself when the boat is heeled 30 degrees on both tacks, either by using footrests or by adjusting the angle of a concave seat that can be pivoted when the navigator is seated. (A pivoting table is another worthwhile feature, although some working area must be sacrificed to accommodate it.) On some well-planned dual-purpose boats, the navigator's station is arranged so the seat can be used during meals and social gatherings below.

There should be a bookshelf for the log, *Light List,* cruising guides, almanac, and other publications. The sextant can be stowed in its sturdy box in a special bracket or in a locker. Add a pencil sharpener and a drawer for pencils, notebooks, calculators, watches, parallel rules, and dividers, and you are in business, ready to go to sea.

Lighting

Illumination should be bright and broad; the lamps should be overhead so a minimum of shadow is cast on the chart while the navigator is working. Fluorescent lights are inadvisable, since they can generate interference with Loran-C.

A good addition is one or two small, gooseneck-type chart lamps, one of

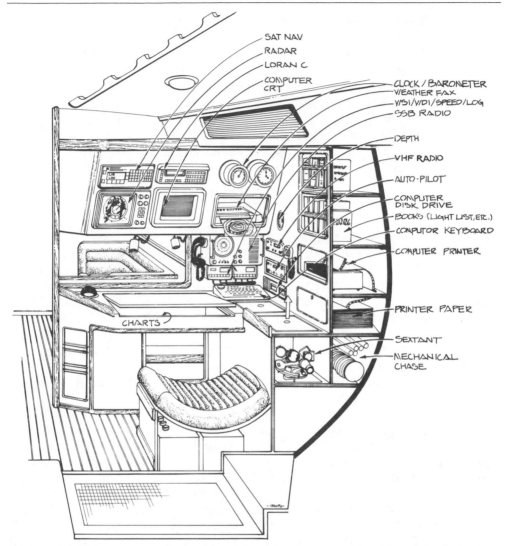

Figure 14-4. This very complete navigator's station has a comfortable seat and plenty of stowage space, as well as a full inventory of instruments. Note that instruments serving the same general function—for example, the radar screen and the Loran-C— are at the same level so that the navigator can read them without turning his or her head very far. Excessive head motion can lead to seasickness.

which should have a red light for night use. However, if part of the chart table extends under the boxes holding the instrument dials, the dial lights may provide enough illumination without the need for additional lighting, which could wake the crew sleeping below and interfere with the night vision of the crew on deck. If necessary, an opaque curtain can be pulled around the navigation station to allow full lighting of the chart table without blinding the helmsman.

Some flashlights for spotlighting hard-to-see dials can be mounted in accessible holders so the navigator can reach them without standing up.

Suggestions for Radio Installation and Use

Having surveyed recent advances in instrumentation, proposed packages for cruising boats, and suggested ways to use them at a navigation station, we would like to end our discussion with some recommendations about installation. Professional help will pay off handsomely in all phases of radio installation, and not just in jobs where it is required by law (such as the setting up of a single-sideband radio). From the planning stage right through post-installation calibration, an owner will be fortunate to secure the best help available. The following material is no substitute for a good radio professional's services, but rather is intended to provide some general background.

Some Basics about Radio Communications

Very-high-frequency (VHF) signals almost always travel in a "line-of-sight" path from the transmitting antenna to the receiving antenna. Since the earth is curved, they can go only so far before the earth gets in the way. This is why VHF-FM radio, like television, is a short-range system. The actual distance the signals can travel depends on the height of the antennas; the higher they are, the longer the path can be.

High-frequency (HF) signals—the kind used in marine single-sideband radios—can bend around the earth for a distance. They also have the very important capability of going to levels high in the atmosphere, where they are reflected back to a point far from the origin of transmission; this means that HF is good for very-long-range communication. Since the atmospheric reflecting layers are generated by sunlight, the ability to communicate from one given point to another depends upon the time of day and other factors (among them, the number of sunspots and solar flares). The frequency in use also affects communication, and SSB instruction manuals list the range for each frequency. Generally, higher frequencies provide very long ranges, especially during the daytime. The foregoing suggests some operating procedures for SSB communication:

- Since the whole process depends on the sun, and since a boat doesn't move very far in 24 hours, what worked at a given time yesterday is a good bet to work at about the same time today.
- Since the reflecting layers up in the sky work both ways, if you can hear another station, it is likely that the other station can hear you.
- A good way to keep posted about conditions is to listen regularly on various frequencies—say, to follow weather reports from different sources.

Antennas

Good antennas are basic to obtaining proper performance from electronic equipment aboard. They require occasional maintenance, can cause windage, and involve appreciable expense. Therefore, careful planning of the antenna system is well worth the effort.

Some equipment, such as VHF-FM, Loran-C, radar, satnav, and Omni, run on special-purpose antennas, one for each instrument. On the other hand, SSB, ham radio, and the communications receiver are all able to operate on the same high-frequency (HF) antenna, using a switch so that one instrument is in use at a time. The classic high-frequency antennas are the insulated permanent backstay, the long whip, and (on two-masted boats) the triatic wire. About 50 feet of wire should be carried aboard for use as an emergency antenna should the boat be dismasted.

This adds up to a lot of antennas, and unfortunately, a yacht—particularly a sloop or cutter—has a limited number of locations for them. All you can do is grit your teeth and find a place for them where they will operate properly. The instrument dealer or a professional radio technician will help you choose the right location.

The HF antenna must be tuned by an antenna tuner, or coupler, which is usually located where the antenna leads into the boat. Without the coupler, the set will not operate and could be damaged. Today's automatic couplers, which sense the frequency coming from the transmitter and tune the antenna to it, can efficiently match the multichannel capability of the newer synthesized transmitters. A coupler can also be used on a ham radio set, although most ham operators prefer to tune manually. When the HF antenna system is used for a communications receiver, the coupler usually should be left out of circuit since it will sometimes weaken incoming signals (by itself, the receiver will not actuate the coupler). Either switch the antenna directly to the receiver while receiving transmissions, or set up a separate receiving antenna altogether using a length of wire hoisted aloft.

Ground Systems

Equal in importance to a single-sideband radio's high-frequency (HF) antenna is the ground system. Since the ocean is a fine ground and is right there, you would think that grounding would be easy. Strangely, it is not, unless the hull is metal. The reason for this is that HF currents are very particular about what they run through. Conductors that would be perfect for carrying direct current (DC) or low-frequency alternating current (AC) may be poor for HF current. Even more strangely, grounds that work for one kind of antenna tuner or coupler may not always work with another kind. A ground system may be built into a fiberglass or wooden hull; it must be carefully designed, and a wooden hull will require substantial work.

The best single piece of advice we can offer concerning the ground is make sure that your SSB is installed by a professional technician who does this sort of work regularly, on the kind of boat you have, with the kind of set that you want.

Noise Reduction

Electrical noise, or "static," is the cause of much poor performance in both Loran-C and radio reception. Such noise can come from the outside, generated by lightning or other external electrical phenomena, or it can be generated aboard the boat by various pieces of equipment—for example, motors and alternators.

The first step to take in cutting static—what is called "raising the signal-to-noise ratio"—is to identify all the on-board sources of noise. Here are the steps:

1. On a clear day, get the boat to a location away from land and other vessels and turn off *all* the equipment.
2. Switch on a radio receiver on the broadcast band, but do not tune it to a station. Turn up the volume until you hear a gentle hiss.
3. One at a time, switch on each piece of equipment on board.
4. Each time, listen carefully to the radio receiver and note the increase in noise.
5. Estimate and log the effect on radio reception of each piece of equipment.

Usually, the on-board static producers will include one or more of the following objects: pumps, alternators and their regulators, refrigerators, motors, computers, Loran-C receivers, fluorescent lights, engine instruments, and loose connections. Have a radio technician examine each piece of gear that affects radio reception. When the technician is finished, there should be a notable improvement in radio and Loran reception. If unacceptable noise remains, make a list of the equipment that must be shut off when the radio or Loran receiver is in use.

As elsewhere in the realm of marine electronics, thinking systematically about the relationship between the instruments, the boat, and the environment will pay big dividends.

CHAPTER 15

Ground Tackle

Clayton Ewing and Stanley Livingston, Jr.

T he comments expressed here are based on the assumption that we are directing our attention to offshore cruising yachts larger than 36 feet that are likely to venture far enough from their home ports so that sooner or later nearly all types of holding ground will be experienced: mud, rock, gravel, sand, weeds, oyster shells, coral, shale, etc. Ideally, one seeks an anchor that will be effective in any bottom condition, and that is a big order. However, a combination of two carefully selected anchors can provide good holding for almost any condition that is likely to be encountered. Quite aside from that consideration, a vessel that ventures far from her home port should have a second anchor aboard for greatest security in the event of extremely severe weather, or the unhappy necessity of anchoring in an exposed area under severe conditions, or as insurance against the loss of a single anchor. Hence, we urge that a minimum of two anchors be carried.

Anchor Types

The Yachtsman or Herreshoff Type

This is an effective and good-holding anchor in any bottom that we have encountered. One of us carried two of them aboard several 55- to 58-foot boats for about 15 years. He became mightily impressed with the Herreshoff anchor when, in November 1960, he rode out a hurricane at Cape Henlopen, New Jersey, with sustained winds in excess of 100 miles per hour, according to the Cape May Coast Guard. The bottom was mud over sand. One anchor weighed 75 pounds and the other 100 pounds. They were each set on 300 feet of nylon line in about 20 feet of water, and buried to a depth that made retrieval very difficult.

On the negative side, the yachtsman-type anchor has one serious deficiency: the anchor cable is very apt to foul the protruding fluke in the event of a change of tide or a wind shift, in which event the anchor loses its holding power and may even become completely dislodged. Also, to be effective, it should be somewhat heavier than some anchors discussed later, and for this reason and because the stock is at right angles to the flukes, it is a difficult anchor to bring aboard.

The yachtsman type is probably the most reliable anchor on a rocky bottom, except for the danger of the upright fluke's being fouled if the boat swings around it in a circle.

All yachtsman-type anchors are not identical. A fine anchor of the type referred to as "yachtsman" was developed by the Herreshoff Manufacturing Company years ago. It is properly called a "Herreshoff anchor." Other yachtsman-type anchors of slightly differing designs are often erroneously referred to as Herreshoff anchors. The design, width, and taper of the flukes of a true Herreshoff anchor are such that it is less likely to foul the anchor rode (cable) if the boat changes heading than some other yachtsman-type anchors. There is a yachtsman anchor so constructed that it can be disassembled for easy stowage. The shank can be removed from the crown and the stock can be removed from the shank, thereby greatly facilitating stowage below without sacrificing efficiency. If one wishes to carry a yachtsman anchor as a second or emergency anchor and wishes to stow it conveniently below, this collapsible version has much to commend it, for each of its three parts can be stowed separately in convenient spaces. In addition, a heavy anchor disassembled into three parts can be brought on deck with ease and assembled there (Figure 15-1).

One advantage of the yachtsman anchor is that in moderate to light conditions it requires less scope than other anchors discussed later. As our harbors are becoming more congested each year, and anchoring with adequate scope therefore more difficult, this becomes an important consideration.

Yachtsman anchors with dull pointed flukes should be avoided in favor of a sharp design. Some people have improved the ability of the yachtsman type to dig in particularly in hard bottom conditions by having a cylindrical piece of

Figure 15-1. (Clockwise from upper left) The most popular anchors are the COR plow, the Bruce, the lightweight Danforth, and the yachtsman (which can be disassembled). The authors recommend the plow as the primary anchor, the yachtsman as the storm anchor, and the Danforth as the third anchor.

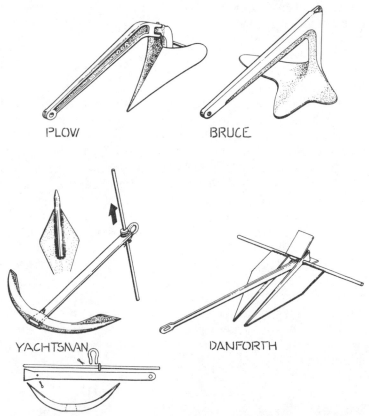

PLOW

BRUCE

YACHTSMAN

DANFORTH

steel with a sharp point welded inside each fluke. This requires that the anchor be regalvanized, but it results in an anchor that is excellent in hard-packed sand. The change does not reduce the anchor's holding power in other conditions.

The Danforth

The Danforth anchor has received more publicity in recent years than any other, a good bit of which has been in the form of commercial advertising. It enjoys a substantial following.

When the bottom conditions are right, the Danforth anchor is very efficient. For example, in sand it is the most efficient anchor. Similarly, in clear mud or in fine gravel it is excellent and reliable. It has the virtue of being light, and it is easy to retrieve and to stow. While it is not apt to foul the anchor rode in the event of a tide or wind shift, it must reseat itself if the boat's heading changes substantially.

The Danforth is excellent in sand or mud, but must be treated with caution in other bottom conditions. It is especially unreliable in heavy weeds because the flukes act as a rake; the weeds ball up between the flukes and the shank and prevent the anchor from penetrating the bottom. While not a frequent occurrence, another problem is that the anchor trips out due to a change of tide or a shift of wind in light-air conditions. If this happens with debris caught between the flukes and shank (can, rock, weed, or other bottom trash), the flukes can point upward and the anchor can become a skate.

As with the Herreshoff, there are a number of copies of the Danforth anchor, and the user should be certain that any copy is as strong as and has design features equal to the original. Danforths come in "Standard" and "High Tensile" versions—the latter advertised to be substantially stronger for a given weight.

The CQR Plow

In our judgment the most reliable all-around anchor is the CQR plow, for many reasons. First, it will penetrate to great depth. Second, it will not foul the anchor cable when the boat's heading shifts. If the current or wind shifts, the anchor does not have to reset itself completely since, due to the pivoting action between the plow and the shank, it remains embedded in the bottom as the boat swings. Third, the plow will not ball up with weeds. Fourth, it has as good a chance as any of fetching up on a rocky bottom, and a better chance than any other (with the possible exception of the yachtsman type) of finding a place to penetrate between the rocks.

The CQR anchor is not very convenient to stow on deck except in a bow roller fitting (which, of course, is not very efficient for an offshore racer). Yet this anchor is more readily stowed below than most other types because it does not have wide flukes or a shank. On many boats it can be stowed in a locker, under the floorboards, or in some other out-of-the-way location.

The CQR plow is made from hot drop forgings of high tensile steel, which makes it very strong. Again, a number of other types of plow anchors are made and the purchaser should compare them to determine that what he or she buys is equal to or better than the original CQR ("secure") brand.

The Northill

This anchor has some adherents because it holds very well, folds up for easy stowage, and is relatively lightweight. But it has some serious disadvantages, the main one being that the shape of the flukes is such that the protruding fluke will almost certainly foul the rode if the boat swings around the anchor. Constructed of stainless-steel plates, the flukes are sharp and can cut the anchor rode unless chain is used.

The Navy Type

A power boat belonging to one of us came equipped with a 250-pound Navy-type anchor and 300 feet of chain. Even with the weight of that chain the anchor was totally unreliable in anything but clear sand. It was replaced with a 40-pound CQR plow. As auxiliary anchors, the boat had a 75-pound Herreshoff and a 40-pound Danforth. It was never necessary to augment the plow with either the Herreshoff or the Danforth anchor. The boat weighed in excess of 70,000 pounds, and she never dragged with the plow.

The Bruce

This anchor was developed for use in North Sea oil-rig operations. It is made of heat-treated cast steel that is galvanized. It has good holding power in most types of bottoms; the large semicircular flukes dig well into soft sand and mud and it holds in many rocky conditions. The heavy shank gives a large weight-for-size ratio, which means that when dug in the Bruce holds on shorter scope than some of the other types. In conditions where the wind changes direction, even as much as 180 degrees, the Bruce is excellent at following around and not tripping out due to the relationship of the shank to the semicircular flukes. In semihard bottom conditions where one fluke may protrude above the bottom, the shape of the fluke makes it very unlikely that the anchor rode will catch and trip out the anchor if the boat swings without exerting a pull on the shank.

Stowage on a bow roller is ideal for the Bruce. Stowage on deck is difficult because there is no satisfactory way to shroud the flukes, and stowage below is cumbersome because the anchor is relatively large.

Anchor Weight

A rough guide often used in determining the weight of the primary anchor is that its weight in pounds should equal the boat's length in feet. However, another rule applies if the boat is used for cruising, and if she has a power winch and the anchor is normally stowed on a bow roller: in that case, *the primary anchor can be as large as can be conveniently handled.* There are several advantages to having a heavier anchor. It will bite in more rapidly than a lighter one, which means that a shorter scope can be used for given conditions. With it, the owner will have an anchor big enough for his or her next boat (which, presumably, will be larger than the present one). And, most important, the extra weight and strength will minimize anxiety when it comes on to blow.

Manufacturers publish tables that indicate the holding power of various types and weights of anchors they make and sell. These tables may be compared with figures given by the American Boat and Yacht Council that summarize loads put on anchors by boats of different sizes (see Table 15-1).

Table 15-1
TYPICAL ANCHOR LOADINGS*

BOAT LOA (IN FEET)	PULL (IN POUNDS)			
	MOORING	STORM ANCHOR	PRIMARY ANCHOR	LUNCH HOOK
25	1470	980	490	125
30	2100	1400	700	175
35	2700	1800	900	225
40	3600	2400	1200	300
50	4800	3200	1600	400
60	6000	4000	2000	500

*Excerpted from *Standards and Recommended Practices for Small Craft,* American Boat and Yacht Council.

Recommendations

We recommend that every yacht carry at least two anchors of different types and sizes. The following summarizes our preferences:

1. For the *primary anchor,* to be used in most conditions, we recommend the CQR plow. Our second choice for this anchor is the Bruce. In either case, we would choose the largest anchor that can be conveniently handled.
2. The *second, or storm, anchor* will be used when the primary one does not dig in, or when two anchors must be set in storm conditions. We believe that this anchor should be a three-piece Herreshoff-type yachtsman of a size equal to or larger than the primary anchor.
3. A *third anchor* should be carried if there is room below for stowage. This should be a Danforth type that is smaller than the primary, for use as a lunch hook when stopping briefly, or as a stern anchor.

That combination should give good protection in nearly all anchoring situations likely to be encountered.

Anchor Cables

A well-found offshore yacht should carry two anchor cables, or rodes, of approximately 300 feet each. Nylon is by far the preferred material because of its strength and stretch, which absorbs the shock loads in a rough sea so that the anchor does not pull out of the bottom. One of these rodes should be on the heavy side—about ¾ inch in diameter for a 50-foot vessel. The second can be substantially lighter for convenience in normal conditions. Used together in tandem with two anchors, with good lengths of chain at the bottom to add some weight to improve digging in, they will provide comfortable security in severe conditions. At both ends of the rodes, there should be eye splices with stainless-steel thimbles to protect the line from the shackles.

Figure 15-2. An all-chain anchor cable is preferred by many cruising sailors because it won't chafe and needs less scope than rope. But chain does not stretch. To put some give in the system, take the strain with a length of heavy nylon secured to the chain with a grab hook.

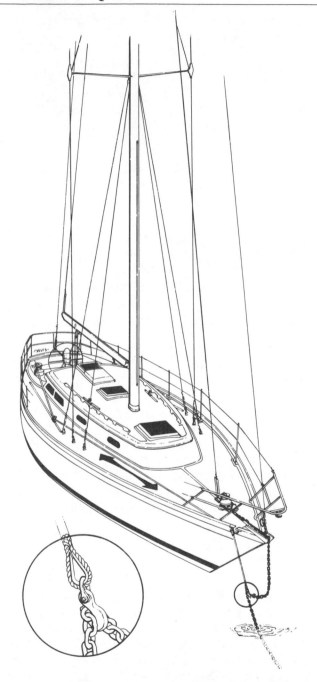

If you are likely to anchor over coral or in a harbor with broken glass on the bottom, it is the better part of good judgment to carry a short (15- to 20-foot) piece of chain which can be bent onto a nylon anchor rode. The likelihood of cutting a nylon cable on the bottom is not great, but it has happened. On many yachts a short length of chain is permanently shackled between the anchor and rode. In addition, rig two pieces of rubber chafe-guard or some equally effective material to prevent the anchor cables from chafing where they pass over a bow chock or through a hawse pipe.

On strictly cruising boats, where weight is not a consideration, an all-chain rode is often used successfully and, with a proper windlass aboard, is easy to stow. Chain will not chafe or cut, and it provides a beneficial catenary factor so that less scope is needed, compared to nylon. But in a hurricane, look out, for if the force is great enough to straighten chain out, there is no stretch and the shock loadings will dislodge any anchor. If you are caught in these conditions and it is not possible to put out a second anchor on a nylon rode, there is a way to alleviate the situation. Hook a chain grab hook, attached to a suitable nylon anchor line, onto the chain forward of the bow, and secure the line aft around the largest winch and to a cleat. Slack off the chain and take the strain on the nylon. The extra length of nylon allows some stretch in the rode (Figure 15-2). The stretch can be increased by further slackening the nylon line (make certain that the slack chain will not run out).

Galvanized chain should last for a number of years if it is rinsed off periodically with fresh water. Unrusted chain can be regalvanized.

Both nylon and chain rodes should be shackled to the anchor, and each shackle should be wired so the pin does not back out. Stainless or galvanized shackles may be used, but be certain that the rated shackle strength is at least as large as the chain and / or nylon rode. With both types of rodes, the bitter end should be stoutly tied to a through-bolted padeye below deck. In case of emergency, the rode can be freed by cutting the rope lashing. Rodes should be marked so the crew can determine the amount of scope used.

Bow chocks, hawse pipes, and hawseholes should be constructed so that they have fair, well-rounded surfaces to minimize chafing and are strong enough to handle severe loads. There should be two large mooring cleats through-bolted to the deck. All of this gear should be placed so that there will not be any acute angles where anchor cables pass by.

Buoys and the Stern Anchor

When anchoring over a foul bottom, the anchor should be buoyed to permit a secondary method of retrieval. Run a strong but fairly light length of line from the crown of the anchor to a small buoy. If the anchor fouls and will not come free when you haul on the rode, it will almost always release when you pull up on the trip line at the buoy.

In some areas, such as California and western Mexico, it is necessary to anchor with the bow into the swell coming into the harbor rather than into the wind. To align the boat properly, run out a light anchor from the stern. On some boats, the stern anchor and its equipment are permanently rigged, ready for use. This rig can also be helpful when kedging off after the boat has run aground.

CHAPTER 16

The Power Plant

George D. Griffith

Most boats are compromises—especially cruising boats, which are expected to be livable, floating homes that sail and can be moved at the whims of their owners. We would never expect similar flexibility in a land-based home. Every aspect of this bundle of compromises is affected, in one way or another, by the boat's power plant. The engine does several things. Foremost, of course, it pushes the boat through the water. On almost all cruising boats, it also makes electricity for lights, navigation instruments, and performance instruments. And on some boats, it helps provide refrigeration, ice, hot water, and potable water.

While power is not necessary for everybody, and some people have cruised many miles (and happily) without an engine, power must be considered a necessity on most cruising boats. As with many other equipment decisions, choosing the power plant for your boat requires that you first establish your own priorities for, and criteria of, successful cruising. The "ideal" boat for you will be as unique as you are. Establishing your special criteria requires thousands of decisions, big and small, and making them is part of the fun of boat ownership.

The process of identifying and meeting your special needs is even more fun if you make the right decisions. The notes that follow are intended to help you avoid mistakes as you analyze and provide for your power requirements.

Diesel or Gasoline?

With the development of small, efficient diesel engines, the question of using gasoline or diesel power has become moot. Still, for the record, we should review the various arguments.

Three negative characteristics of gasoline engines make the choice of diesel the most practical one for a cruising boat. First, gasoline is highly volatile and presents a constant safety problem. Second, gasoline engines have a much higher fuel consumption than diesel engines. And third, the electronic ignition system in a gasoline engine is susceptible to corrosion and other ravages of a saltwater environment.

While those arguments should convince you to prefer diesel over gasoline, just in cast you have your doubts consider some others. While gasoline engines are lighter and initially less expensive than diesels, these advantages are offset by the added fuel tankage needed for the less fuel-efficient gasoline engines, by the lower cost of diesel fuel, and by the higher resale value of a diesel-powered boat (the increase may well exceed the initial cost of the diesel).

Diesels come in low-speed and high-speed models. Low-speed, heavy-duty diesels have a record of lasting longer than high-speed engines, although some new high-speed, low-cost, lightweight diesels may well be just as enduring.

Performance

A typical displacement cruising boat can be easily powered to a speed in knots equal to 120 percent of the square root of her waterline length (LWL):

Speed under power $= 1.2\sqrt{\text{LWL}}$.

For example, a boat with a 25-foot waterline length should do 6 knots; one with a 36-foot LWL should do 7.2 knots.

At this speed, the boat will be building a pattern of bow wave and stern wave. Pushing the hull harder will increase the speed a little. However, the size of the bow-wave/stern-wave pattern will increase so rapidly with higher speed that the cost in fuel consumption and engine size will be very high. If your engine and propeller can push your boat at this speed without too much effort, they are right for her. But if your cruising criteria demand a higher speed, then you should opt for a different boat—either a longer one with a higher speed or one that is especially designed for powering with a large engine.

On the other hand, if your power package does not achieve this speed, it is quite possible that minor changes—for example, in propeller size and shape— would affect performance.

The Propeller

Engine performance is only as good as the propeller. The first consideration should be to deal with the mismatch that can occur between efficient engine speed and efficient propeller speed. Most engines for cruising boats run efficiently in the 1800–3000 rpm range, while propeller tip speed and blade areas work best at about one-half those speeds. The solution to this problem is to install a reduction gear on the engine to cut the shaft speed. But, as we said at the beginning of the chapter, compromises occur everywhere with cruising boats. The compromise here is that reducing shaft speed (and, with it, propeller rpm's) means that a larger propeller must be installed so that thrust is not lost, and a larger propeller adds drag and reduces sailing speed.

However, propeller drag while sailing can be dramatically reduced (Figure 16-1). On an exposed strut installation (typical in a modern separated-rudder, fin-keel design), use a folding or feathering propeller. If the yacht has a full-length keel with the propeller in an aperture, a good compromise between good thrust and low drag is to use a two-bladed solid, nonfolding or nonfeathering propeller, whose blades can be aligned with the keel when the boat is under sail.

If you see, or have in mind, a propeller installation that is uncommon, question someone about it. There has been considerable progress in this area both for racing and for cruising boats. Cruising people have benefited by the development of the low-drag folding or feathering propellers for racing yachts, and modern folding and feathering propellers are nearly as efficient as solid ones. However, some owners elect to have both kinds of propellers—the feathering

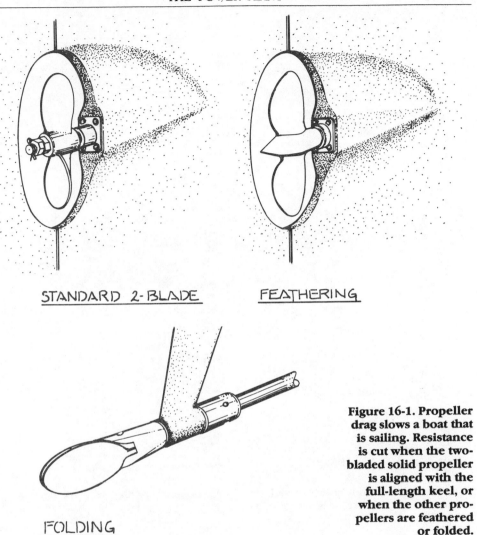

STANDARD 2-BLADE   FEATHERING

FOLDING

Figure 16-1. Propeller drag slows a boat that is sailing. Resistance is cut when the two-bladed solid propeller is aligned with the full-length keel, or when the other propellers are feathered or folded.

or folding type to be installed before a cruise that will be made mainly under sail, and a solid type for a long passage that will require a lot of powering. If the two propellers have matched machining, they can be changed in a quiet harbor without the necessity of an expensive haul-out.

Engine Location, Maintenance, and Insulation

The engine must have tender loving care, and that means good access so that you can easily change the oil and check the oil level, the water strainer, the belt drives, the shaft packing gland, and all the other important items. If you don't have easy access, you won't perform even the minimum maintenance. It is especially important to be able to reach a lost tool in the bilge. It's not enough to say, "I'll never drop a tool," because one of your friends eventually will.

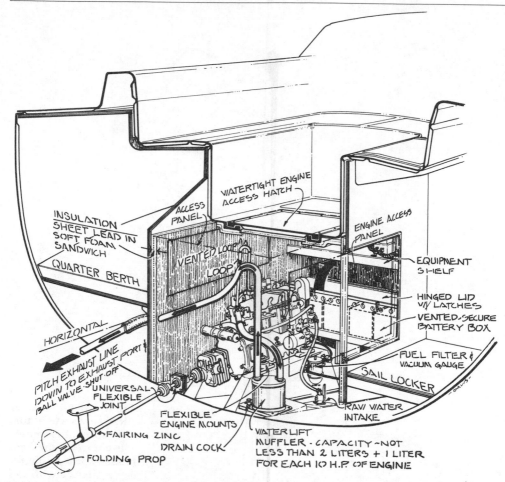

Figure 16-2. In a good engine installation, there is plenty of air and working space, and water flow is free and easily traced.

Unfortunately, the logical location for the engine—toward the middle of the boat where the motion is least and the beam, light, and general accessibility are greatest—is also the logical location for bunks and other people accommodations. This is a hard compromise to make in any design. Since guests aboard a boat generally find a way to adapt to less than perfect accommodations, and your engine won't, you should give priority to the engine so you can enjoy the comforts of a reliable power plant in a low-maintenance installation. The engine must have ventilation and cooling. A good installation will provide the engine with plenty of air space, and with a freshwater cooling system using a heat exchanger so that the engine never comes in contact with salt water (Figure 16-2); the best engine coolant generally is a rust-inhibiting antifreeze like the coolants used in automobiles.

The engine should lead to the propeller shaft either directly or though a **V-**

drive. Belt drives and hydraulic drives have been used to get around awkward installations, but they should be avoided because they are inefficient.

A key concern is that the engine must have clean fuel. Since fuel tanks collect sediment, many yachts have experienced fuel problems in rough weather, when sloshing about stirs up dirt. Of course, tanks should be cleaned periodically and before long passages, but it is just as important that fuel filters be installed in the line in an accessible location, along with water/particle separators. So you can monitor the filter's efficiency, it's a good idea to rig a pressure differential gauge or a vacuum gauge between the fuel filter and the engine.

One commonly accepted measure of a well-installed engine is the following: it should be capable of being operated safely and efficiently on either tack at an angle of heel of not less than 28 degrees for at least 2 hours. That is another way of saying that you should be able to charge batteries in a gale of wind without worrying whether the engine will overheat and burn out.

Exhaust and Noise

The exhaust system has to work well both while the boat is lying at anchor and while she is sailing at a severe angle of heel in rough weather. This means that there must be a high loop in the system to keep water from backing up into the engine, as well as a pine plug to shove into the pipe in the transom when you're running in heavy seas.

Like the ideal child, the engine must be seen but not heard. The best installation leaves the engine so quiet that you must look at the instruments to make sure that it is running.

This degree of quiet requires some special equipment. First, there should be a constant velocity coupling between the engine and the shaft. This type of coupling tolerates a large amount of misalignment and reduces problems with the packing gland. Second, the engine should be installed on soft mounts, which reduce vibration and noise transmission into the hull and propeller. Third, air intake and outflow should be through sound labyrinths, and there must be an air inlet silencer mounted on the engine. Of course there should be a good muffler—a dry-break or some other good type—and the exhaust hose should be insulated from vibration in the hull and accommodations. Finally, the engine space itself should be 100 percent insulated with a combination of sheet lead and soft foam sandwich; even a small crack in this insulation will leak considerable noise.

All of these factors are considered when making an engine installation. Many installations, however, fall far short of ideal for one reason or another and sometimes for several reasons. Many can be improved, but in some cases an all-out effort to perfect the installation may not be worth the expense if the engine is used only infrequently in order to charge batteries and power into the marina. Once again we see that the owner's priorities make all the difference.

Engine Auxiliaries

Most boats have a 12-volt direct-current (DC) electrical system for running lights, refrigeration, and other amenities. Some larger boats are equipped with the so-called "cruising alternator," which will generate 120 volts DC or AC (household electricity), which is fine if you want to use household appliances but has the serious disadvantage of turning out lethal amounts of electricity, whereas 12-volt DC is inherently safe. In our discussion below, we are assuming that 12-volt DC is the system of choice.

The technology as well as many of the parts come straight from the automobile industry. Of course, there are a few basic differences between a boat and a car. Since an automobile seldom uses electricity unless its engine is running, it can get away with utilizing the starter battery for the radio and lights for short periods of time. Not so with a boat.

On a cruising boat, electricity is used for long periods of time without the engine running. Therefore, sailors require a house battery system so that one battery is reserved and kept charged solely for the purpose of starting the engine. There is nothing more useless than an engine with dead batteries. A few small engines are equipped for a hand-cranked start, but they usually lack the gorilla needed to turn the crank.

The house system should be sized to carry a continuing electrical load. To determine the load, you must calculate the ampere-hours that you plan to use. Here is how to determine that figure:

1. Find the number of amperes used by each piece of equipment.
2. Multiply that number by the number of hours the equipment will be used between chargings.
3. Add up all the products.
4. Multiply the sum by 150 or 200 percent. The product is the desired total battery capacity, with a safety factor of 1.5–2.

The safety factor is necessary since batteries never seem to produce their rated capacity, especially if they age and the load is heavy.

One other reason for the safety factor is that owners often do not recharge batteries completely, as the last increment of charging can be time consuming. Automotive electrical systems use a voltage regulator to control the alternator as the battery is charging. As the system's voltage increases, the alternator's output decreases. This may work well in an automobile, but it is not successful in a boat because it only extends the time needed to recharge. You may want to install a manual alternator control, which permits you to override the voltage regulator and continue a large charge as the battery nears its full charge, thereby shortening recharging time. However, the alternator and battery can be damaged if this system is misused.

An increasing number of long-distance cruisers are using solar cells and wind-driven generators to charge their batteries. These chargers take up deck space, but work quite well when the conditions are right.

Batteries are heavy and need to be secured carefully so they will not go adrift and capsize in severe weather. They also must be well ventilated, as they may give off hydrogen gas, which is highly explosive, while being recharged.

At sea, there is no electrician to call when the lights go out. *You* are the electrician; know how to troubleshoot your electrical system. This means knowing the system's intricacies. Make sure that the systems are clearly labeled and that all connections are well made. If your boat comes with a wiring diagram, study it, preserve it, and take the time to trace all circuits. If for some reason you do not have a wiring diagram, make one. Every load connected to the system, every connection or terminal, is a battery discharger. A poor connection is a resistance and will use current just as well as a filament in a light globe.

Extra devices don't always place large demands on the system. A good example is a hot-water system, in which the running engine's cooling system is used to heat a water tank with no loss of power to the engine itself or to the batteries. However, refrigeration (covered in detail in Chapter 9) and watermakers take power from the plant to drive compressors and high-pressure desalinating pumps. Still, the power loss can be low in an efficient system. A watermaker can produce 20–25 gallons of fresh water for a gallon of diesel fuel. (A word of caution: do not make fresh water in a harbor, as the local water may contain contaminants that the watermaker's filter is unable to remove.)

Summary

In conclusion, we would like to emphasize that making a realistic evaluation of your priorities, needs, and cruising criteria is the first and perhaps most important step in developing a suitable power system. Even then, the chances are that the criteria will grossly underestimate the importance of the engine and the auxiliary equipment. Once you have enjoyed the pleasures of a quiet engine and ice cubes in your drinks, you won't want to go back to "the good old days" of wooden ships and iron men.

Wallace J. Stenhouse, Jr., contributed to this chapter.

CHAPTER 17

Emergency Equipment

Stanley Livingston, Jr.

I f and when you encounter a true emergency at sea, almost every aspect and part of the boat is, in some sense, emergency equipment. Therefore, the advice about hull and rig design and construction given in the other chapters in this book should be considered from the point of view of surviving potential disasters such as holings, fires, and man-overboard. Anything aboard that is not helping to solve the problems presented by emergencies is either superfluous, in the way, or a handicap. If it's not part of the solution, it's part of the problem itself. Here we will talk about specific items of gear that you should take aboard in anticipation of a serious problem. The emergency may never occur, but you don't know that.

Careful preparation is everything. Once you're out at sea, it will be too late to change your mind and order that extra-large life raft, those new flares and batteries, those good Type I life preservers. You will only be able to use the gear that's on board, and it had better be suitable, in working order, and located where anybody can find it (Figure 17-1).

Emergency Avoidance

Let's begin with some gear that is perhaps more properly thought of as safety equipment used to *avoid* emergencies.

Radar Reflector

One of these is a good radar reflector, which is essential when you are sailing anywhere near other vessels. The best kind is shaped like a canister: it presents many facets for another boat's radar to reflect off of, and, unlike the simple fold-up reflector, it has a smooth surface that won't tear your sails. Once you've hoisted it, ask somebody with a radar receiver to tell you how large the blip is at various distances.

Safety Harness

Another vital piece of emergency avoidance gear is a good inventory of safety harnesses, one for each crew member (not simply one for each person on deck) so that everybody on board has his or her own good harness to wear on deck at night, in rough weather, or when alone. The best safety harnesses are built like parachute harnesses, with wide webbing that is heavily and repeatedly stitched at attachment points in a way that distributes loads over the entire upper body. They should be easy to put on quickly in the dark over heavy clothing and foul-weather gear. The tether or lanyard should be as strong as the harness straps,

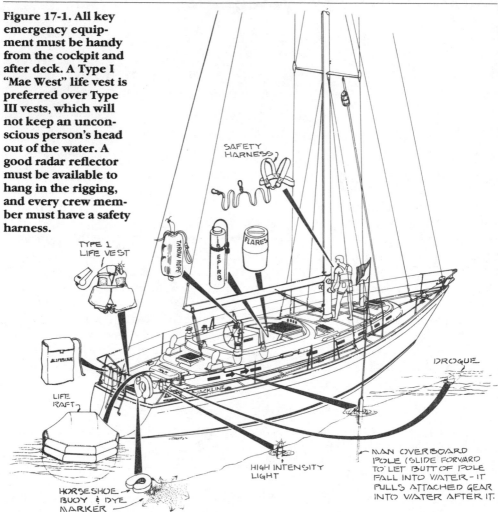

Figure 17-1. All key emergency equipment must be handy from the cockpit and after deck. A Type I "Mae West" life vest is preferred over Type III vests, which will not keep an unconscious person's head out of the water. A good radar reflector must be available to hang in the rigging, and every crew member must have a safety harness.

SAFETY HARNESS

TYPE 1 LIFE VEST

THROW ROPE

EPIRB

FLARES

DROGUE

LIFE RAFT

JACKLINE

LIFE SLING

HIGH INTENSITY LIGHT

MAN OVERBOARD POLE (SLIDE FORWARD TO LET BUTT OF POLE FALL INTO WATER - IT PULLS ATTACHED GEAR INTO WATER AFTER IT.

HORSESHOE BUOY & DYE MARKER

and its hook should be a strong carabiner type that will not open when under strain. Some people prefer to have two hooks on a 6-foot tether, one at the end and another halfway to the end, so they can shorten up; others prefer the simplicity of one hook, which they double back to the harness when the whole length of the tether is not needed.

The harness works only if the attachment point is strong. Lifelines definitely are *not* good attachment points; while the stanchions on a well-built boat should of course be through-bolted to the deck and constructed of heavy stainless steel, that is no guarantee that the wire in the lifeline itself will take the 2000-pound-plus load of a body thrown to the full length of the harness tether during a wild roll. Rather than snapping on to the wires, hook on at deck level to strongly welded stanchion bases, through-bolted padeyes and cleats, and sturdy plastic-covered jack wires or rope jack lines led between them. If the wire or line runs the length of the boat above and outside all running rigging (but inside the shrouds and lifelines), a crew member can hook on at the stern and go all the way to the bow without unhooking. Some people object to wires because they act like roller bearings when stepped on. A ⅜-inch or ½-inch line, such as a long docking line, is less likely to cause a spill and has more give to absorb some of the strain of a hard fall.

Batteries

A key ingredient in any safety or emergence gear that has an electric light is a reliable battery, so it deserves a discussion all its own. Batteries must be fresh, which means that they must not be allowed to die out. A good policy is to use only one kind of battery in ship's gear and lanterns so batteries can be interchanged: put brand-new ones in emergency gear and recycle old ones into on-deck flashlights and, eventually, into the light you use at home when walking the dog.

To remind you to change batteries on a scheduled basis—say, every 6 or 12 months—it's a good idea to write the date of installation on the cases with a marking pen.

Man-Overboard Gear

For rescue of a crew member who has fallen overboard, the first priority is to launch horseshoe buoys and poles with automatic high-intensity lights, drogues, and marker flags, all of which should be tied together with buoyant line. Some inflatable gear has recently appeared on the market, and it looks strong and handy, but unfortunately the Coast Guard has not yet approved it. Be sure to inspect the man-overboard gear frequently and replace it if it looks weak or worn. This gear must be accessible to the helmsman, who, in a two-person watch system, will be the only person left on deck after somebody falls over. He or she should be able to get it in the water within a few seconds, with no foul-ups and no lines to untie or cut.

At the same time, the gear must be stowed securely so it will not go overboard accidentally. The best system is to have a tube for the man-overboard pole set into the transom, but that is often impossible. Next best is a system using two large tubes secured to the outside of the lifelines. Everybody should try it out so they know which way to pull to release the pole. The horseshoe ring, light, and drogue should hang in special brackets on the stern pulpit—of course, connected to the pole by a line.

The "Seattle Sling"

A man-overboard rescue system recently developed by members of the Seattle Sailing Foundation has been thoroughly tested and has received favorable support as an innovative and successful retrieval system. It is now available on the market and is called the Lifesling (Figure 17-2). The unit has a ruggedly made flotation harness in the shape of a horsecollar, attached to 150 feet of ⅜-inch polypropylene line. The unit is similar to the hoisting sling used by helicopters

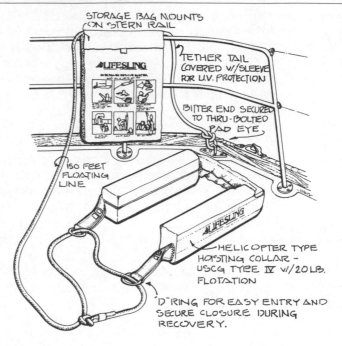

Figure 17-2. The "Seattle Sling," sold under the trade name Lifesling, is stowed on the aft pulpit.

with the addition of flotation. The harness is secured in a storage bag to the stern rail with the end tied to a stanchion.

When needed, the harness is thrown overboard and streamed astern (Figure 17-3). The boat is stopped as quickly as possible and then circled around the overboard member of the crew. The action is similar to that of a water-ski boat that returns the line to a fallen water-skier. When the flotation harness is within reach, the person in the water slips it under his or her arms. At this point the boat must be stopped *immediately* so that the person in the water is not dragged under. One or more of those aboard pull the line in and bring the swimmer alongside. The line is made fast to a cleat so that the person's head is clear of the water. The overboard person can then be hauled aboard by attaching a halyard directly to the harness. If the halyard is not long enough, there should be a specially dedicated length of line with snap shackles at each end to go between the halyard and the harness. Another method that can be used is to rig a 4:1 tackle between a raised halyard that is cleated and the harness (Figure 17-4). The tail is lead through a block on the rail to a cockpit winch. One person can pull another heavier crew member out of the water with either hoisting system, particularly when using a self-tailing winch. However, in rough conditions it is better to have at least two—one to winch and the other to assist the victim in keeping clear of the side of the boat and the lifelines. The victim may also come aboard via a stern ladder.

It cannot be said enough times that a key ingredient to rescuing somebody who goes overboard is the crew's ability to use the gear at hand quickly and efficiently. That means *practice*. Extensive experimentation with various man-

Figure 17-3. Steps in using the sling.
(1) Boat sailing on course.
(2) "Man overboard!"
(3) Boat is slowed by being steered into the wind as the sling is thrown astern.
(4-5-6) Using sails to help (backing jib to head off), boat is steered around the swimmer in the way that brings the sling closest to him or her (in either a circle or an ellipse). Swimmer should be able to reach the sling by the third circle.
(7) Swimmer grabs the sling. The sails are immediately doused. One end of a tackle is rigged to the main halyard shackle, which is hoisted 10 feet above deck. The halyard is cleated.
(8) The other end of the tackle is rigged to the sling, which is hoisted from the water with the swimmer.

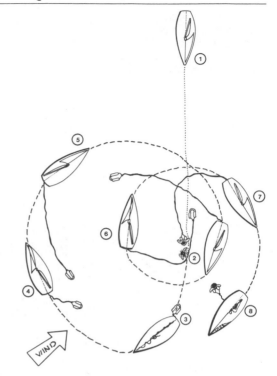

overboard drills by the Seattle Sailing Foundation and the U.S. Naval Academy proves that, with the right equipment, a competent, well-trained crew—even a solitary person—can recover a victim of this much-feared accident. The boat must be stopped immediately; the gear must be deployed; the boat must be returned to the proximity of the swimmer; and the swimmer must be brought aboard. All that is possible if the crew knows what they're doing.

Heaving Line

A good requirement for participation in offshore racing made by the Offshore Rating Council is to carry heaving line at least 50 feet in length readily accessible to the cockpit. Many yachts have met this requirement by carrying a unit made of a deck tennis quoit with 50 feet of light polypropylene line attached and neatly housed in a container screwed to a bulkhead. In an emergency, such as man-overboard, these units are extremely poor if not useless. Only if the line is uncoiled and carefully recoiled is there a chance that a heave with distance and accuracy can be attained. A second method used is a flexible line with a weighted monkey fist on the end. To obtain distance and accuracy with this requires skill and a great deal of practice.

Recently, a new system has been developed under the very active safety testing program of the U.S. Naval Academy. In this device, 60 to 70 feet of floating polypropylene line is stuffed into a small bag. There is a loop at each end of the line that sticks out of the bag. One end of the bag is open. The thrower grips the

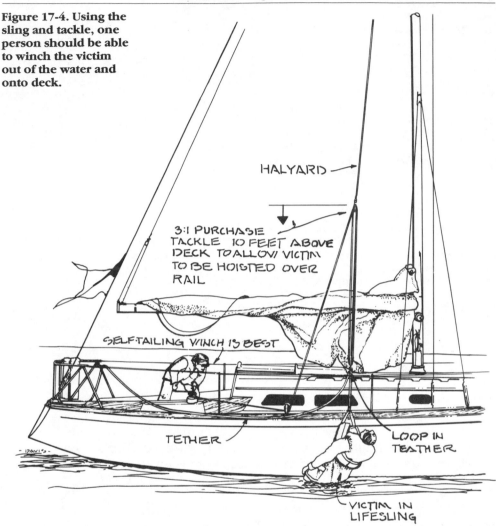

Figure 17-4. Using the sling and tackle, one person should be able to winch the victim out of the water and onto deck.

HALYARD

3:1 PURCHASE TACKLE 10 FEET ABOVE DECK TO ALLOW VICTIM TO BE HOISTED OVER RAIL

SELF-TAILING WINCH IS BEST

TETHER

LOOP IN TEATHER

VICTIM IN LIFESLING

loop at the open end in one hand and throws the bag with the other. As the bag goes through the air the line feeds out smoothly. With practice it is possible to be fairly accurate and to attain relatively good distance. Repacking the rope in the bag for future use also requires practice. At least one version of the throw-line rescue bag is commercially available (Figure 17-5).

Fire Extinguishers

At sea, most fires are caused by mishandled cooking fuels, short circuits in the electrical system, or overheated exhaust lines near carelessly stowed combustibles. Obviously, prevention is the best cure; in Chapter 10, Tom Young has much to say about the importance of good ventilation in preventing fires. But if you can't prevent a fire, second best is to have the right kind of fire extinguisher. The simplest is a pot of water to dump on an alcohol fire. Next is a fiberglass or

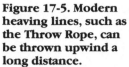

Figure 17-5. Modern heaving lines, such as the Throw Rope, can be thrown upwind a long distance.

Figure 17-5. Modern heaving lines, such as the Throw Rope, can be thrown upwind a long distance.

asbestos blanket stowed in a handy location near the galley so it can be quickly thrown over any fire.

Then there are the containers of liquid, foam, and carbon dioxide extinguisher to be sprayed on fires. The U.S. Coast Guard requires that fire extinguishers be carried on all boats equipped with engines (except boats smaller than 26 feet that have outboard motors without compartments in which fumes can be trapped). Regulations about type and size are quite specific, though multipurpose extinguishers provide the best all-round coverage for sailors. For information, see *The Annapolis Book of Seamanship* or *Piloting, Seamanship, and Small Boat Handling,* or contact your local Coast Guard Auxiliary flotilla.

Selecting the type of extinguisher is easier than finding good places to mount them permanently. Here are the basic rules for mounting extinguishers:

1. Each extinguisher should be accessible from two different directions, either from fore *and* aft or from above decks *and* below.
2. There should be an extinguisher near each potential fire source: the galley, the engine, and the main electrical switches.
3. Extinguishers should be located in open lockers, not closed ones.

Damage Control

Wheel-steered boats should have some way of rigging an emergency tiller, which should be strongly built and stowed in a handy location. Of course, every boat will have tools for ordinary repairs and emergencies, as well as a good bosun's chair with deep pockets for tools and a strap to secure a person aloft to the mast.

If the boat is dismasted, you'll need some or all of the following special tools to clear away the rigging to keep a broken mast from poking a hole in the hull: a sledge and spike to drive clevis pins out of turnbuckles; a hacksaw to cut rigging; and bolt cutters to cut through rigging. In addition, you should carry a spare propeller. There also must be a soft wooden plug for each hole to stopper broken through-hull fittings. (It's a good idea to tie each plug to the through-hull with a length of light line so it doesn't float away.)

Abandoning Ship

This is the big emergency. Typically, pump failure is the first step in this grim business. You should carry backups, but, still, there is no such thing as a pump that is too good. Clogging is the biggest pump problem; it is usually caused by paper, can labels, and other trash in the bilge. Obviously, care in housekeeping can prevent much clogging, but you should know how to clean a pump out before it jams up. There must be a deep sump where water can collect to be pumped out. Too many modern racer-cruisers lack this extremely important design feature, and the crew's socks get wet with even a cup of water.

It is hard to say anything constructive about life preservers except that, when you need one, you need the very best. While vest-style Type III life jackets are Coast Guard approved, the Coast Guard itself does not use them as they do not have sufficient buoyancy to keep an unconscious person's head afloat. That can be an important consideration in cold weather and water, when hypothermia can make a person unconscious. It's a good idea, therefore, to carry a set of Type I "Mae West" life preservers. They're uncomfortably bulky when worn in normal weather, but you won't need them in normal weather. They may save your life in an emergency. Obviously, they should be kept dry and given a frequent airing. Survival suits should be aboard boats sailing in very cold waters.

Flares

If you're going down, you should try to get help. With radio communications and the EPIRB expertly covered by Dick McCurdy and Tom Young in Chapter 14, I will skip to pryotechnics, A full set containing every type of flare is smart insurance. If you are in need of rescue, you will need red flares for signaling; if you are the rescuer, you will need white for answering. The worst thing about flares on most boats is that they are usually stowed in the lowest spot in the ship, which almost guarantees that they will be damp and hard to get at (assuming that anybody knows where they are). Flares deserve better. So do the crew members.

Flares must be kept dry—which means watertight boxes painted with a unique color so they are distinct from toolboxes and first-aid kits. They must be fresh—which means that they should be replaced *at minimum* every three years. And they should be accessible—which means stowing them in handy lockers.

The Life Raft

The life raft is the last and most important item on the emergency equipment list. If you're going offshore, spend the extra money on a good one that is *really* large enough for you and your crew (capacity figures sometimes are optimistic) and have it inspected annually by a professional. Stow the raft properly either in an on-deck canister (for example, on the cabin roof) or in an accessible cockpit locker that is not used for anything else. Stowing it below may clear up the cockpit, but you may never be able to get it back on deck when you really need it. If winch handles, light sheets, spare shackles, cameras, knives, tools, or other gear are stowed in the same place, there are bound to be problems either because the gear punctures the raft or because somebody closes the locker hatch on it, pinching it along the hinge.

Know the Locations of All Gear

As I have suggested in various places, a major problem with emergency gear is that, since it is rarely (if ever) used, it is taken for granted and left lying around in obscure corners of the boat. You must be able to find it if you want to use it.

An excellent practice is to draw an overhead picture of the boat on which all the lockers are clearly shown; the designer's accommodations plan will do nicely. On this chart, mark the location of every piece of emergency gear, then hang the chart in a visible location—say, next to the bookcase in the navigation station. Keep a couple of photocopies of the filled-out chart in a dry, secure place, just in case.

Alan McIlhenny and Richard C. McCurdy contributed to this chapter.

FIVE GOOD BOATS

1. *Adele,* by Ted Hood

Designer's Comments by Frederick E. Hood

Adele is a Little Harbor 50, designed in 1968 for fiberglass semiproduction boats. The hulls were molded to Lloyd's Scantlings at Tyler Boat Company in England and shipped to Maas Brothers in Breskens, Holland, to have the interior work done, and then finished off at Little Harbor in Marblehead. *Adele* was hull number three and was built for my own personal use and was raced extensively on the East Coast. She was sold to Richard Burnes in 1970. Mr. Burnes's previous boat was a Little Harbor 45, built in 1962 at the same yard, but with a steel hull covered with fiberglass and wooden decks covered with fiberglass. She was also a very successful racing boat in her day; her sister ship won the St. Petersburg to Ft. Lauderdale Race in the SORC in 1962. *Adele* was designed for offshore racing and cruising, as well as for shallow-water cruising; therefore she has a 5-foot draft and a centerboard. Three different models were tank tested at Davison Institute to get a good, all-around boat before hull lines were finalized.

The "split yawl-rig ketch" was chosen specifically for racing purposes rather than cruising, as it was slightly favored under the rule in most ocean racing conditions, of course, to the detriment of around-the-buoy racing. The split yawl-rig ketch was also helpful in cruising conditions before the days of roller-furling sails. The mizzen location in the cockpit just forward of the wheel is very handy to hang on to in a seaway and makes it very easy to trim the mizzen sail and mizzen staysails from the cockpit. The cockpit seats are long and wide enough to sleep on. Access to the main cabin is easy with no bridge deck to climb over, but with a high sill to keep out most cockpit water. It is very convenient for people working in the galley to communicate with people in the cockpit.

The flush deck in the way of the mast partners gives added strength and workability around the base of the mast when hoisting sails, reefing, and setting spinnakers. The small, raised cabin trunk forward makes it possible to keep all the hatches up, off the main deck, and gives the added headroom needed forward below deck, making the walking area of the deck very clear and free of toe-stubbers. At the same time, the edges of the small cabin trunk give extra, secure footing when crawling forward in heavy sea conditions.

The rig was considered to be a tall, high-aspect rig for its day, and proved to

257

be successful when racing as well as in giving good light-air performance when cruising with smaller jibs. The mainsheet is trimmed to a traveler just forward of the companionway dodger, keeping the mainsheet completely clear of the cockpit and other sheet winches. A roller reefing main was standard in the late 1960s, but was later changed to slab reefing.

Underwater, the centerboard is a high-aspect board with a thin cross section that proved very successful when going to windward. At one time the keel had 7 inches of draft added to it to give it a little more stability for offshore passages, which Mr. Burnes so frequently makes. The rudder configuration was half skeg and half balanced, which proved to be very successful and a good compromise. Experiments were made, full-size, on many of these boats with full skeg, half skeg, and large and small skegs. It was concluded that the half-skeg and half-balanced configuration gave the best and easiest control for steering the boat. In recent years it has been proved still further that the completely balanced rudder is most effective for sailing performance.

All in all, *Adele* is a successful offshore cruising boat; her sisters are often sought after in the secondhand market.

Owner's Comments by Richard M. Burnes

We have owned *Adele* for over fifteen years and have traveled up and down the coast and back and forth across the ocean numerous times. We have, naturally, met with almost all possible weather conditions, from boring calms to the excitement of a hurricane off to the east of Nantucket, and have gone through them all with ease and comfort.

The key to understanding *Adele* as an ocean-cruising boat is the strength and lines of her hull. She was designed in the late 1960s near the end of the CCA Rule prior to the extremes that the IOR has encouraged. There is nothing extreme about *Adele* except comfort. Her classic keel / centerboard hull, with long overhangs and ample beam carried well aft, give her a great deal of stability. The relatively low ballast-to-displacement ratio and soft chines create a hull that is easy to sail in a wide variety of sea conditions. She is easily driven with greatly reduced sail so that even in 35 knots of wind she can go to weather at 6 knots, with the off-watch sleeping comfortably below. Another factor about the hull is its terrific strength. In the worst sea conditions it is quiet below with very little banging or creaking.

The rig is straightforward and very strong with a single spreader. *Adele* was designed before all of the finicky gadgets that have been developed in the 1970s and 1980s and she therefore is a lot easier to sail than a more modern vessel, especially in difficult conditions at sea.

The cockpit arrangement is particularly conducive to ocean cruising. It is deep, with high-backed seats, and there is a large dodger that keeps everyone in the cockpit dry. An interesting feature is the forestay from the mizzenmast, which comes down to the middle of the cockpit and provides an excellent place to hold on. There is no bridge deck and one can move directly from the cockpit into the cabin down four easy steps. The galley is immediately on the starboard side and a large head with a separate shower is to port. This arrangement is

LOA: 49′8″
LWL: 37′6″
Beam: 13′1″
Draft: centerboard up, 5′3″ (with keel addition, 6′); centerboard down, 11′6″
Displacement: 42,000 pounds
Ballast: 12,000 pounds
Sail area: 1026 square feet

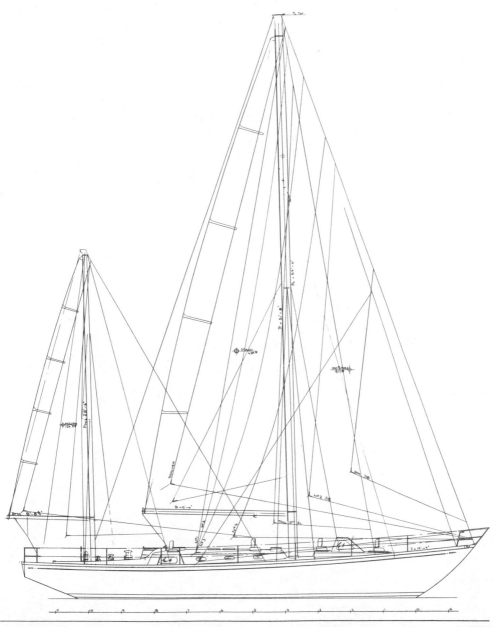

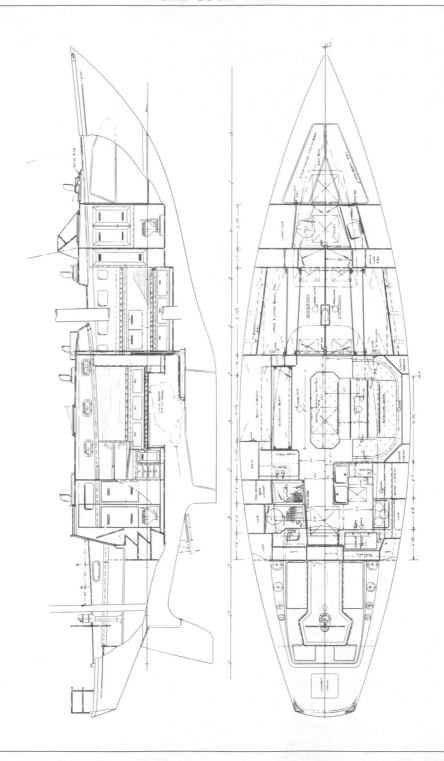

particularly satisfactory in rough conditions when the shower is used for stowing wet foul-weather gear.

The layout below has a large head forward, followed (moving aft) by two double cabins, one on either side, then the main saloon. It works well at sea because there are always a minimum of three leeward bunks available for the off-watch. In addition, the off-watch can sleep during the day, away from the galley and those talking in the saloon. *Adele*'s ample displacement allows room for a great deal of storage area; there are enough lockers and/or drawers to stow all of the gear for nine people for a month.

The engine is located under a midship's bench in the main cabin. This not only provides excellent access, but it also serves as an ideal bunk amidships during really rough going.

The galley is L-shaped, with the sink in the middle of the boat, so that people can work at it from both sides. A strap across the entrance makes it possible to brace yourself to cook at the stove in any sea conditions.

The light and air in the cabin are key features. There is a hatch with a canvas hood over it in the forward head which can be left open in all but the roughest sea conditions, meaning that there is through ventilation. The boat rarely gets stuffy, even in the hottest weather. There also are numerous opening ports and four Dorade ventilators. The main cabin has a large Plexiglas hatch, letting in light, and windows on either side. There is ample headroom, but it is possible—even for a five-foot-six person—to see out the windows. She is not a deep, dark boat.

Because *Adele* was designed before they began putting accommodations back under the cockpit, there are large sail and storage lockers in that area, making most gear readily accessible. In more modern boats, designers have built in so many accommodations that the layouts become awkward. This is not the case with *Adele;* she is a graceful lady throughout.

2. *Compadre,* by Bill Lapworth

Designer's Comments by C. William Lapworth

The story of Howard Wright's *Compadre* begins in 1958, when the late Hale Field was cruising a 50-foot yawl back to Newport Beach, California, after the Acapulco Race. The uphill course from Mexico requires a lot of motor sailing under mainsail and diesel. For one reason or another, the diesel packed it up. Hale sailed into one of the Mexican ports, tore the engine down, and sent to the States for parts. When the parts arrived, the engine was reassembled and the cruise was completed without further problems. However, there was one difficulty faced by the two couples on board during the engine overhaul: the engine was located just below the cabin sole. So when Hale later came to me for the design of a new cruising boat, among the several clear-cut requirements that he had was that the engine be located aft in an engine room, where it could be serviced, maintained, and, if necessary, repaired without disrupting the lives of all the human creatures on board.

Hale envisioned an arrangement that he fondly called a "wheelhouse sloop." Launched in 1965, this boat, which was named *Fram,* had a wheelhouse that contained the galley, the dinette, and a complete inside steering station where one could stay out of the wet and cold when that sort of thing was necessary. Under the wheelhouse was a room that housed the fuel tanks, batteries, and galley stores. In the most commodious area of the boat, between the wheelhouse and engine room, was the owner's "apartment," complete with head, walk-in shower, sofa bed, and a couple of berths for use at sea. The guest cabin forward of the wheelhouse was complete with its own head, but it was on a smaller scale so that, as Hale put it, "the guests won't stay too long."

In *Fram,* Hale cruised from California to Maine and back. She was the prototype for the Cal 46, and the hull was later used for the Cal 2-46. In 1975, Hale sold *Fram* to Howard and Jane Wright. After cruising in her for several years, the Wrights began thinking about a somewhat larger version that would give them a little more speed and comfort for the extended cruising that they were planning to do after Howard's retirement. In the new boat, we incorporated *Fram*'s best features, eliminated her faults, and added things that were missing.

First of all, *Compadre* is a larger boat. We increased the overall length by 9 feet, the waterline by 7 feet, the beam by 2 feet, and the draft by 1 foot. She has the same general layout as *Fram* except for a considerably larger guest accommodation and, forward of that, the crew quarters. *Compadre* was planned with the idea of living aboard for long periods of time while cruising. Her facilities are complete to the extent that at ports of call she need only take on food and fuel. A reverse osmosis watermaker eliminates worry about taking on questionable drinking water; it has enough capacity to take care of cooking, bathing, and use of the on-board laundry. The fresh hot-water system has a circulating pump so that hot water is available instantly at the tap, hence negating wastage of heat and fresh water. Air conditioning was not desired, but there is a hot-water heating system for all cabins in addition to the Luke fireplace in the owner's stateroom. Her hull and decks are of foam-sandwich fiberglass construction, which, in addition to stiffness and strength, provides both sound and heat insulation.

Compadre has proved to be a fine sailboat. She is strong, stiff, and comfortable, and has demonstrated good speed under power and—in spite of her motorsailer appearance—under sail. The dual-station hydraulic steering system has an auto pilot; a Luke feathering propeller minimizes drag when the boat is sailing. She has a Hood Stoway mast and Sea Furl system for the headsails, and her working sails are handled from the cockpit. An internal extension allows the main boom to be used as a cargo boom to lift the 11-foot Boston Whaler dinghy. To handle any mooring problems, anchors, 300-foot lengths of chain, and windlasses are located both forward and aft. If one wanted to race her to Bermuda, the only improvement I can think of right now would be a centerboard to reduce her leeway angle.

Owner's Comments by Howard Wright

Compadre has lived up to every expectation that we envisioned when we commissioned Bill Lapworth to design a stretch version of the marvelous *Fram* as a long-range cruising yacht. Since she was launched in 1983, we have sailed her from Los Angeles to the Panama Canal, through the western Caribbean and the Gulf of Mexico to the Intracoastal Waterway, and then up the east coast to the reversing falls at St. John, New Brunswick. We then went back to Charleston, South Carolina, and thence to Bermuda, the Azores, Gibraltar, and the western Mediterranean.

During these wanderings, we have not had winds much over 40 knots and seas larger than 10–12 feet, so *Compadre* has not been tested under storm conditions. The Atlantic crossing was, in every respect, delightful, and her behavior and treatment of her crew in what weather we did experience have been exemplary. Prior to the crossing, we made a few preparations for heavy weather. We fabricated removable Lexan storm windows for the pilot house and lower cabin ports. We also made provision for two extra berths in the lower cabin so the crew could move out of the forward cabin should we meet head seas.

As our voyage continued, the virtues of the arrangement became increasingly apparent. The accessible engine, generator, watermaker, and tool storage made at-sea maintenance and repairs very easy to perform. There is great merit in being able to see what's going on while cooking, eating, or navigating in the spacious pilot house, which also offers an escape from the weather. And the easy motion of the lower cabin makes for quiet off-watch sleeping. The large midship cockpit at deck level, with its opening aft, is most convenient in port, at anchor, and under way. The Whaler on deck serves as an additional storage locker, and the sizable open deck area aft is a great place to land a big fish—we've even caught a small marlin back there.

One rigging detail that we carry, and that no other boat I know has, is a gantline—a relatively heavy length of line running through a masthead cheek

LOA: 55′
LWL: 45′
Beam: 12′6″
Draft: 6′
Displacement: 50,000 pounds
Ballast: 15,000 pounds
Sail area: 1223 square feet

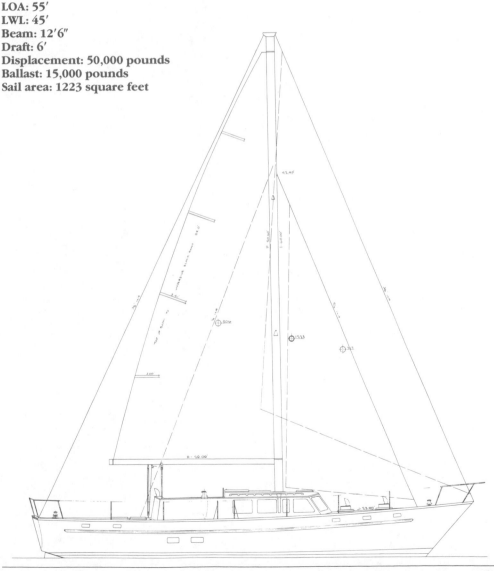

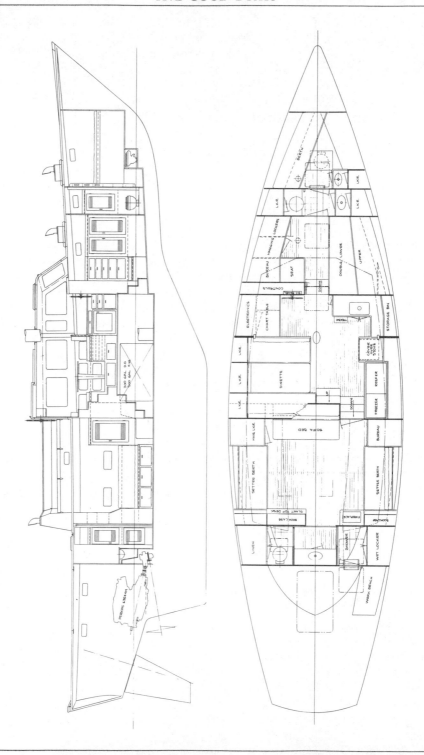

block down to an electric winch at the forward end of the cockpit. We lead the gantline through a sheave on the main boom extension to a sling in order to put the Whaler, the Avon inflatable, or the gangplank over the side or on deck.

We are delighted with *Compadre*'s sailing ability. We raced only once, in the Chesapeake, and were doing fine until we ran aground, and in other situations where we could compare speed we found that she was often faster than comparable-size boats, and sailed surprisingly well with larger IOR boats. She carries the sail plan quite comfortably, with reefing becoming advisable above 25 knots. With the Hood roller-furling systems, all working sails can be set, furled, or reefed from the cockpit; interestingly, we seem to set, hand, or reef sails sooner than experience has shown would be the case with conventional rigs.

The Perkins 6-3544 diesel gives a solid 8 knots at 1800 rpm. Including equal use of the 8-kilowatt Entech generator, our fuel consumption is about 2.3 gallons per hour. On the transatlantic trip, when we cut back to 1650 rpm, the speed was 7 knots and the fuel consumption (with the generator running) was 1.7 gallons per hour (an 18 percent improvement in efficiency). Thanks to the 15-gallon-per-hour watermaker, we seldom took on any fresh water. We did have trouble with the refrigeration compressor running off the main engine, but we were able to use the separate generator-powered 110-volt reefer unit, which worked fine.

In summary, after cruising and living aboard *Compadre* for the better part of two years and 25,000 miles, I can think of nothing of significance that I would change in her design.

3. *Wissahickon,* by McCurdy & Rhodes

Designer's and Owner's Comments by James A. McCurdy

In 1973 we were asked by a Canadian to design for production a fast cruising boat of sound construction. The proportions and details of the design were to be free of IOR influence. Our client felt there was a market niche for such a boat, particularly if built to first-class standards. This opinion was substantiated by a strong response to advertising. However, the usual problems of a new company, principally financing, delayed production for two years or so and in the end about twelve boats were produced under the name of Heritage 35 before the enterprise failed. Efforts by some Heritage 35 owners to revive the project were not successful and ultimately the tooling was bought by Cape Dory Yachts in Massachusetts.

Cape Dory produced five boats under the name of Intrepid 35 before a marketing decision terminated production. *Wissahickon* was the fifth and last boat. She has a custom rig by Hall Spars and other custom features put in both before and after delivery—all done with a view toward suitability for offshore use and local racing.

Displacement is on the heavy side (the displacement-to-length ratio is 352), sufficient to carry the weight of sound construction, complete cruising amenities and interior, and enough ballast for good stability. Ballast is externally mounted in a fin keel. The ballast-to-displacement ratio is 39.2 percent. The separate rudder is skeg-mounted. Beam is moderate by racing standards.

These design proportions produce a boat with good performance to windward that is at home in a seaway. Another result is quite good capsize resistance for such a small boat. The range of positive stability is 129 degrees and the capsize screening value is 1.61, well below the 2.00 limit that has been proposed to the Offshore Racing Council.

The hull is of conventional fiberglass construction, rather heavily built of single-skin E glass mat / roving pairs. Interior joinerwork is principally oiled teak plywood with a deck liner and a minimum hull liner mostly below the waterline. The hull-deck joint is an inward-turning flange with a teak toerail through-bolted. The engine is a two-cylinder Volvo Penta MD 11 C, 23 horsepower at 2300 rpm.

The heart of the electrical system is two separate 120-ampere-hour, 12-volt Surrette batteries. One hour's charging per day takes care of lights and electronics. There are no electric pumps and no pressurized water. The electronics consist of Datamarine sailing instruments, VHF radiotelephone, and Loran-C. The galley stove is a two-burner gimballed alcohol Hillerange with oven. The 6½-cubic-foot refrigerator is cooled by ice. There is sufficient stowage space for a transatlantic passage with a crew of five. Five berths including a double stateroom forward are provided. There is a full-size sit-down chart table. High fiddles and grab rails are provided throughout the interior.

The sloop rig has single spreaders and double lower shrouds. All standing rigging is Navtec rod with internal tangs. The backstay adjuster is an integral Navtec hydraulic model. Winches are Lewmar aluminum. The primary winches are self-tailing No. 44's. Steering is by Edson pedestal through a radial drive. The head of the rudder stock is squared and readily accessible for quick installation of an emergency tiller. Cockpit length is 8 feet, generous for a 35-footer.

Writing as her owner, I had *Wissahickon* built because we had been given such a free hand in the design that the boat fitted closely most of my own preferences for a cruiser-racer of her size. Although the design was 6 years old at the time she was built, fundamentals, as compared to fashion, change only slowly.

In the 7 years I have owned her she has done everything required of her. The traditional trophies of our yacht club have been won in local racing. We have enjoyed coastal cruising between Long Island Sound and Maine waters. The boat is very easy to handle and on many occasions the crew has been limited to my wife and myself. It is a pleasure to have others along because one would like to and not because it is necessary. The size and arrangements are right for five to cruise in comfort and for two to enjoy the boat alone. In the summer of 1985 we had planned a passage to the Azores in connection with a Cruising Club cruise to and in that archipelago. Circumstances made it impossible for my wife and me to make the passage so the boat was turned over to my daughter Sheila, who with my son Ian, Harvey Loomis, and John Rousmaniere made the 1900 or

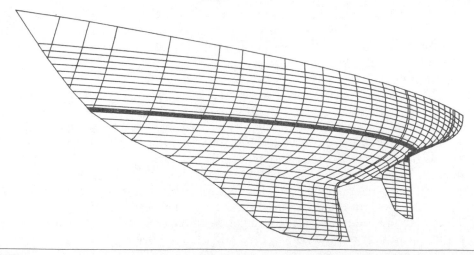

LOA: 35′
LWL: 27′3″
Beam: 10′1½″
Draft: 5′7½″
Displacement: 15,930 pounds
Ballast: 6250 pounds
Sail area: 570 square feet

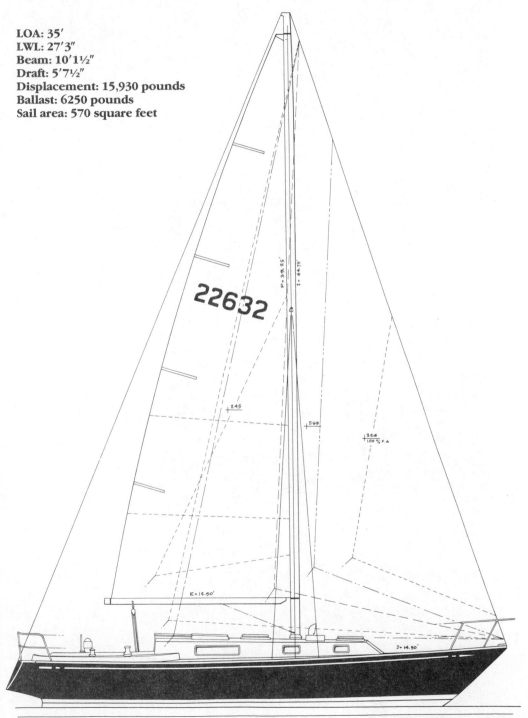

so miles in 14 days. They enjoyed themselves and I think *Wissahickon* did too, in a well-behaved way.

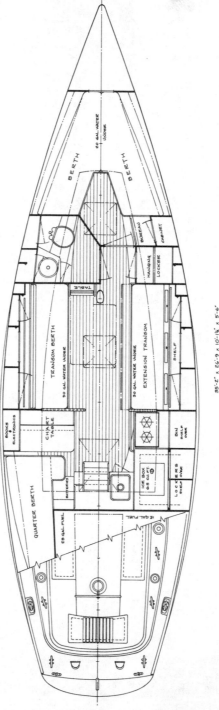

4. *The Pearson 386,* by Bill Shaw

Designer's Comments by William S. Shaw

The classic specifications for the design of a good cruising boat contain the elements of ease of handling, crew safety, good steering control, balance, ample stability, speed, and accommodations that are both functional and comfortable. The integration of these factors has taken on many forms over the years, often changing with technological and socioeconomic developments. Present-day materials, such as aluminum, fiberglass, stainless steel, Dacron, Kevlar, and high-strength plastics, have revolutionized yacht construction. Their use has made possible lighter, stronger, stiffer hulls, sails, and rigs capable of withstanding tremendous loads. Meanwhile, improvements in systems, especially sail handling, have made it possible for the small crew to control larger boats with relative ease.

As a designer of production boats for Pearson Yachts, I find challenging the task of melding these desirable characteristics into a given hull in a manner that will appeal to a number of owners as opposed to a single client. The Pearson 386, a design I did a few years ago, illustrates one solution to the very diverse requirements of cruising-boat owners.

The original specifications for this design called for a boat under 40 feet LOA with a keel draft of 5½ feet. The rig was to be masthead, of moderate proportions for ease of handling, but large enough to ensure fairly good light-air performance. Accommodations had to sleep two couples in separate areas, with provision for two additional guests in the main cabin. Both the galley and navigation center were to be located aft near the companionway and out of the traffic pattern going on deck. The power was to be diesel with the emphasis on performance, especially maneuverability. A separate stall shower was high on the want list, having proven to be a successful feature on previous designs. Since the boat was intended for cruising and possibly some live-aboard usage, locker and drawer stowage was emphasized.

The final design incorporates a number of features that deserve mention.

Today's harbors and anchorages are becoming increasingly congested, so a high degree of maneuverability is important. This was accomplished by using a separated keel/rudder combination, a form that I particularly like. This type of underbody is highly maneuverable under both sail and power, and boats still track well. Under power, they can be steered in reverse, which is especially important when working in tight quarters. There might be some criticism of the exposed propeller and shaft that is inherent with this type of underbody; however, when one considers the thousands of yachts in use today with this installation, the positives outweigh the negatives.

So much time is spent in the cockpit both under sail and swinging on the hook that particular attention was paid to comfort and safety when designing it. Fiberglass allows us to translate shapes heretofore impractical in other materials into contoured shapes suiting the human form. For example, the edges of the cockpit seats have large radii instead of sharp corners. The seats themselves are sloped outboard to meet high, angled backrest coamings, not unlike the shape of a well-designed chair. The top of the cockpit coaming is very wide and angles outboard, providing a comfortable place to sit, especially on a long beat to windward. On the deck, the side and foredecks incorporate a substantial bulwark rail with a teak cap. This configuration provides an excellent foothold when someone must go forward to leeward.

The rig is a simple, single-spreader masthead type, with the option for a removable forestay and running backstays. The main boom sheeting is attached to a traveler, which has become almost universal today as it permits better sail control. This is an important consideration as a cruising boat should be capable of a good turn of speed. Should the occasion arise when it becomes necessary to outrun a storm, good speed is certainly welcome. The traveler was located on top of the sea hood, which removed a major obstruction from the cockpit. In this location it is possible to rig a cockpit dodger and sun awning even when under sail.

Further refinements to the rig are possible with the addition of headsail furling and reefing systems. When sailing shorthanded, jib-furling systems make striking the jib or reducing its area a simple task compared with going forward and trying to smother the sail, unhank it, and stuff it into a sailbag that is always too small.

My last point on the subject of rig is the forestaysail. For the serious cruiser, this is a must. Under storm conditions, a headsail in this location provides better balance and it is safer to set than an outer jib. When sailing under normal conditions, especially when the forestaysail is fitted with a club, you have the luxury of tacking the boat without having to tend sheets.

Below decks, the arrangement follows the classic form for boats of this size and for good reason. For example, the galley is aft and close to the cockpit, making it easier to pass food on deck. Communications are better and the motion of the boat is less at this point, which helps keep pots on the stove and the cook much happier. The galley is U-shaped, which places the stove, sink, icebox, and lockers within easy reach and keeps the cook out of the traffic coming below or going on deck. The icebox lid is L-shaped in cross section, which means that part of the opening is in the vertical face of the box. This design makes it much easier to reach items at the bottom, especially for short people.

The navigation station is also close to the companionway for better communication with the cockpit and ease of access to the deck for taking bearings. While it would be nice to have a separate seat for the navigator, the layout did not permit this luxury. Sitting on the end of the quarter berth works quite well as a compromise. The large quarter berth also is an ideal spot for the navigator to curl up on between fixes, and provides stowage for duffle and sleeping bags.

Main cabin layouts can take many forms, such as uppers and lowers, a dinette

LOA: 38′3½″
LWL: 30′
Beam: 11′7″
Draft: 5′6″ (centerboard version, 4′4″)
Displacement: 16,915 pounds
Ballast: 7000 pounds
Sail area: 684 square feet

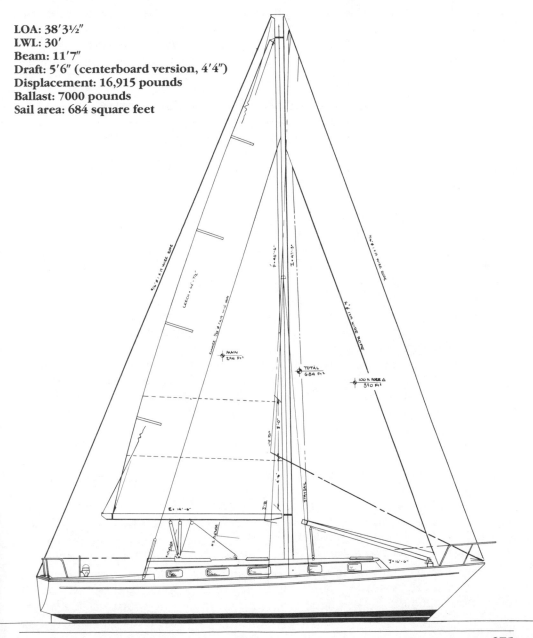

with single settee opposite, or, as we elected to do here, single settee berths port and starboard. This arrangement provides tremendous storage space behind the removable backrests. Also, there are additional storage compartments above, with locker doors and open bookshelves. The centerline drop-leaf table is fixed and has storage compartments in its center section for condiments, napkins, etc. For extensive offshore work, a gimballed table would be preferable as it would provide a relatively level platform.

Finally, the head has a separate stall shower, which is a very desirable feature if it can be worked into the arrangement. By providing a separate compartment, the rest of the area stays dry when someone takes a shower. It also provides a space to hang wet clothing, foul-weather gear, and bathing suits so they can dry off without getting other areas wet.

Owner's Comments by Thomas Hazelhurst

When God made the world I think He said, "I'm going to create a lot of beautiful harbors specifically for boats that draw less than six feet." So for those of us who derive a lot of cruising pleasure from gunkholing, a relatively shallow draft boat that has enough lateral resistance to minimize leeway and produce good upwind performance is a must.

With a draft of 5'6" *Baggywrinkle,* a Pearson 386, is that kind of boat and more. Following is what I was looking for and what I found in this Bill Shaw design. If the emphasis seems to be on sailing quality, that elusive ingredient that some boats have and others don't, I guess it's because I value that the most.

Extremely important is the ability to stand up in a breeze yet be nimble enough to ghost through the light spots and accelerate quickly. Heavy-displacement boats are terrific in over 20 knots of apparent wind, and light displacement will run away and hide from them in under 5 knots. The trick is to achieve that happy balance of form stability, ballast, and sail area that provides the ability to sail well over a wide variety of wind ranges.

My second criterion speaks to the first but from a different point of view. It has to do with the ability of the boat to be balanced up and down the Beaufort scale. Generally this means superlative steering and control, an easily adjusted traveler that is located out of harm's way, and simple reefing controls that, for the most part, can be handled from the cockpit.

I've never enjoyed being the last to cocktail hour so good to excellent speed potential on all angles of sail is a given, and, since I can't seem to get racing out of my system, the Pearson 386 allows me to be competitive under rules other than the IOR.

On deck, the cruising boat I like is somewhat conservative by today's standards. *Simple* is probably the best way to describe it. Sure, the coach roof and decks should be crowned slightly to accommodate water runoff, but they must also be flat and roomy enough for safety and good footing while providing room for an inflatable dinghy or, in its absence, a sun deck. I like moderate bulwarks, long and properly positioned handrails, good-size cowl vents, and a clean uncluttered look—all the tools you need to get the job done—no more, no less.

Cockpits are a favorite of mine. You spend a lot of time there. I like them big,

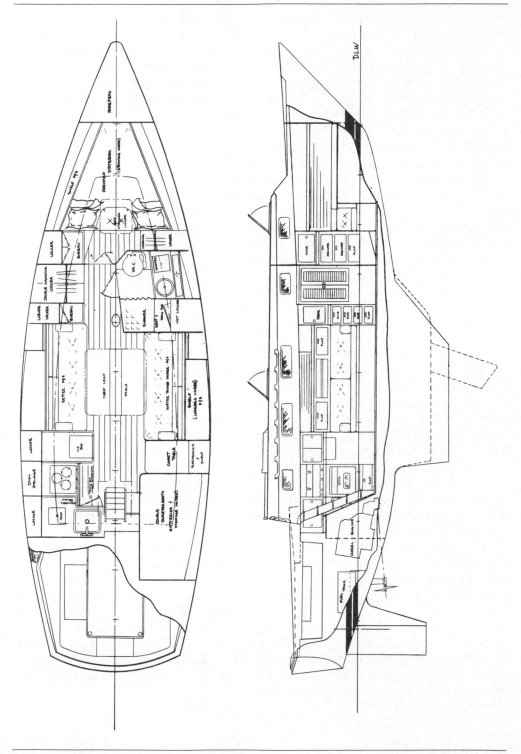

deep, and as anatomically designed as you can make them. For example, radiused corners, angled backrests, and a helmsman's seat that remembers that you don't often sail at no angle of heel. More than adequate cockpit drains are, obviously, essential, as is a deep bridge deck and easily installed drop slides. I used to like the steering pedestal forward enough to allow the helmsman to take advantage of the spray dodger's protection but the other advantages provided by placing the wheel further aft outweigh that consideration. It's fun to see the entire boat in front of you. And finally, I think winch and cleating islands should be wide enough for good footing and to sit on. After all, don't most of us sit up there anyway once the heel angle exceeds 15 degrees?

Below decks, again, I guess I must admit to my more traditional and conservative personal tastes. For offshore cruising purposes, I am partial to the wide-open spaces provided by what I guess is now referred to as a conventional layout: V-berths forward, followed by head and hanging locker, main saloon with settee berths, galley with navigation station opposite, and a quarter berth aft for instant access to the cockpit. This plan opens the boat up, makes passage fore and aft easier in a seaway, provides a big seating area for après sail gatherings, and puts the chef and the navigator where they ought to be—within hailing distance of the cockpit. And when the helmsman and navigator are one and the same, as I am most of the time, neither workshop is very far from the other.

Then there are the details that separate pleasure cruising from an adventure. Adequate tankage is a must: no less than 50 gallons of diesel and 150 of water. A separate shower may be considered hedonistic by some but, believe me, it's a delight after a day's sail and keeps the rest of the head from looking like a public locker room. Proper storage is obvious though too often neglected and, although none of us likes to admit it, water does have its way of seeping into the boat even if a loose stuffing box is the only orifice, so I'm somewhat fond of deep bilges and self-contained clothing lockers.

When engines weren't so reliable, great consideration was given to access to machinery for obvious reasons. Today I again revert back to my more traditional thinking and vote for a return to easy, complete access to all of the ship's systems. Half the aggravation of a failure offshore is caused by difficult or impossible access to the problem.

To summarize, I'm reminded of a delightful book by Farley Mowat titled *The Boat Who Wouldn't Float*. I've been fortunate to have had the opportunity to steer a lot of different boats. Comparison of sailing qualities is inevitable. *Baggywrinkle* is a boat who *will* sail magnificently. She more than meets the test of "tilt"—the ability to be easily worked and comfortable at a 15-degree angle of heel for hours or days at a time. She also meets the aforementioned criteria.

Would I change anything? Sure. In retrospect I'd like to have a pilot berth, more for lining up seabags on short cruises than for sleeping. I'd also like through-gunwhale chocks that would force dock lines to be run consistently and preclude spring line chafing that, in turn, precludes varnish.

5. The Seguin 44 *First Light,* by Sparkman & Stephens

Designer's Comments by Roderick Stephens, Jr.

First Light, owned by James C. Pitney, is a Seguin 44 built by Lyman-Morse Boatbuilders, Thomaston, Maine. When Cabot Lyman and S&S began working together on the concept of the Seguin 44 in the spring of 1980, we agreed that fiberglass construction offered the greatest flexibility for our purpose, which was to provide a fast, seaworthy, easily handled offshore boat on a semi-custom basis so that certain features could be tailored to an owner's special requirements. The hulls would be constructed from Airex-cored fiberglass using the same mold, thus saving time and money in both lofting and tooling. However, we came up with four innovative ways to customize the boat for individual owners.

One of these customizing methods was to leave the hull molds open at the aft end so that an owner could choose between reverse and traditional transoms in either of two lengths. With the short reverse transom, the overall length is 43'1"; with either the traditional or the extended reverse transom, the LOA is 45'9½". Second, the mold was made so that it could accept either one of three different external keels: a keel-centerboard with a draft of 5'3"; a cruising keel with a draft of 6'3"; or a fin keel with a draft of 7'9". A third way to allow owners some freedom of choice was to provide for houses and cockpits of different lengths and shapes by building separate molds for the deck, cockpit, and house. The owner can select a long or short house, and couple it with a T-shaped, midship, or traditional cockpit. Finally, owners living in light-air regions could order a special tall rig 24 inches higher than the regular rig. For *First Light* Jim Pitney opted for the extended reverse transom, the deep fin keel, the short house, and the tall rig.

Sparkman & Stephens has produced more than 2500 designs over a 58-year period, and among the concerns that go into any new boat is the accumulated experience of sea trials and racing. One of the goals in the design of the Seguin 44 was to provide a handsome boat; another was to give her a good turn of speed; and a third was to make her strong. The aesthetic intent was to design a distinctly American-looking cruising boat with a large sweep to the sheer and graceful overhangs. The bow overhang provides reserve buoyancy should the boat be forced into a bow-down condition—say, when surfing down large waves. The stern overhang is proportioned to balance the bow overhang visually; and as the boat heels, her effective waterline is lengthened. The house was kept low and short to accentuate the gracefulness of the hull.

The Seguin 44's hull has fairly rounded sections, which provide low wetted area and help light-air performance. Displacement is considered to be moderate. In terms of performance and construction, the boat has met her design criteria: in the 1985 Marion-Bermuda Race, handicapped under the Measurement Handicap System (now the International Measurement System), Class B was won by *Alert,* a centerboard 44. Constructed to American Bureau of Shipping scantlings, Seguin 44's have held up well offshore and through hard groundings; during Hurricane Gloria, one 44 wasn't even holed when she dragged onto the Amtrak stone roadway at Stonington, Connecticut.

Another important goal was to build an offshore cruiser that could be handled easily by a couple. Therefore, the cutter rig was chosen, two small jibs being easier to handle than one big one. For light-air sailing, to allow a large genoa to be tacked with minimum interference, we made the forestay readily removable so it could be taken back to the mast. Although the inertias of the double-spreader rigged mast are sufficient to withstand the loads imposed by the righting moment and sail area, running backstays are provided in order to give it extra support in adverse conditions.

The running rigging and sails are as recommended in Chapters 12 and 13, but we would like to emphasize certain features:

- Halyards are led internally in the mast in order to cut windage, and are made of low-stretch rope (instead of wire) to make handling easier.
- The mainsail, jib, and forestaysail winches are placed on the mast in order to facilitate raising and dousing jibs in shorthanded situations.
- To make it easier to walk forward, the spinnaker pole stows against the mast instead of on deck.
- The boom vang is a 6:1 rope tackle, which works more quickly than a hydraulic vang and does not leak fluid. The preventer runs from the end of the boom, in order to minimize load on the system, to a block forward of the main chain plate, and then back to secondary winches on the forward end of the cabin roof.
- The storm forestaysail is set on the forestay with its tack on a 24-inch pendant so that the foot will not catch and be burst by a wave breaking across the deck. This sail trims to the same lead block that the regular forestaysail uses; when making a sail change, the crew does not have to spend time adjusting the lead position.
- The mainsail and the storm trysail are set with slides on the mast on separate, parallel luff tracks so that the trysail can be rigged early and then set easily.

The cockpit is smaller than would be expected on a boat of this size so that it will drain quickly if filled by a wave. It does not have a bridge deck. The two 10-pound propane tanks are stored in a molded-in locker in the cockpit.

LOA: 45′9½″
LWL: 33′6½″
Beam: 12′10″
Draft: 7′9″
Displacement: 27,400 pounds
Ballast: 10,500 pounds
Sail area: 958 square feet

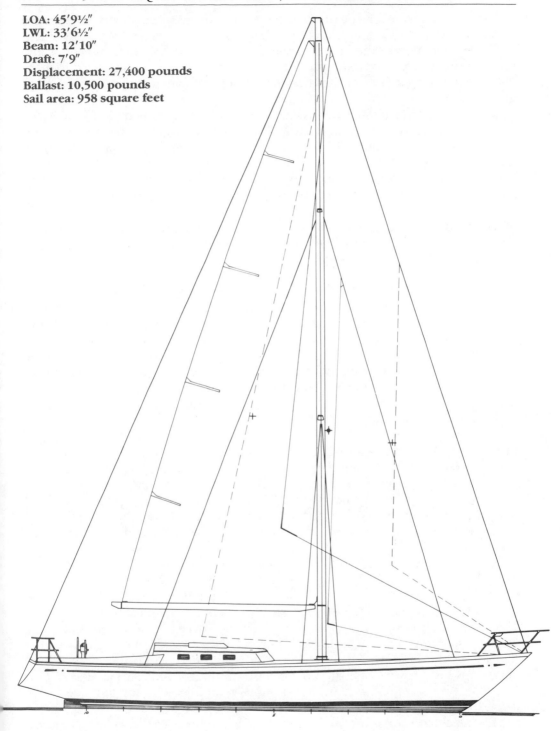

Ventilation has received considerable attention. Five 6-inch Dorade vents are in place, and there are several deck hatches placed on or close to the centerline. With the exception of the lazarette hatch, the hatches have their hinges on the forward side so that a wave from the bow cannot get under the lips and rip them off. For heavy weather, the hatches have Dacron tent-type covers using edge grooves.

Below, the arrangement was designed with offshore cruising in mind. A wet locker and seat are placed adjacent to the companionway so that foul-weather gear can be pulled on and off while sitting down, close to the cockpit. The galley and head sinks are located close to the centerline so they will drain properly if the boat is heeling considerably. In the bilge is a sump fed by large limber holes so bilge water drains to one central point, where the intake for the bilge pump is led. Bilge pumps can be operated both on and below deck. The engine is hidden under the centerline counter, with good access provided by large removable panels on all four sides. The entire box over the engine can be removed for major engine work, if necessary.

Owner's Comments by James C. Pitney

In 1982 my wife, Mimi, and I were looking for a boat to replace our Swan 40, on which we had enjoyed many happy and memorable cruises for the ten years that we owned her. We wanted a slightly larger and more powerful vessel with more stowage space and ease of access to the engine and equipment below deck. We had some very definite ideas, few of which were available in any stock boat on the market. Then we learned of the Seguins designed by Sparkman & Stephens and built by Lyman-Morse Boatbuilding Company. A total of twelve Seguins have been built, of which ours is Number 9.

The boat is rigged as a cutter. We chose the tall mast ($I = 57$ feet) for speed in light air. A double-head rig and jiffy reefing enable us to shorten sail with relative ease even when shorthanded. We have avoided roller-furling sails out of fear (perhaps through inexperience with it) that it may sometime jam on an offshore passage when the need to reduce sail in a hurry is greatest. Instead, we have rigged old-fashioned lazyjacks on the boom; they have simplified the handling and furling of a slippery, resin-impregnated mainsail. We have never regretted the choice.

We also opted for a short coach roof giving our vessel a flush deck from approximately 4 feet abaft the mast forward to the bow. This not only makes for a commodious deck area; it also makes for a beautiful profile. The boat is reminiscent in appearance to *Yankee Girl,* surely one of the loveliest boats ever built. The flush deck is not without its trade-offs, however, all of which had to be worked out well in the final design. There is 6'4" of headroom throughout the interior of the boat, which is achieved by a step down into the main saloon amidships just forward of Station 6. Because of this, the tankage on *First Light* is less than on the other Seguins, but is more than adequate for our needs. We carry 133 gallons of water and 77 gallons of fuel.

The deck and the top of the coach roof are both teak planked, making for superb footing in the roughest and wettest weather. The cockpit is T-shaped with seats that are 6 feet in length, enabling crew members who are on watch to sleep comfortably and yet be available to the helmsman on a moment's notice. Under the port seat is an enormous sail locker and a separate compartment for two propane tanks for the stove. An eight-man Avon life raft is mounted on top of the coach roof. Rod Stephens persuaded us not to have any break for a gangway in the lifelines for safety reasons. The two oversize primary winches (Lewmar three-speed 65s) are mounted outboard of the cockpit. The two secondary winches (Lewmar 55s) are mounted on the forward part of the coach roof. The starboard secondary winch doubles as a windlass, there being a clear run to the bow roller. This has proved to be a wonderful feature enabling us to pull up nylon anchor rode and 20 feet of chain (clear of the deck) without effort. In this way, we handle our 45-pound CQR plow anchor and our 75-pound Luke three-piece anchor (which we used constantly in the summer of 1984 on our cruise to Labrador) with ease. As a result, the electric windlass on the foredeck sees relatively little use.

The boat is extremely well ventilated. There are five Dorades, one in the forward part of the forward cabin, two amidships, and two in the coach roof. One of the midships Dorades is over the head and one of the after Dorades is over the galley. There are five hatches, one 31½ by 31½ inches over the forward cabin, one slightly smaller over the saloon, plus three smaller hatches—one over the head, one over the galley, and one over the aft cabin. We have four opening ports on each side of the coach roof, and two opening ports on the starboard side of the cockpit well (which open into the after cabin).

The interior of *First Light* is a custom job and reflects the owners' concepts under the guidance of the builder and the designer. One basic decision made early on was to have only one head. Although some of the other Seguins have two heads, we felt that this was an enormous waste of space. (How often are two heads on a 46-foot boat in use at the same time?)

The interior gives the appearance of a wooden boat. The predominant wood is ash with teak trim. Since the ceilings, bulkheads, and overhead are all made of ash, the boat looks distinctly Scandinavian. Drawers, doors, drip rails, grab rails, overhead beams, and vertical corners at the junction of bulkheads are for the most part made of teak, as is the companionway ladder.

There are lockers immediately aft of the main companionway under the cockpit sole in which our Avon dinghy and compressor for refrigeration are located. To the left of the companionway and aft is a seat on top of the deep freeze where one can take off sea boots. Immediately aft of the seat is a large hanging locker for foul-weather gear and boots. The U-shaped galley on the port side is designed to simplify cooking at sea. Outboard aft is the refrigerator, immediately forward of which are the stove and a dry locker. Twin sinks form the bottom of the U and the engine box furnishes the cook with support when on the port tack. The engine box itself is worthy of the master craftsman who built it. It is made entirely of wood. By undoing two catches, we can have complete access to the Perkins 4:108 diesel below.

Immediately to the starboard of the main companionway is an enclosed cabin which contains a double berth extending under the seat on the starboard side of

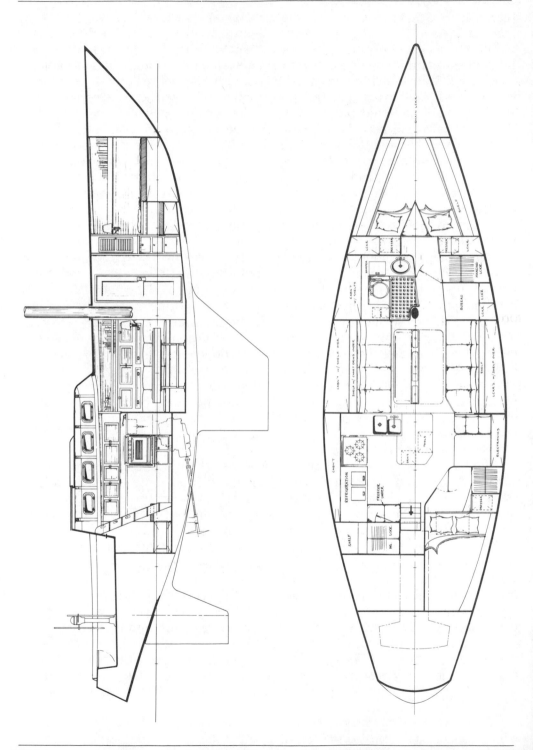

the cockpit. The cabin has its own closet and dresser. Forward of the after cabin is the navigator's station facing aft to simplify communication with the helmsman.

There is a passage between the engine box and the navigator's station on the starboard side with a step down into the main saloon. In the main saloon are two large bunks which pivot on the forward end to increase their width aft. The backrests of these bunks give access to six lockers for clothes. Above them are cupboards fore and aft with bookshelves in between. On the port side immediately above the backrests are two deep lockers for chart storage on extended cruises.

A large head is on the port side. Opposite it are a bureau and hanging lockers, with a passage in between. The forward cabin contains lockers and dressers and a double berth. Under the berth is sufficient space for a spinnaker and a variety of other sails.

Because we intended to do further cruising in northern waters (Nova Scotia, Newfoundland, and Labrador), we installed two Espar diesel forced-hot-air heaters which have outlets in the foul-weather gear locker, aft cabin, main saloon, head, and forward cabin.

First Light is a joy to sail and lovely to behold. On her shakedown cruise in November 1983 the two of us brought her down alone from Maine to New Bedford in a breeze gusting up to 40 knots. The following summer we took her as far as the Mugford Tickle (two days beyond Nain) in Labrador and returned. For most of that cruise we had one or two other couples aboard. The boat is capable of taking us in comfort and with speed anywhere in the world. In our book, she represents the best possible compromise between a standard hull and a custom boat, and reflects great credit on the designer and builder, both of whom guided the owners throughout the period of construction.

APPENDIXES

A Checklist for Offshore Sailing

At minimum, the following equipment checks should be carried out before you head out on an offshore passage.

Hulls and Decks

Hull

Check all through-hull fittings and sea cocks to see that they are lubricated and operating freely. Make a wooden plug for each hole and secure it to the through-hull fitting with a lanyard (also make a plug for the engine exhaust). Examine hoses and hose clamps, and replace them if they are worn or cracked.

Pumps, Drains, and Watertightness

There must be a sump for bilge water in the deepest part of the bilge into which is led the intake hose of a hand-operated, high-capacity bilge pump in excellent operating order. There must also be at least one backup manual pump. The bilge must be cleared of paper, sawdust, and any other objects that might clog either the intake or the limber holes between compartments. Inspect bilge pumps and try them out at various angles of heel. If necessary, install additional intake hoses to reach corners of the bilge. Make certain that spare parts and handles are aboard and accessible. Pump handles on deck should be secured to the boat with lanyards to prevent accidental loss. Fill the cockpit with fresh water to test its draining speed and to look for leaks.

Steering

Examine every component of the steering system. If it works with a cable, the wire should be properly tensioned (with the tensioning device locked) and unfrayed. The cable sheaves should be well lubricated so they turn easily. If the boat has a wheel steering system, mark the king spoke and make sure it is vertical when the rudder is centered, and be sure that the emergency tiller fits and can be worked.

Lifelines

Make sure that stanchion bases are bolted through the deck. Test the lifelines by tying a line to the middle, halfway between stanchions, leading the line to a block on the rail and then to a winch, and pulling down so there is 200–300 pounds of strain on the wire. The lifeline should take the pull. At the ends of the lifelines, rig toggles so the turnbuckles do not bend. Double-check all clevis and cotter pins as well as the security of stanchion set screws. Rig jack wires or lines on deck for safety harnesses.

Below

Stowage

Make sure that all heavy items, such as the stove, the ice-chest lid, storage batteries, tools, and the spare anchor, will not come loose or fall out if the boat is rolled over.

Watertightness

With a hose, spray dodgers, ports, hatches, vents, and the mast boot to test for leaks. In anticipation of heavy seas, carry deck plates to fill vent holes and shutters to cover windows.

Companionway

The hatch boards (slats) must be sturdy and must be secured against falling out when the boat is rolled. The ladder must be secured positively.

Rigging and Sails

Standing Rigging

Carefully inspect all shrouds, turnbuckles, toggles, and spreaders for signs of chafing, fatigue, or failure. No rough edges should be exposed to wear on sails and lines. With 1 × 19 rigging, visually inspect the lower swaged fittings for longitudinal cracks or rust lines caused by water penetration of the swage. Cracked fittings should be replaced. Give the "blind man's test" to 1 × 19 wire: run your fingers up and down to detect any loose wires that protude abnormally. The diameters of clevis pins should match those of the holes in which they fit. Be sure that all cotter pins are in place and properly taped. Carry a spare upper shroud with an eye in one end and mechanical fittings for making an eye in the other end.

Mast

Make certain that the heel of the mast is fastened to the mast step.

Running Rigging

Inspect halyards, sheets, reefing lines, and shackles for signs of wear, fatigue, and failure. Halyards and reefing lines should have Flemish eyes to allow the attachment of messenger lines for reeving. If sheet and halyard leads are bad or inefficient, relocate them. Check winches for smooth operation and proper lubrication. Make sure there is a lock-in handle for winches mounted on the mast and boom.

Sails

Carefully inspect all stitching and hardware for fatigue and wear. If in doubt about a sail's strength, send it to the sailmaker for repair well before your departure date. Raise and lead the sheets for the storm jib and storm trysail to make certain that everything works.

Auxiliary Equipment

Instruments

Run all electronic equipment, checking for noise as described at the end of Chapter 14. Double-check connections. Make sure there are plenty of extra fuses. Have the EPIRB checked out. Renew batteries and bulbs in all man-overboard lights and flashlights. Carry plenty of extra batteries and bulbs below. Equip the navigation station with the requisite number and types of navigation publications.

Ground Tackle

Make sure that you are carrying the right types of anchors and sufficient lengths of rode (including plenty of chain) for the harbors in which you will anchor. Be prepared to lay out two heavy anchors on long rodes in a storm.

The Power Plant

Renew fuel and lubrication filters. If possible, drain the fuel tanks dry to remove any accumulated water and sediment. Check storage batteries to be certain that they are sturdily secured and in good condition.

Emergency Equipment

Carefully examine all man-overboard gear for wear; try it out several times in a variety of conditions so the crew knows how to use it. Have a professional inspector (name available from the manufacturer) inspect the life raft. Stow the life-raft container on deck so one person can quickly drop the raft overboard and inflate it from approximately amidships, so it is in the lee of the house. There must be a strong safety harness and buoyant life jacket for each person on board. With a physician's advice, compile a good first-aid kit; ask crew members if they have any special medical needs. Renew flares and stow them in an accessible, dry, and clearly marked locker below. Provide an emergency water supply in a separate, sturdy, and clearly marked plastic container.

Gear to Carry

Following are introductory lists of general and spare equipment to be carried. The locations of nonfixed equipment and spare parts should be clearly marked on an overhead boat plan posted near the chart table.

General Equipment

Bags or pouches for holding small items
Banding kit with tensioning device and roll of ½-inch stainless-steel
    strap
Bosun's chair or sling
Buckets with lanyards (for emergency bailing)
Diving mask and swim fins (for inspecting underwater)
Drift pins and a large hammer or sledge to knock out clevis pins

Emergency compass
Emergency radio antenna
Emergency running lights (battery powered)
Emergency tiller
Engine oil and filters
Grease, spray, and liquid lubricants
Lead line
Light line (marline, nylon, and Dacron)
Matches
Messenger lines and assorted long, small-diameter lines
Paper towels (one roll per day)
Radar reflector
Rigging knives (at least one with a dull tip)
Sailcloth for repairs
Sail stops (at least nine, 6 feet in length)
Sailmaker's kit, rigging tape, and waxed twine
Sharpening stone for knives
Tape (duct, electrician's, and Rip-Stop)
Timepieces
Tools, with screwdrivers and wrenches to fit every fastening on board,
   and a sturdy hacksaw with extra blades

Spares

Battens
Blocks and shackles for every function on board
Clevis pins, cotter pins, and fastenings of the right sizes
Gaskets for hatches and windows
Halyards and sheets
Hose clamps and hosing
Propeller
Sail slides and jib hanks
Turnbuckles and toggles
Winch handles

Stanley Livingston, Jr., Richard C. McCurdy, John Rousmaniere, and Roderick Stephens, Jr., contributed to this appendix.

Illness, Injury, and Accidents at Sea: Recommended Procedures, Basic Medical Supplies and Their Use

George H. A. Clowes, Jr., M.D., Fleet Surgeon, CCA

Although serious illness is unusual among healthy people who make up the crews of oceangoing yachts, and fatal injuries are rare, they do occur. Knowledge of certain procedures, securing medical advice by radio (if none is available aboard), and medical supplies adequate for treatment may save a life or prevent serious complications. From the practical standpoint of the skipper and crew at sea, medical situations can be classified into three types:

- *Acute life-threatening emergencies* requiring immediate action to prevent death: strangulation (blockage of the airway at the larynx), cardiac arrest, severe hemorrhage, and respiratory arrest (asphyxia, drowning, etc.).
- *Urgent problems requiring medical advice and treatment* to avoid complications and to relieve pain include: lacerations and wounds, fractures, dislocations of joints, burns (usually in the galley), and severe head injuries. Illnesses in this category are severe abdominal pain (appendicitis, intestinal obstruction, etc.), chest pain (heart attacks), stroke, severe diarrhea (food poisoning or bacillary dysentery), and, more commonly (in men), urinary (prostatic) obstruction.
- *Of lesser significance but painful or debilitating* are bruises, minor lacerations, sprains, cough, sore throats, earaches, toothaches, boils, impetigo, and fungus infections (athlete's foot, "jock itch," etc.). Seasickness can be a serious problem because of dehydration, rendering a crew member ineffective and a danger to her- or himself and others on deck.

Procedures

1. Carry out procedures to save life if necessary (see below).
2. Call for medical aid by radio to obtain instructions from a physician.
   A. Call on Channel 16 to nearby yachts or steamers that may have a physician on board. Report position.
   B. Call the Coast Guard on AMVERS duplex channel 8241.5 (ship transmit) and 8756.4 (ship receive), which will put caller in communication with a U.S. Public Health physician or other source of medical advice. Report position.

In seeking medical assistance by radio, report clearly the clinical problem and answer the doctor's questions to help him or her make the diagnosis and formulate suggestions for treatment. Inform the doctor as to what drugs or supplies are available and appropriate for treatment, and request instructions on how to carry out the treatment. If emergency evacuation of the patient is deemed essential, it will be necessary to maintain communication with the Coast Guard or other rescue system to assure contact.

Treatment of Acute Medical Emergencies that Must Be Carried Out Immediately to Save Life

Strangulation (obstruction of larynx) by meat or other foreign body is recognized by the patient's grasping the throat and inability to breathe or talk. The Heimlich maneuver is performed by standing behind the patient. Wrap your arms around the waist. Make a fist with one hand and grasp it with the other. By a quick hard squeeze, force the fist into the pit of the stomach to induce exhalation of air and vomiting, which will usually dislodge the foreign body in the larynx. Remove the foreign body from the pharynx with the fingers or a forceps.

Cardiac Arrest and Respiratory Arrest: Cardiac massage and mouth-to-mouth breathing. Determine that there is no pulse, heartbeat, or respiration. Place the patient flat on the back on a hard surface. Kneel on his or her right side. Place the heel of the right hand on the lower end of the sternum (breastbone). Place left hand over the right. With your shoulders over the patient's chest, compress the sternum forcefully by applying your weight and straightening both arms. Repeat 60 times per minute. A second person should tip the head back with a hand behind the neck to assure a clear airway. Pinch the patient's nose, and by applying the lips directly to the patient's mouth, exhale into the patient's mouth to inflate the lungs 20 times per minute.

Control of Hemorrhage: Extensive bleeding from a surface wound is usually best controlled immediately by application of direct pressure to the wound itself. The pressure should be exerted by the fingers on sterile gauze packed into the wound. Although bleeding arteries are clamped with hemostats by a surgeon, great damage to nerves and other tissues can be caused if this is done blindly in the presence of massive hemorrhage. A tourniquet is useful only if it can be applied to an extremity above the site of injury, and it must be tight enough to produce a pressure greater than that in the arteries. It can only be left in place for 2 hours without causing serious tissue injury.

Treatment of Urgent and Lesser Injuries and Illnesses

Sprains are tears of one or more ligaments, the fibrous structures which hold a joint in its normal position yet let it move. Commonly, sprains are caused by abnormal motions of joints associated with twists or blows. They are recognized by localized tenderness and swelling of joints, accompanied by pain on motion. Unfortunately, severe sprains of the ankle, knee, wrist, elbow, and fingers or toes are frequently accompanied by fractures, which usually cannot be diagnosed accurately without X-ray. However, treatment remains essentially the same and consists of mild compression with an Ace bandage and splinting in a position of comfort. Always check to be certain that swelling of an extremity does not take place beyond a circular compression bandage. If this should occur, the bandage must be loosened. When possible, rest of the injured joint should be continued for several days, followed by increasing motion and use, provided that pain on motion is not severe. Back strain is similar in nature to a sprain and causes marked pain by inducing muscle spasm. Rest with the knees and head elevated; in the acute stage may require sedation with aspirin or codeine if pain is unremitting. Subsequently, motion and walking can be resumed, provided that severe pain is not provoked.

Dislocations of joints are recognized by abnormal configuration of the joint and loss of function. Reduction of a dislocation is often accomplished with the greatest ease soon after the injury before muscle spasm occurs. Gentle traction accompanied by a variety of special maneuvers is required to reduce a dislocation, followed by early immobilization of the joint with a sling, bandage, etc. It must be remembered that fractures sometimes accompany dislocations, especially of the humeral neck in injuries involving the shoulder joint. Therefore, excessive force must not be used unless one is certain that no fracture exists. Failure of efforts to reduce the dislocation will require splinting and immobilization of the joint until medical help may be obtained.

Fractures are recognized by an abnormal position of an extremity or by very severe pain on motion of the broken bone. The emergency treatment of fractures is to restore as nearly a normal position as possible by gentle traction followed by immobilization. The latter is accomplished by padding the limb with soft material and then applying splints, which are held in place by elastic or other bandages. Sail battens serve well as splints. Because of swelling or bleeding into tissues around a fracture, it is important always to check for swelling and numbness beyond the point of injury, in which case the bandage securing the splints must be loosened and the affected limb elevated. It is seldom possible to set a major fracture in an ideal position for healing, but a patient may be kept comfortable with good splinting until definitive treatment becomes available.

Compound fractures pose a difficult problem because of infection at the site where bone ends protrude through the skin. In the absence of medical assistance, it is best not to close the wound. Before reducing the fracture, as above, clean the skin around the wound with Betadine solution. Following reduction, place sterile gauze pads over the wound. Hold the dressing in place with a bandage before splinting. An antibiotic (Keflex or erythromycin) should be administered as recommended below.

Lacerations: After cleaning the surrounding skin with Betadine solution, most skin wounds and lacerations can be closed or pulled together with strips of adhesive or loosely tied sutures. This must be done promptly after bleeding has stopped in order to avoid infection. To suture a skin wound, inject novocaine into the skin around the wound. Use a cutting needle with a triangular section to insert a stitch (suture) into one side and out the other side of the wound. A sterile dressing should be applied. With all but superficial wounds, an antibiotic should be administered for at least 3 days.

All surface burns should be treated with Silvadene cream to prevent infection. Cover with a dressing if practical. The pain of severe sunburn can be relieved with surfacaine ointment, but prevention of sunburn by a good "blocker" or sunscreen ointment is better.

Constipation is best avoided by drinking extra water. A tablespoon of salt or Epsom salts in a quart of water is effective. However, *abdominal or chest pain* which does not disappear promptly must be taken seriously. If tenderness is present when pressure is applied to the abdomen, it is a sign of visceral or peritoneal disease. Do not use cathartics. Severe diarrhea may be treated with Bactrim by mouth supplemented with paregoric to relieve cramps. Mefoxin is included as an antibiotic for intramuscular injection if, after consultation with a physician, peritonitis or appendicitis is thought to be present.

Urinary Retention: Prostatic enlargement in older men may result in acute urinary retention with severe discomfort in the lower abdomen. To relieve this situation, the penis should be thoroughly cleaned with soap and water. Wearing sterile gloves, apply sterile lubricating jelly to a rubber catheter, which must be boiled if not previously sterilized. The catheter tip is inserted into the urethra. It must be gently but firmly pushed until the tip enters the bladder to allow urine to flow freely out. Following evacuation of the urine, the catheter should be withdrawn. The procedure may be repeated once or twice a day as needed.

Keflex or erythromycin may be used for treatment of skin, ear, or airway infections, again after radio consultation with a physician. Adrenalin may be called for in acute asthma or other allergic situations (drugs, etc.). Pronestyl is included as an aid to controlling unusual heart rhythms in the event of a heart attack. For foreign bodies and injury to the eye, do not use anesthetic ointments, since permanent corneal damage may result. Rely on Bacitracin ophthalmic (*not* the regular kind) or other antibiotic eye ointment.

Crew members who are on chronic medication with insulin, digitalis, diuretics, etc., should bring their own drugs in quantity sufficient for the voyage. Most such patients are fully aware of their own requirements and will deal with them.

References

Bergan, John. *Sailing and Yachting First Aid,* 45 pages, USYRU, Newport, Rhode Island, 1977.

The Ship's Medicine Chest and Medical Aid at Sea, Department of Public Health Services, U.S. Government Printing Office, Washington, D.C., 1978.

Suggested Medical Supplies

In considering the items in the list of drugs, an attempt has been made not to include dangerous drugs. Or, if they are included, only small quantities of narcotics or toxic antibiotics are suggested. These will be sufficient for several days, when presumably some help may become available.

A skipper or other person responsible for outfitting a vessel for sea who is desirous of securing the items on this list should consult his or her own doctor to obtain prescriptions for certain of the drugs and syringes. A doctor may also have valuable suggestions in terms of other supplies or immunizations needed for your special voyage. In any case, don't worry about the possibility of sickness, which is uncommon at sea. It is just easier to be prepared with a few essentials if injury or illness should strike.

INSTRUMENTS AND EQUIPMENT	USE
1 scalpel with disposable sterile blades	Incision of abscess, etc.
1 splinter forceps	Removal of splinters
1 needle holder	Suturing wound
Sutures (pre-sterilized in glass vials)	Suturing wound
Skin: 00 silk with curved cutting 1-inch needles	Suturing wound
Subcutaneous: 000 chromic catgut with curved round 1-inch needle	Suturing wound
Ligatures: spool 00 silk	Suturing wound
1 surgical mayo scissors curved	Suturing wound
1 thumb forceps smooth	Suturing wound
4 hemostats	Suturing wound
1 long curved forceps laryngeal	Removal of foreign body, throat
1 urethral catheter rubber (French #16)	Urinary obstruction
1 urethral catheter rubber (French #14)	Urinary obstruction
1 Levine nasogastric tube	Removal of gastric secretion
Lubricating jelly	
Disposable plastic hypodermic needles: 3 2-cc syringes (sterile disposable)	Injection of drugs or local anesthetic
3 10-cc syringes (sterile disposable)	Injection of drugs or local anesthetic
Intravenous and hypodermic needles: 12 #21 1½" (sterile disposable)	Subcutaneous or intramuscular injection
12 #19 2" (sterile disposable)	Subcutaneous or intramuscular injection
2 pairs surgical rubber gloves (size 8)	
Fever thermometer	

SUPPLIES	USE
Gauze bandages, 1", 2", 3", each 3	Dressings
Gauze sponges, 4" x 4" (sterile) 12 packs	Dressings
Adhesive tape, 3", 3 rolls	Dressings, sprains, etc.

"Bandaids," selection of sizes	Minor lacerations, etc.
Elastic bandages, 3″ and 4″, 4 each	Sprains, dressings
Sterile cotton	Application of disinfectant
Oral airway	

Drugs

ANTIBIOTICS	USE
Bactrim tablets (standard size), 40 tablets (dose: 2 tablets every 12 hours)	Urinary tract infection, diarrhea
Keflex (cephalexin), 60-ml oral suspension (dose: 250 mg [2 teaspoons] every 6 hours)	Sore throat (strep), earache, skin infection, upper respiratory tract
or:	
Erythromycin, 250-mg tablets, 50 tablets (dose: 1 tablet every 6 hours)	Same as Keflex
Mefoxin (Cefoxitin), 1-gram vials, Number 12, with sterile water for mixing (dose: 1 gram every 8 hours)	For intramuscular injection to treat peritonitis, appendicitis, etc.

ANTIFUNGAL AGENTS	USE
Desenex powder (feet, etc.)	Feet
Cruex powder aerosol (groin, etc.)	Jock itch
Tinactin cream 1%	Athletes' foot

ANTIHISTAMINE	USE
Benadryl, 50-mg capsules, 50 capsules	Hay fever, other allergies
or:	Warning: may induce sleepiness
Chlortrimetron, 4-mg tablets, 50 tablets (dose for either: 1 every 6 to 8 hours)	

PAIN (ANALGESICS)	USE
Morphine sulfate, 15 mg, 5 Tubex-prefilled cartridge units with tubex syringe. To be used only with medical consultation	For severe pain; to be injected subcutaneously not more often than every 4 hours
Codeine, 30-mg tablets, 20 tablets (dose: 1 not more often than every 4 hours). Take with aspirin for greater effect	By mouth for toothache, headache, or other severe pain
Aspirin, 325-mg tablets, 100 tablets (dose: 2 tablets every 4 hours)	May be used with codeine

MOTION SICKNESS	USE
Dramamine, 50-mg tablets, 100 tablets (dose: 1 tablet every 4 hours; take ½ hour before activity begins)	Prevention of seasickness
Dramamine suppositories, 100 mg, 12 suppositories. Insert one not more often than every 12 hours	To treat ongoing severe seasickness

Bonine, 25-mg tablets, 100 tablets (dose: 1 or 2 tablets every 24 hours)	Prevention of seasickness

Warning: These motion-sickness drugs may induce drowsiness

LOCAL ANESTHETIC	USE
Procaine hydrochloride, 1%, 5 vials of 10 cc	

SEDATIVES (not to be used for personnel on duty at sea)	USE
Valium, 5-mg tablets, 25 tablets (not more than 1 tablet 2 times daily)	For severe psychological disorders
Dalmane, 15-mg tablets, 25 tablets (for sleep—1 tablet at bedtime)	For sleep

CARDIOVASCULAR	USE
Adrenalin (epinephrine) solution 1:1000, 1 vial 10 cc	Acute asthma or allergy; not more than 1 cc (intramuscular)
Pronestyl (procaine amide), 250-mg capsules, 50 capsules	Control cardiac arrythmia; 1 tablet every 3 hours

EAR, NOSE, AND THROAT	USE
Afrin (nasal) solution 0.5%, 30-cc bottle with dropper (dose: not more than 4 drops 2 times daily)	Relieves nasal congestion and sinus or ear pain

EYE	USE
Bacitracin ophthalmic ointment, 1 tube	For corneal or conjunctive injury or pain

GASTROINTESTINAL	USE
Laxatives: Epsom salts, milk of magnesia	Constipation
Maalox	Gastritis or ulcer pain
Anusol suppositories, 1 box (24 suppositories). Use 1 twice daily	Painful or itching hemorrhoids
Paregoric, 16 ounces (dose: 1 teaspoonful 4 times daily)	Diarrhea and cramps

GENITO-URINARY	USE
Gantricin, 500-mg tablets, 50 tablets (dose: 1 g/day for cystitis)	Cystitis
Urispas, 100-mg tablets, 50 tablets (dose: 1 tablet 4 times daily)	

MUSCULOSKELETAL	USE
Norflex, 50 tablets (dose: 1 tablet every 4 hours)	For muscle spasm and backache

or:

Parafon Forte, 100 tablets (dose: 2 tablets 4
   times daily)

SKIN	USE
Betadine solution, 16 ounces	Skin sterilizing for surgery, etc.
Silvadene cream, 50-g jar	For skin burns—keep burned area covered with layer of cream $\frac{1}{16}$ inch thick
Fly dope	
Sunburn preventive: sunscreen, Piz Buin, etc.	

Further Reading

The authors and editor recommend the following forty-odd books as supplementary reading.

Naval Architecture and Yacht Design

American Boat and Yacht Council, Inc. *Standards and Recommended Practices for Small Craft.*

American Bureau of Shipping, *Guide for Building and Classing Offshore Yachts.*

Atwood, E.L., and H.S. Pengally. *Theoretical Naval Architecture.*

Kinney, Francis S. *Skene's Elements of Yacht Design,* 8th edition.

Marchaj, C.A. *Sailing Theory and Practice.*

———. *Seaworthiness: The Forgotten Factor.*

Roberts, John. *Fiberglass Boats.*

Russell, H.E., and L.R. Chapman (eds.). *Principles of Naval Architecture.*

The *Reports* of the United States Yacht Racing Union and the Society of Naval Architects and Marine Engineers Joint Committee on Safety from Capsizing, April 1983, June 1984, June 1985. Available from USYRU, Box 209, Newport, RI 02840.

Cruising Yachts

Beiser, Arthur. *The Proper Yacht.*

Henderson, Richard. *The Racing-Cruiser.*

Maté, Ferenc. *Best Boats to Build or Buy.*

Roth, Hal. *After 50,000 Miles.*

Schlereth, Hewitt. *How to Buy a Sailboat.*

Spurr, Daniel *Upgrading the Cruising Sailboat.*

Street, Donald. *The Ocean Sailing Yacht,* 2 vols.

Worth, Claud. *Yacht Cruising.*

Sails and Maintenance

Donaldson, Sven. *A Sailor's Guide to Sails.*

Duffet, John. *Boatowner's Guide to Modern Maintenance,* 2nd edition.

Maté, Ferenc. *Shipshape: The Art of Sailboat Maintenance.*

Ross, Wallace C. *Sail Power,* 2nd edition.

Auxiliary Equipment

Bamford, Don. *Anchoring.*

Beyn, Edgar J. *The Twelve Volt Doctor's Practical Handbook.*

Hobbs, Richard R. *Marine Navigation 2: Celestial and Electronic,* 2nd edition.
Jeffrey, Nan, and Kevin Jeffrey. *Free Energy Afloat.*
Kotsch, William J. *Weather for the Mariner,* 4th edition.
Miller, Conrad. *Engines for Sailboats.*
Ogg, Robert D. *Anchors and Anchoring.*
Practical Sailor magazine.
Zadig, Ernest A. *The Complete Book of Boat Electronics.*
————. *The Complete Book of Pleasure Boat Engines.*

Seamanship

Coles, K. Adlard. *Heavy Weather Sailing.*
Dashew, Steven, and Linda Dashew. *The Circumnavigator's Handbook.*
————. *Bluewater Handbook.*
van Dorn, William G. *Oceanography and Seamanship.*
Henderson, Richard. *Sea Sense.*
Maloney, Elbert S. *Piloting, Seamanship, and Small Boat Handling.*
Rousmaniere, John. *The Annapolis Book of Seamanship.*
————. *The Sailing Lifestyle.*

History

Howland, Waldo. *A Life in Boats: The Years Before the War.*
Loomis, Alfred F. *Ocean Racing.*
Members of the Cruising Club of America. *Far Horizons: Adventures in Cruising,*
    2 vols.
Nutting, William N. *Track of the Typhoon.*
Parkinson, John, Jr. *Nowhere Is Too Far: The Annals of the Cruising Club of
    America.*
Pinchot, Gifford B. *Loki and Loon.*
Robinson, Bill. *The Great American Yacht Designers.*
Rousmaniere, John. *"Fastnet, Force 10".*
————. *The Golden Pastime.*
Vilas, Charles H. *Saga of Direction.*

Index

Adele (Hood design), 257–61
aft cabin arrangement, 117–18
air supply to cabin, 150–52, 158
Alden, John (yacht designer), 24–26
alternator, 241–42
American Boat and Yacht Council, 155
American Bureau of Shipping, 97, 280
American Radio Relay League, 219
American Society of Heating, Refrigerating, and Air Conditioning Engineers, 150
anchor, *see* ground tackle
anhydrous lanolin (lubricant), 170, 171, 173
Annapolis Book of Seamanship, The (Rousmaniere), 155, 251
antennas, 217, 226–27
Archer, Colin (yacht designer), 46
Awlgrip paint, 166

babystay, 164, 165
backstay, adjustable, 163, 173
ballast, 96
    construction and, 96, 99–100
    inside, 46, 65
    roller furlers and, 202
    stability and, 40, 46, 54, 71–73
barometer, 216, 222, 223
Baruna (Sparkman & Stephens design), 33
battens, 198
battery, 241–43, 247
beam, *see* stability range, stability
bedding compound, 109
Bermuda Race, *see* Cruising Club of America
berths and bunks, types and dimensions of, 128–32
bilge, *see* pump, sump
binoculars, 209, 222
"blind man's test" (rigging), 290
blocks, 141–42, 187
Bolero (Sparkman & Stephens design), 33

"bomb" (meteorological term), 67
boom, main, 167
boom pad, 163, 183
boom vang, 163, 173, 181, 183–85, 280, *see also* preventer, reefing equipment
bowline hitch, 176
bridge deck, 106, 107, 122
broach, 90–91
Brown, Warren, owner of *War Baby,* 130
bulkhead, 96
bunks, *see* berths and bunks
buntline hitch, 176, 186
Burgess, W. Starling (yacht designer), 26–27
Burnes, Richard M., owner of *Adele,* 257, 258

cabin:
    arrangement of, 127–29
    heaters in, 155–56
    ventilation of, 145–58
cabin trunk, 106, 113
cable, anchor, *see* rode
Cal 29 (Lapworth design), 124
Cal 2-35 (Lapworth design), 122
Cal 40 (Lapworth design), 37, 118
Cal 46, 2-46 (Lapworth design), 263
calculators, navigation, 210
Capsize Project (SNAME / USYRU), 57–82
capsize, 46–47
    factors in, 54
    history of, 45–47
    hull shape and, 51, 69–71
    knockdowns and, 79
    masts and, 61–63, 67–69, 76
    moment of inertia and, 53, 61–62, 67–69
    positive stability range and, 47–48
    turtling, problem of, 63–64
    waves and, 65–67, 76
    weather changes and, 67
    yacht size and, 53, 62, 75–77

capsize (*continued*)
  see also capsize length, stability, stability range
capsize length:
  definition of, 62–63, 76
  recommended, 76
capsize length formula, 82
capsize screening formula, 76–78
Carina (McCurdy & Rhodes design), 141
Carter, Dick (yacht designer), 37
cat rig, 162
celestial navigation equipment, 209–10
center of gravity, 40, 46, 50, 51, 54, 82, 85–88, *see also* stability, stability range
centerboard, 258
  as undesirable feature, 99
  CCA Rule and, 31–36
  pendant for, 190–91
chafe:
  on anchor cable, 235
  on halyard, 178, 180
  on sheets, 182–83
chain hook, anchor, 110
chain plates, 96, 171
Challenge (Sparkman & Stephens design), 42
children, 127
chocks, 109–10, 235, 278
cleats:
  Clam, 188–89
  horn, 188
  mooring, 110
  halyard and sheet, 188–89
  see also lock-offs
clothes, stowage of, 128, 131, 140–41
Coast Guard, U.S., 155, 251, 252
Coast Guard Auxiliary, 155, 251
cockpit:
  aft, 117, 120
  construction of, 123
  cushions in, 124
  deck and, 112–13
  design of, 112–113, 274
  drains in, 122–23
  lockers in, 125, 128
  midship, 117–18, 121, 263–67
  seats in, 113, 123–25
  sole of, 124
  stowage in, 125, 131
  volume of, 122
comfort, importance of, 115
communications instruments, *see* radio
communications receiver, 218, 223, 227
Compadre (Lapworth design), 121, 263–67
companionway, 106, 107, 108, 119–22, 145

companionway boards (slats), 108, 119–20, 290
companionway ladder, 129, 290
compass, 222
  deviation in, 209
  hand-bearing, 209, 222
  location of, 125
computer, on-board, 220–21, 223
Concordia yawl (Hunt design), 37, 108
condensation, 153–55
construction, yacht:
  aluminum, 97, 98, 101, 106
  centerboard type, 32, 34
  cockpit, 123
  ferrocement, 102
  fiberglass (GRP), 36, 97, 98–99, 100, 101–2, 106, 109
  importance of strong, 54, 76, 105
  Kevlar, 97
  mast, 76
  rudder and skeg, 93, 99
  steel, 97, 102
  wood, 26, 31, 97, 102, 106–7
corrosion, 100, 101
cotter pins, construction and use of, 170, 171–72
Crowninshield, B. B. (yacht designer), 23–24
Cruising Club of America (CCA):
  Bermuda Race, 11, 12, 26, 36, 37, 39, 45, 53, 58, 76, 120, 122
  history and publications of, 11–13
  rating rule of, 28, 31–36, 37, 258
  Technical Committee of, 11–13, 57–58
cutter rig, 161, 198–99

Decca (navigation instrument), 207, 214, 223
deck, 105–15
  as structural member, 95–96, 105–6
  cockpit and, 112
  -hull joint, 96, 98, 106, 114
  size of, 124
depth sounder, 210–11, 222
deviation, finding and correcting:
  in compass, 209
  in radio direction finder, 212
dinghy, 110
directional stability:
  factors in, 83–89
  hull shape and, 91–92
  keel and, 91, 92
  rudder and, 91, 92–93
discontinuous rigging, 163

displacement, *see* stability
distance meters, 211
dodger:
    construction of, 148–50
    importance of in ventilation, 145
    water and, 120
Dora IV (later *Tenacious* and *War Baby*,
        Sparkman & Stephens design),
        130
Dorade (Sparkman & Stephens design),
        29–31, 32, 33, 34, 38, 145
Dorade vent, 145, 146, 148, 156–58
double-headed rig, 161, 198–200
Dri-Vent vent, 145
drogue, 81

electrical system, 241–43
emergency bag, 215
emergency equipment, 125, 215, 245–53,
        291, 292
emergency position-indicating beacon
        (EPIRB), 215, 222
emergency tiller, 252
emergency tools, 252
engine:
    filters for, 241
    fuel for, 237–38, 240
    insulation of, 241
    performance of, 238
    propellers for, 238–39
    location of, 118, 239–41, 263
    ventilation for, 240

fans and blowers, 132, 153
"Fastnet, Force 10" (Rousmaniere), 19, 58
Fastnet Race, 45
    1979, 12, 45, 46–47, 58, 60, 67, 80, 108
    1985, 12–13
Field, Hale, and wheelhouse sloop, 263
Finisterre (Sparkman & Stephens design),
        34–36, 39, 41
fire, 148
fire extinguishers, 250–51
first aid procedures and equipment, 293–
        300
First Light (Sparkman & Stephens design),
        279–85
fisherman type schooners, 24–26, 46
flares, 252–53
Flyer (Sparkman & Stephens design), 41
floors, structural, 96
food, stowage of, 139–40
foot blocks, 111, 187, 189

forestay, 163–66
forestaysail, 198, 274, 280
forward lower stay, 163, 165
fractional rig, advantages of, 162–65
Fram (Lapworth design), 263
frames, structural, 97
fuel, engine, 237–38, 240
fuel, stove, 134–35, 147–48

Galerider drogue, 81
galley:
    location of, 132
    shape of, 128, 132
    stowage in, 139–40
    ventilation of, 146–48
garbage, stowage of, 140
genoa jib, in rough water, 199
Gleistein Cup Sheet rope, 175
Global Positioning System (GPS), *see* satnav
Greeff, Ed, owner of *Puffin,* 158
ground tackle:
    anchor weight, 232–33
    bow roller for, 112
    Bruce anchor, 230, 232, 233
    buoys for, 235
    cable (rode), 175, 233–35
    chain hook for, 110, 234
    chocks for, 109–10
    Danforth anchor, 112, 230, 231, 233
    lunch hook, 233
    Navy type anchor, 232
    Northill anchor, 232
    plow anchor (CQR), 112, 230, 231, 233
    stern anchor, 235
    storm anchoring, 291
    yachtsman (Herreshoff) anchor, 229–
        31, 233
*Guide for Building and Classing Offshore
        Racing Yachts* (American Bureau
        of Shipping), 97–98

halyards:
    arrangement of, 176–79, 181
    internal, 177–78
    length of, 178–79
    maintenance of, 180–81, 290
    marks on, 194–96
    materials for, 176–76
    replacement of, 181–82
    spinnaker, 189
ham (amateur) radio, 218–19, 227
Hand, William H. (yacht designer), 24
hanks, jib, 196–97, 198

hatches, 106, 108, 125, 146–47, 152–53, 156
Hathaway, Reiser, & Raymond (drogue manufacturer), 81
Hazelhurst, Thomas, and Pearson 386, 276
head, ventilation of, 148
headroom, 113–14, 128
headstay, construction of, 196
heaters, danger of, 155–56
heaving line, 249–50, 251
heavy-weather tactics, 80–81
Herreshoff, Nathanael (yacht designer), 24, 33, 229–31, 233, *see also* Universal Rule
Hood, Frederick E. (yacht designer), 257
hot water system, 243
hull deflection, 100–101
hull shape:
    capsize and, 51, 69–71
    directional stability and, 89, 91–93
    stability and, 48–51, 54–55, 65, 69–71
hull to deck joint, 96, 98, 106, 114
Hunt, C. Raymond (yacht designer), 37
Hyfield lever, 165
hydraulic adjuster, 163, 165, 172–73, 183–84
hypothermia, 252

Imron paint, 166
insulation, hull and engine, 154, 241
International Measurement System (IMS), 119:
    history of, 42–44
    need for, 43
    Velocity Prediction Program, 220
International Offshore Rule (IOR), 34, 73, 258
    characteristics of boats designed to, 41–42, 52
    cockpits in, 122–23
    history of, 39–42
    stability and, 40, 53, 71–72
International Rule, 23, 71, 72
International Technical Committee (IOR and IMS), 39, 43
inertia, moment of, *see* capsize
Intrepid (Sparkman & Stephens design), 37

jacklines, safety harness, 111, 114, 246
jib attachment, 196–97
jib, storm, 200, 201

keel:
    directional stability and, 85, 91, 92
    propellers and, 238–39

size of, 36–39, 92
    speed and, 38
    steering and, 39
Kerwin, Jake, and IMS, 42
ketch rig, 161–62, 164, 257
Kevlar:
    in hulls, 97
    in rope, 175–77
    in sails, 193
Kirkman, Karl L. (naval architect), 11, 38, 59
knockdowns, 79

Lapworth, C. William (yacht designer), 11, 37, 112, 263, 264
lazyjacks, 202, 282
lead line, 210
leaks, 109, 167
Lewmar turnbuckle, 171
Life-Caulk (sealant), 109
life raft, 246, 253
life vest, 246, 252
lifelines, 124, 289, *see also* stanchions
light, below deck, 113, 224–26
Light List, 224
Lippincott, Wells, and rating rules, 28
lockers:
    cabin, 139
    cockpit, 125, 141–42
    condensation in, 154
    ventilation of, 148, 153
    wet, 128
lock-offs, 188–89
Loomis, Alfred F., and story of slow boat, 12
Loomis, Harvey, and *Wissahickon,* 13, 271
Loran-C (navigation instrument), 207, 214, 223, 225, 227, 228
lubricants, 170, 171, 173
luff-fed sails, danger of, 196–98
Lymann-Morse Boatbuilding Co., 279, 282

McCurdy, Ian, and *Wissahickon,* 271
McCurdy, James A. (yacht designer), 11, 13, 42, 269
McCurdy, Richard C., and navigation station, 142
McCurdy, Sheila, skipper of *Wissahickon,* 13, 271
mainsail attachment, 197–98
mainsail, cut of, 198
mainsail luff gauge, 182, 195
mainsail stowage, 202
Malabars (Alden designs), 25–26, 29
Malay (Hunt design), 37

man-overboard rescue equipment, 246, 247–49, 250, 251
mast boot, 167
mast design and construction, 166–67
mast, leaks around, 167
mast loss as factor in capsize, 61–62, 67–69, 75–76
mast step, 290
masthead rig, 162–63, 179
Measurement Handicap System (MHS), *see* International Measurement System (IMS)
Memory (Herreshoff design), 26, 46
Merriman turnbuckle, 171
messenger line, 180–81, 185–86, 190
Mitchell, Carleton, and *Finisterre,* 34, 36
mizzen, advantages of, 162
Mylar sail cloth, 193

Naval Academy, U.S., 60, 249
Naval Academy Sailing Squadron, 81
navigation:
	basic equipment for, 207–10, 222
	instruments for, 209, 211–15, 223, 225
	station for, 128, 142, 224–26
Navstar, *see* satnav
Navtec (equipment supplier), 170, 171
Nicro-Fico vent, 148
Nye, Dick, and clothing stowage, 141
Newman, J. Nicholas, and IMS, 42, 61
New York 32 (Sparkman & Stephens design), 32, 41
New York 40 (Herreshoff design), 23, 24, 26, 46, 72
New York 48 (Sparkman & Stephens design), 43
Niña (Burgess design), 26–27
noise reduction of marine radio, 227–28
Nutting, Bill, and early cruising, 45–46

odors, removal of, 154–55
Offshore Rating Council, 122–23, 249, *see also* International Offshore Rule
Omega (navigation instrument), 207, 214–15, 227
One-Ton Class, 39–40, 41
Omni (navigation instrument), 212
outhaul, 185
overflow vents, fuel and water, 153

Palawan III (Sparkman & Stephens design), 38

passageway, 117–18
Pearson 386 (Shaw design), 273–78
pendants, 178, 180, 190, 198, 202
Performance Handicap Rating Fleet (PHRF), 44
performance instruments, 219–21, 223
pilotage, *see* navigation
Piloting, Seamanship, & Small Boat Handling ("Chapman's"), 155, 251
Pitney, James C., owner of *First Light,* 279, 282
plugs, 252, 289
polar curves, 220–21
ports, 107, 113, 153
positive stability range, *see* stability range
Practical Sailor magazine, 148
Pratt, H. Irving, and IMS, 42, 119
preventer, 183, 280
prisms, deck, 113
propeller and shaft, 96, 98, 238–39
Puffin (Sparkman & Stephens design), 158
pump, bilge, 125, 252, 289

Rabbit (Carter design), 37
racing, influence of on design of cruising yachts, 27, 31, 45, 39–44
radar (navigation instrument), 212–13, 223, 225, 227
radar reflector, 245, 246
radio, marine:
	antennas for, 226–27
	basic principles of, 226
	ground systems for, 227
	installation of, 226–28
	noise reduction in, 227–28
	types of, 217–19
radio direction finder (navigation instrument), 211–12, 223
range of positive stability, *see* stability range
rating rules:
	characteristics of, 28–31, 71–73
	history of, 27–44
	influence of, 27, 31, 93
	measurement under, 28–29, 48
	see also Cruising Club of America, International Measurement System, International Rule, International Offshore Rule, Royal Ocean Racing Club, Universal Rule
reaching strut, 168
reefing equipment, 181, 185–87, 188, *see also* roller furlers
reefs, mainsail, size of, 198
reefs, jib, 198

reel halyard winch, danger of, 189–90
refrigeration, 132, 217, 135–38
rig, *see* capsize, mast, sail plan
rod rigging, 168, 171
rode, anchor, *see* ground tackle
roller furlers, 200–202
rope, types available, 175–76
Rousmaniere, John, 58, 271
 Annapolis Book of Seamanship, The,
  155, 251
  "Fastnet, Force 10," 58
Royal Ocean Racing Club (RORC), 29, 39, 60
rudder:
 characteristics of, 38–39
 construction of, 92–93, 96, 99
 directional stability and, 84–88, 91, 92–
  93
 separate, 36–39
 skeg and, 93, 99
 spade, 93
Rugosa II (Herreshoff design), 24, 26
running backstays, 162–65
Running Tide (Sparkman & Stephens
  design), 71–73

S & S, *see* Sparkman & Stephens
safety harness, 110–11, 125, 245–47
Safety Standards for Small Craft (American
  Boat and Yacht Council), 155
sail plans:
 cat, 162
 cutter, 161, 198–99
 fractional, 162–65
 masthead, 162, 179
 schooner, 162
 sloop, 161, 198
 split (yawl and ketch), 161–62, 164,
  200, 257
sail inventories, recommended, 198–200
sails:
 care of, 194
 fabrics in, 193–94
 luff-fed, danger of, 196–98
 storm, 200, 201
 stowage of, 128, 141–42, 194
satnav (navigation instrument), 207, 215,
  223, 227
schooner, 162
screens, 155
scuppers, 109, 114
sea cocks, 289
seats, cockpit, 113, 123–25
"Seattle Sling" (man-overboard recovery
  device), 247–50

skeg, 93, 99
skylights, 113, 146
sloop rig, 161, 198
"snake" (line retriever), 187
"sniffer" (fuel leak detector), 135, 147
Society of Naval Architects and Marine Engineers (SNAME), 59
Sparcraft shackle, 165
spare equipment, 292
Sparkman & Stephens (yacht designers), 32,
  33, 36, 37, 38, 41, 42, 44, 279, *see*
  also Olin J. Stephens II, Roderick
  Stephens, Jr.
spars, 166, *see also* boom, mast, reaching
  strut, spinnaker pole
speed, as factor in seamanship, 11–12, 46,
  52–53, 80–81
speed meters, 211, 219–21, 222
spinnaker:
 crane for halyard of, 163, 178
 cut of, 198, 203
 dousing systems for, 203
 lock-offs and, 188–89
spinnaker pole, 168, 280
stability:
 ballast and, 40, 46, 54, 71–73, 79
 beam and, 48–51, 54–55, 65–71
 benefits of good, 52–53
 center of gravity and, 40, 46, 48, 50, 51,
  54
 definition of, 47–48
 displacement and, 48, 51, 54–55
 freeboard and, 54
 hull shape and, 54–55, 65, 69–71
 importance of, 52–53
 initial, 51, 69–71
 righting moment and, 51
 ultimate, 51, 69–71
 yacht's age and, 48–51
 yacht's size and, 48–51, 53, 75–78
 see also capsize, stability range
stability range:
 calculation of, 73–74
 deck structures and, 73–74
 definition of, 47–48, 69
 factors in, 48–51, 54, 69–73
 improving, 79
 recommended, 65, 79
 trends in, 48–51, 71–73
 see also capsize, stability
stanchions, 98, 124, 246, 289
static, radio, 227–28
stays:
 construction of, 168–69
 discontinuous, 168

rod and wire, 168, 171
 terminals for, 168–69
 see also babystay, forestay, headstay,
  running backstay
steering, 76, 80–81, *see also* directional stability
steering gear, 190, 289
Stephens, Olin J. II (yacht designer), 11, 13,
  59, 145
 early sailing career of, 23–27, 45–47
 sailboards and, 44
Stephens, Roderick, Jr. (yacht designer), 11,
  23, 145, 152, 279, 283
storm sails, 200, 201, 280, 290–91
storm shutters, 107, 114
storm tactics, 80–81
stove:
 construction of, 134
 fires and flare-ups in, 148
 fuel for, 134–35, 148
 location of, 132–33
 size of, 127–28
stowage:
 in cabin, 128, 131, 139
 in cockpit, 125
 in galley, 139–40
 in navigation station, 224–25
 of blocks, 141–42
 of books and charts, 131, 142–43, 224
 of cooking fuel, 135
 of heavy items, 290
 of sails, 141–42, 194
 of tools, 42
stringers, structural, 96, 98
Strohmeier, Daniel D., and Capsize Project,
  37, 59
sump, bilge, 125, 252, 289
Swan 43 (Sparkman & Stephens design),
  111
Sydney-Hobart Race, 1984, 13

table, cabin, 138–39
tactics, rough-weather, 80–81
tape, rigging, 173–74
Tartan 41 (Sparkman & Stephens design),
  40–41
Teflon spray, 173, 190
temperature indicators, 216–17, 223
Tenacious (ex-*Dora IV,* Sparkman & Stephens design), 130
timepieces, navigation, 210, 222
toggles, construction and use of, 170, 171
tools, 142, 252, 291–92

topping lift, 184–85, 186
Transpacific Yacht Club, 122
trigger-type shackle, 165
Tru-Lock stay terminal, 169
trysail, storm, 200
turnbuckles, construction and use of, 169–
  72
Turner, Ted, and *Tenacious,* 130
turtling, 63–64, 71

United States Yacht Racing Union (USYRU),
  42, 59, 76, 82
Universal Rule (Herreshoff), 23, 26, 71, 72

vang, *see* boom vang
Velocity Prediction Program (IMS), 220
ventilation:
 cabin heaters and, 155–56
 Coast Guard requirements for, 155
 gear and systems for, 145–46, 152–54
 minimum requirements for, 150–52
 of engine, 155, 240
 of galley, 132, 146–48
 of head, 148
 of lockers, 148
ventilators, 145–46, 149, 153, 154, 156–58
very high-frequency-FM radio (VHF-FM),
  215, 217–18, 222–23, 226, 227

War Baby (ex-*Dora IV,* ex-*Tenacious,*
  Sparkman & Stephens design),
  130
watermaker, 243
watertightness, testing for, 290
waves, large:
 capsize and, 65–67, 78–79
 steering in, 80–81, 89–91
 see also stability
weather changes as cause of capsize, 67
weather facsimile machine, 218, 223
weather forecasts, 217–18
WEST system, 97
wheelhouse sloop, 263
Williams, Lynn A., and CCA Technical Committee, 12–13
winch handles, lock-in, 290
winches, 189–90
wind indicators, 216, 219–21, 223
Wissahickon (McCurdy & Rhodes design),
  13, 269–72
Wolfson Unit (University of Southampton),
  60, 81

Worldwide Marine Weather Broadcasts, 217
Wright, Howard, owner of *Compadre,* 263,
    264

Yacht Cruising (Worth), 45
yacht design, trends in, 23–47, 57–58
Yankee Girl (Sparkman & Stephens design),
    40–41, 282

yawl rig, 161–62, 164
Young, Tom, and ventilation and instru-
    ments, 122, 142, 250

Zest (McCurdy & Rhodes design), 119